ADVANCE PRAISE FOR BOY WITH A KNIFE

"Through skillful storytelling and rigorous research, Jean Trounstine shows us why young people engage in crime and violence, and how we can create rehabilitation and redemption for those caught up in the system. This book is an argument for why youth justice should move to the top of our national priorities if we want safe and equitable communities for all Americans."
—**Piper Kerman**, author of the *New York Times* bestselling *Orange is the New Black: My Year in a Women's Prison*

"Jean Trounstine tells Karter Reed's story with warmth, with complexity, with nuance. She weaves in his background, trial, conviction, imprisonment in the context of larger contemporary public and scholarly debates about punishment and especially, adolescents. She frames a critical contemporary debate with a very human face. We see through Karter the mistakes that we have made and critically, how much more needs to be done. This is essential reading for anyone who cares about justice."
—**Nancy Gertner,** former U.S. federal judge, named one of "The Most Influential Lawyers of the Past 25 Years" by *Massachusetts Lawyers Weekly*

"Jean Trounstine has delivered a searing wake-up call about the need to reform and redeem our juvenile justice system. Sentencing children as adults is neither productive nor morally sound, and the tale of Karter Kane Reed exemplifies that truth."
—**Shon Hopwood,** author of *Law Man: My Story of Robbing Banks, Winning Supreme Court Cases, and Finding Redemption*

"*Boy with a Knife* is a masterful narrative rooted in the tragedy of a life lost and another launched into a complex journey of transformation. It is a must read—a compelling story and a deep reflection for teachers and students, advocates and policymakers, parents and youth on the meaning of justice."
—**Robert Kinscherff,** PhD, JD., William James College, National Center for Mental Health and Juvenile Justice, and the Center for Law, Brain and Behavior at Massachusetts General Hospital

"Gripping and important, Jean Trounstine's real-life account about a boy thrust into an adult prison unfolds is heart-shattering drama. Written with deep compassion and grace, Trounstine brilliantly proves that people can—and do change—and so, too, can the system. A must-read for anyone who cares about justice and forgiveness—and that should be all of us."—**Caroline Leavitt,** *New York Times* bestselling author of *Is This Tomorrow* and *Pictures of You*

"*Boy With A Knife* is a devastatingly detailed indictment of a criminal justice system that routinely sends youth to adult jails and prisons, yet it's a story infused with much needed hope. A must read for anyone interested in criminal justice reform."
—**TJ Parsell**, author of *Fish: A Memoir of a Boy in a Man's Prison*

"With meticulous research, Jean Trounstine mirrors what I've seen in U.S. prisons for over thirty-five years as a speaker and workshop facilitator, where I witnessed an increasing number of troubled youth being thrown away, abused, and in too many cases, prepared as higher-end criminals, all at taxpayers' expense. Read this book and take action. Anybody can be saved. Anybody can change. It's time our laws and justice systems aligned to this moral and biological fact."—**Luis J. Rodriguez**, author of *Always Running, La Vida Loca, Gang Days in L.A.* and *Hearts & Hands: Creating Community in Violent Times*

"Jean Trounstine has opened a window into the disaster of American juvenile justice. The story of Karter Kane Reed serves not only as a cautionary tale of what can happen to kids who commit serious crimes, but of how American juvenile justice policies actually hamper rehabilitation and the correction of flawed character. Hands down this book is certain to be a top criminal justice read for 2016. Also certain is that Trounstine will leave her readers with deeply personal questions about how best to deal with juvenile justice."
—**Chris Zoukis**, award-winning incarcerated writer and author of *College for Convicts: The Case for Higher Education in American Prisons*

BOY
WITH A
KNIFE

BOY WITH A KNIFE

A STORY OF MURDER, REMORSE, AND A PRISONER'S FIGHT FOR JUSTICE

JEAN TROUNSTINE

ig PUBLISHING

NEW YORK, NY

Printed in the United States
First Edition
10 9 8 7 6 5 4 3 2 1

Ig Publishing
Box 2547
New York, NY 10163
www.igpub.com

Library of Congress Cataloging-in-Publication Data

Names: Trounstine, Jean R., 1946- author.
Title: Boy with a knife : a story of murder, remorse, and a prisoner's fight for justice / Jean Trounstinc.
Description: New York, NY : Ig Publishing, 2016.
Identifiers: LCCN 2016005389 | ISBN 9781632460240 (paperback)
Subjects: LCSH: Reed, Karter Kane. | Murderers--Massachusetts--Biography. |Prisoners--Massachusetts--Biography. | Criminal justice, Administration of--Massachusetts. | Youth--Effect of imprisonment on--Massachusetts. | Social justice--Massachusetts. | BISAC: SOCIAL SCIENCE / Penology. | SOCIAL SCIENCE / Sociology / General. | LAW / Criminal Law / Sentencing. |TRUE CRIME / Murder / General. Classification: LCC HV6248.R44 T76 2016 | DDC 364.152/3092--dc23
LC record available at http://lccn.loc.gov/2016005389

ISBN: 978-1-63246-024-0 (paperback)

For Karter Kane Reed and his family

CONTENTS

INTRODUCTION

There is another Lady Justice, less well-known than the fair-minded goddess that adorns our courthouses. She is "Lady Justice Red," a distortion of the icon in robes and blindfold. Lady Justice Red is not the impartial arbiter of cases that come before her.[1] Instead, she looks away from whatever she is judging. Her robes are blotted with blood. She "sees what she is paid to see," her vision blurred behind bright red goggles.[2] Her sword lacks the acuity to cut through the evidence for and against those who appear before her. Rather than reason, Lady Justice Red relies on dice, cupped in one side of the Scales of Justice, which she rolls when judging the unfortunate.

And so it was, in a country ruled by Lady Justice Red, that sixteen-year-old Massachusetts high school sophomore Karter Kane Reed was charged with first-degree murder and ultimately sentenced to life in an adult prison. According to the *Boston Herald*, on April 12, 1993, Karter "stormed" into a high school classroom and stabbed an unarmed boy named Jason Robinson, also sixteen years old.[3] The reasons why evolved for Karter as he understood more about himself, but the facts were distilled by many news sources into this: Karter Reed, along with two friends, arrived at a local high school to finish an earlier fight, and their actions set off a firestorm in the quiet town of Dartmouth, Massachusetts. Something had, as Karter himself later professed, gone "horribly wrong" in his life.[4]

While Karter's stabbing of Jason Robinson is not in dispute, the penalty for the crime is. Karter was tried and convicted as an adult, sent to prison for the rest of his life, with only the possibility of obtaining his freedom after serving fifteen years. At the time of Karter's sentencing, the United States was a country that set controversial boundaries where childhood ended and adulthood began in terms of criminal responsibility.[5] Until 2005, the US was the only nation that still sanctioned the death penalty for youth.[6] Unlike 194 other countries, the United States, along with Somalia and South Sudan, were the only ones (and still are) not to ratify the Convention on the Rights of the Child, an international treaty designed to protect children from a variety of abuses—including forbidding a life sentence without the possibility of parole.[7]

At the time of Karter's arraignment, prosecutors could suggest, and even insist, that sixteen-year-olds were incapable of change, ignoring what science has since proved: that teenagers are not little adults, psychologically, physically, or socially.[8] Teens who killed could be transferred to the adult system, where they would mix with the general prison population—that is, if they weren't kept in solitary confinement, to protect them from rape and other bodily harm. Notably, these imprisoned youths were often refused the benefit of education or therapy, programs that are more available in the juvenile system; nor were they protected from psychological harm.

Today, more than twenty years later, we have learned that it is wrong to treat kids as if they were little adults, no matter what crime they may have committed. Yet many of the same policies that impacted Karter Reed back in the 1990s continue to affect incarcerated youth today. On average, approximately 250,000 youths are currently processed in adult courts each year, a large number for drugs, burglary, theft, and property crimes, as well as for violent acts.[9] While the age of adulthood in all states but New York and North Carolina (as of 2015) is eighteen, juveniles as young as twelve in Colorado can be tried as adults for capital crimes.[10] Of the 250,000 facing adult imprisonment, the Sentencing Project reported in 2013 that 10,000 had been convicted of crimes that occurred before they turned eighteen, and subsequently resulted in life sentences behind bars.[11] These are boys and girls, barely having earned their driver's license, too young to vote, too young to legally buy alcohol or cigarettes, who are locked away with adult men and women. This, in spite of the fact that 90 percent of juveniles, even those convicted of murder, grow out of criminal behavior as they age.[12]

Part of what makes this practice unconscionable is that teens who are convicted and sentenced as adults actually have higher recidivism rates than those sentenced to juvenile jails; that is, they are rearrested and returned to prison more frequently.[13] It is not that juvenile jails don't have their problems too, but teens in adult prisons suffer dire consequences. They are thirty-six times more likely to commit suicide than those in juvenile detention facilities.[14] They are one hundred percent more likely to face physical assault by staff than those in juvenile placements.[15] They are often labelled "felons" for life, receive less support from families, and far less in the way of counseling, medical care, and education; and when they're released, finding jobs is more difficult.[16] Putting young people in state prisons essentially silences them, or as Massachusetts Juvenile Justice Jay Blitzman wrote, "Most committed juveniles do not have access to prisoner rights projects, institutionalized methods of legal redress, or other advocacy; their association with court appointed counsel, in most instances, ends when they are sentenced and the lawyer has filed for his/her reimbursement."[17]

Karter Reed at sixteen was a pretty ordinary figure—slight build, dirty-blonde hair, meticulously groomed, wearing the style of the era in baggy pants and an oversized shirt. A skateboarder who often bombed with girls, he was being raised by his mother Sharon; his father, Derek, was in prison for dealing cocaine. In his own words, Karter was a "good kid." He wrote in 2008, "I didn't drink, smoke, sell, or use drugs. I'd never been suspended from school, wasn't in a gang, and certainly wasn't known for getting into fights. I occasionally made the honor roll, and usually had perfect attendance. I often babysat my two little sisters, and had been an altar boy, and was poised to become the first in my family to attend college."

Because of his youth, Karter Reed at age sixteen was not so different from many of the other 250,000 young people who today face adult courts. Their criminal responsibility is real, but it must be framed by age, as well as how race and class have impacted the US punishment system. In *The Growth of Incarceration in the United States,* scholars Jeremy Travis and Bruce Western, give us insight into Karter's crime, writing that such acts must be "embedded in the context of social and economic disadvantage."[18] However, the kind of harsh sentencing that Karter faced as a young white man—in his case, a life sentence—has been meted out most unfairly to youth of color across the US.[19] At every step of the process, beginning with arrest and ending with whether or not a juvenile will be held in an adult state prison, blacks, Latinos, and Native Americans receive harsher treatment than whites. Black youth comprise 62 percent of those sent to adult courts, and are nine times more likely to receive an adult prison sentence than white defendants.[20] In spite of the fact that states have been collecting data on these inequities since 1974 through the Juvenile Justice and Delinquency Prevention Act, most have still not taken the important extra step to address preventing racial injustice in our punishment system.[21]

Although Karter is not a person of color, his story is still important, as it is deeply rooted in the landscape of juveniles facing harsh sentencing and punishment. The researcher and activist Nell Bernstein found that "between 80% and 90% of all American teenagers in confidential interviews acknowledge[d] having committed a delinquent act serious enough under the law to get them incarcerated."[22] Karter's crime was no simple delinquent act, but his story shows the universality of young people swept up in the madness called "tough on crime." Karter faced a justice system where a Massachusetts juvenile judge once said: "You ask why detention is so high. Some judges would say they use it as a teaching tool for kids."[23] However, as studies have shown, such "lessons" have backfired: sending juveniles to adult prisons doesn't make us safer.[24]

Karter's trial occurred almost twenty years before *Miller v. Alabama,* the 2012 decision in which the Supreme Court declared that sentencing juvenile murderers to life behind bars with no possibility of parole violated the Constitution's ban on cruel and unusual punishment. The importance of *Miller* to Karter's case—and to many others—is that juveniles often take plea bargains so they won't end up in prison for life, or face jury trials where the prosecutor seeks a first-degree murder conviction. Under *Miller,* the mandatory sentence of life without parole is no longer required by law for juvenile first-degree murder.[25] In spite of this ruling, as of 2015, fourteen states still set no minimum age in their bylaws for trying and sentencing children as adults.[26]

Joshua Rovner, State Advocacy Associate at the Sentencing Project, has pointed out that of the fourteen states that allow the sentence of juvenile life without parole (JLWOP), not all use it, including New York, Maine, and Rhode Island.[27] But some states changed their laws after *Miller,* adding many years before parole eligibility, and could be seen as out of compliance with a ruling that inferred that young people have the capacity to change.[28] Requiring a boy or girl to serve a minimum of forty years before they become parole-eligible hardly seems in the spirit of giving juveniles a serious chance at release.[29] This is the case in Texas and Nebraska. Almost as bad are the thirty-five years required by Florida, Pennsylvania, and Louisiana. (The international standard for incarceration of juveniles for the most serious crimes is ten or fifteen years prior to parole eligibility.[30]) Thirty-five or forty years prohibits a meaningful opportunity for review to those youth who demonstrate that they have earned parole.[31]

There has been some positive change in this country's attitude towards harsh policies for youth since Karter went to prison. The inhumanity of juveniles serving time in solitary confinement is an example. Solitary, where one can spend at least twenty-two out of twenty-four hours a day locked up, gained particular attention after the case of Kalief Browder shocked the nation. Browder was arrested at age sixteen for robbery, a crime he said he never committed.[32] He spent two years in solitary confinement during his three years at New York's notorious Rikers Island jail complex, where he tried to hang himself twice; he had been abused by guards and other prisoners, not to mention the agony he suffered from isolation—all this despite the fact that he had never been convicted of a crime.[33] After his release from Rikers in 2013, he wrestled with all of the scars suffered from being a youth incarcerated with adults, and he hung himself less than two years later.[34] While California passed a bill to limit youth solitary in 2015, as of this writing, only seven other states limit its use.[35] Likewise, as policymakers struggle with how to treat juveniles in light of recent Supreme Court rulings, the use of practices designed for adults (e.g. shackling kids when they are transported to or appear in court) have come into question.[36]

By November 2007, Karter had served nearly fifteen years of his life sentence and was someone who Robert Kinscherff, a psychologist who testified on Karter's behalf during his trial, called "a poster boy for success."[37] While behind bars, Karter had educated himself, read hundreds of books, stayed away from the troublemakers and sexual predators, and succeeded in every program he could participate in, from barbering to emotional awareness. He dreamed of what he would do if he earned parole: become a sociologist, help his stepbrother grow up, find someone to love and start a family with. And, every day, he thought of the boy he had killed. A few weeks before his parole hearing in 2008, he wrote, "I am torn between the dreams I have for myself and my family, and the thoughts of dreams I've stolen from another family."

Karter's story itself makes the argument why we must stop incarcerating juveniles in adult prisons. Kids are hardly incapable of change. This has led many activists, families, prisoners, and organizations like the Annie E. Casey Foundation to ask if our society will ever give up its incarceration model for youth and embrace "a more constructive, humane, and cost effective paradigm for how we treat, educate, and punish youth who break the law."[38]

The trend has been mixed in many states, which have continued to pass bad laws in response to brutal crimes.[39] This is, in part, because a horrendous crime draws outrage from the press and an outcry from the public, and then we tend to legislate by anecdote.[40] Stories can be used for political advantage by the powers that be, and before we know it, the need for change, and in some cases, vengeance, turns too quickly into ill-conceived laws.[41] For example, in 2014, Massachusetts passed harsher juvenile sentencing laws for first-degree lifers, setting parole eligibility between twenty and thirty years, allowing that a youth as young as fourteen could receive thirty years before parole eligibility if he was found guilty of a heinous murder.[42] This was a reaction to the

Diatchenko v. District Attorney ruling, the groundbreaking 2013 decision by the Massachusetts Supreme Judicial Court which struck down all sentences of life without parole for juveniles.[43]

In 2014, Karter went with me to see State Senator William Brownsberger, then head of the Judiciary Committee, to protest the impending changes in the law. Karter told Brownsberger that many of those youths sentenced to JLWOP will grow up and age out of criminal behavior while others will dramatically change behind bars. He spoke out for second chances. But he was unable to stop the punitive attitude that still has hold all across this country.

I first met Karter Reed by mail in November 2007. He'd come across a book I'd written, *Shakespeare Behind Bars: The Power of Drama in a Women's Prison,* and wanted to know if I could help a friend, a female prisoner who wanted information about parole.[44] I was no longer working at the women's prison in Framingham, Massachusetts, where I taught and directed plays for almost ten years, but Karter could not have known that. He was merely reaching out to a name on a book jacket. Although he did not say so, when I received that first letter, I thought that perhaps Karter wanted help for himself, too.

For more than twenty years I'd worked with women in the criminal justice system and believed the theory of the journalist Adrian Nicole LeBlanc, who coined the phrase "a woman behind bars is not a dangerous man."[45] I was suspicious of male prisoners, imagining them to be stereotypically brutal and aggressive, i.e. *dangerous*.[46] I had never received a letter from a young man sentenced to prison for second-degree murder. I thought long and hard about whether to answer someone who said he had recreated himself in prison but who in news articles had been condemned as a "monster," carrying out a "methodical crime."[47]

Perhaps I would send just one reply. But then another letter followed, and soon another. Pulled in by his language, a little awed by the quality of the books he'd read, and genuinely shocked that a sixteen-year-old could be sentenced to life with only the possibility of ever getting out of prison, I began to correspond with Karter. We each wrote more than one hundred letters after that first one in November 2007. The content of Karter's letters inform much of this book, and his thoughts and insights helped me understand what a person sentenced as a child goes through behind bars. The discrepancy between the man I saw in his letters and the boy described by prosecutors, the press, and school officials in the town of Dartmouth urged me to reconsider how I thought about juveniles who kill.[48]

While writing this book, I met Karter in person five times. The first was in January 2008, when I took students to the state prison for men in Shirley, Massachusetts, to hear Karter and several other convicted murderers talk about their botched lives, what brought them to crime, and the difficulty of change behind bars. It was that meeting, and the swirl of questions about justice that resulted from it, that drew me in to writing *Boy with a Knife.* I wondered: Would these once-juvenile murderers ever get out of prison? Or would they face parole boards that felt pressured to respond to victims' rights advocates who resisted paroling prisoners, and to the communities who wanted no part in their return? And: Would these prisoners ultimately end up living behind bars for the rest of their lives, even if they had not been sentenced to life without parole? What would it mean to take on a system that insisted on keeping young people locked up in spite of personal transformation?

But it was the doggedness of Karter Reed, the way he kept at his own case, his self-development, and his belief that everyone deserves a second chance, which persuaded me to share his story, and show how it connects to our country's harsh policies for juveniles who commit violent crimes. Karter refused to settle for anything less than what he felt was justice. He had the support and inner strength to face the consequences of his actions and was not crushed by unjust punishment. In some circles, one might call him just plain lucky. But those who know Karter and the criminal justice system would argue that he is an example of overcoming the odds. He floundered and failed along the way, but eventually he was able to beat Lady Justice Red at her own game.

I

If you can look into the seeds of time,
and say which grain will grow and which will not,
speak then unto me.

William Shakespeare, *Macbeth*

1. MEETING KARTER

For many kids in New Bedford, Massachusetts in the 1980s and 1990s, the world was a minefield. They saw fights in school and at home. In a 2009 letter, Karter wrote that it was "common" for high school students to attack junior high kids. Even when he was jumped in school—and he was jumped five times before he got to high school—Karter said, "I just took a beating . . . I never threw a punch." As a result of this environment, however, Karter felt he needed a knife for protection.

Karter's first knife was given to him by his father. It was a double-edge non-folding style with a leather sheath. Karter later obtained other knives. Once he stole a paring knife from a silverware drawer at a friend's house because he had to walk home through an unknown neighborhood and didn't feel safe without it. The knife he owned when he was sixteen was a buck knife, a folding type with a fixed blade. Karter had gotten it from a friend in a casual exchange for a couple of donut holes. It was four or five inches long, and Karter preferred to carry it with the blade open in the pocket of his pants or shirt. He didn't mind if it stuck holes in his clothes; he knew that this knife—advertised as being designed for opening boxes or cutting twine—was his security.

With a knife in his pocket, Karter took his place among the one in three adolescent boys who, in 1993, were armed when they went to school.[1] Some students felt that school had become a frightening place and saw weapons as the answer to bullying; others carried a knife to harass or to intimidate; still others relied on weapons to please their friends or to command respect.[2] Before the proliferation of security monitors, metal detectors, and emergency notification systems in schools, a few students in the nearby town of Mattapoisett kept sticks with a ball and chain in their lockers.[3] Across the country, others stashed guns in their cars.[4] While Karter was fascinated with guns, he wrote in 2008, that "to get one in his neighborhood, you needed money and to know the right people." Thus, he settled on a knife in his pocket, making what he later called in an essay he wrote behind bars, "a devil's bargain."[5]

In January 2008, when I first visited Karter in prison, I knew little about knives and even less about the rough-and-tumble lives of teenagers from New Bedford. I had received five letters from Karter in which he wrote freely about all that he had done to transform himself in prison over the past fifteen years. In one of his letters, Karter invited the community college class I was teaching, *Voices Behind Bars: The Literature of Prison,* to visit him in prison. Several of the students, a culturally diverse group struggling financially as well as academically, agreed to take the hour trip, in spite of the fact that the semester was close to ending. They wanted to meet Karter Reed, a convicted murderer. And, I have to admit, so did I.

It was a bitterly cold winter day and we were bundled up in parkas, boots, and an abundance of wool as we piled into cars to head for the Massachusetts Correctional Institution–Shirley, forty-two miles northwest of Boston. At the time, MCI-Shirley held 1219 of the approximately 11,000 men and women serving state sentences in Massachusetts; the facility was meant to accommodate slightly more than half that capacity.[6] The prison had opened its doors in the 1970s, and by 1991, it housed prisoners who were considered minimum- and medium-security risks.[7]

My students and I had been invited by Karter to take in a presentation by Project Youth, a statewide program run by prisoners. The program functioned as a more civilized version of the popular 1970s documentary *Scared Straight!*, which aimed to frighten kids from committing crimes by having them come face to face with prisoners. Participants in Project Youth meant to educate, they told us, not terrorize. Karter was one of the organization's leaders at MCI-Shirley. The visit was authorized by prison authorities who wanted the public to believe that the punishment system was able to rehabilitate prisoners. But, as former prisoner Ronald Day said to graduates at a 2014 Cornell prison education ceremony behind bars, "Few people are rehabilitated in prisons. Fewer still are rehabilitated by prisons. But a few rehabilitate themselves in spite of prison."[8]

The prisoners gravitated to Project Youth for several reasons: to face their crimes; to gain value from teaching others; to experience humanity amid the prison's stone walls; and to share remorse. Prisoners told their stories to students, who, frankly, were some of the only people who would listen to them. Correction officers allowed the programs, though some quietly sent the message that we should be suspect of everything we were told. I was fairly certain the participants in Project Youth would be forced to screen out any controversial comments that disparaged the prison. Still, I hoped that the men might dispel the stereotypes of hardened convicts, and that my students might see the faces behind the crimes.

Upon arriving at the prison, we found a squat building that served as the entry point where visitors were searched. My students joked with one another that they were grateful not to be asked to lock up their hats, gloves, and scarves along with their jewelry and wallets. Crossing a patch of frozen yard, we entered the main prison block. Inside, the space was boxy and barren, far from noise and commotion; more like an anteroom, but typical of the undistinguished modular units popular these days in prison construction. Nothing but an occasional instructional poster hung on the walls. Cold light shone on the row of hardback chairs set up for the prisoners. In this no man's land, between inside and outside, the prison held programs with students from the free world.

We took our seats across from a row of nine prisoners who sat about twenty feet away, all dressed in prison blues. Karter sat at the end of the row. I recognized him immediately from photos I'd found while searching the Internet about his crime. At thirty-one, he was not much older than my students, though his face had aged from that of the fair-skinned, sandy-haired boy he was when he was first sentenced to life in an adult institution. He watched us with curiosity.

The event began with a man who identified himself as "Boogie." Boogie strolled back and forth in the space in front of us, and, like a comic, tried to loosen up the somber-faced audience with a few jokes about being incarcerated. He said he was a thirty-eight-year-old, 100-percent black man—that made everyone laugh. He then gave us a rundown on what we were going to hear. We settled in, enrapt, as if watching a show. Boogie didn't say why he had shot and killed a rival gang member at age nineteen in a turf war over drugs. Just that he had done it. Then he said he had been sentenced to life with no opportunity of parole. That revelation took the air out of the room, the fact that this man in front of us would likely die in prison. That year, 8.7 percent of state prisoners in Massachusetts were serving a life sentence without parole, four times the national average.[9] By 2015, 1009 prisoners out of 9670 were serving a first-degree life sentence in the state, close to 9.5 percent.[10] It was difficult for some of my students to comprehend death, much less death behind bars.

After Boogie was finished, an Asian man stood. I guessed him to be about twenty-two, though his unravaged face suggested that he could have been as young as seventeen. At that time, Massachusetts still prosecuted seventeen-year-olds in adult courts, and if found guilty, the boys did their time in adult facilities.[11] This would change in 2013, when the criminal age of responsibility would become eighteen.[12] (As of 2015, nine states are still holdouts on this point.[13]) The young man did not move from the front of his chair as he unwound a story of gangs, guns, and drugs, and of being turned in by his buddies, who made a deal with the federal authorities. I'd heard this story before, of young kids who got involved in drugs, with one tapped to turn in the supposed kingpin. He also said he had shot someone in a drive-by in Lawrence, Massachusetts. The admission elicited audible gasps in the room, as Lawrence was next door to Lowell, not far from many of my students' homes.

We heard several more stories like this. Some of these men had been incarcerated for more years than many of my students had been alive. Most had come from poor families; drugs and alcohol permeated their lives. Almost all had been abandoned by someone—parents, children, or spouses. They were not making excuses. They recognized that their actions had killed another person. But it was hard to know the losses they caused and to see their humanity at the same time. A kind of grief permeated the room as the stories unfolded. One speaker stated it simply when he said that if he had only one word to describe what prison life was like, that word would be *loneliness*.

Karter watched each man closely, and I watched Karter. He alternated between nervously hunching over in his chair, eyes darting around the room, and seeming relaxed and comfortable. He nodded and smiled when a fellow prisoner's line provoked laughter, enjoying this space outside his daily life, away from the early wake-up, chores, chow, and isolation.

By the time Karter rose, the last to tell his story, everyone knew who he was. He moved silently to the center of the room. He had rolled up the sleeves of his light-blue shirt very precisely. He still looked so much like the boy in the courtroom whose picture I had seen—a teenager in an overly large striped shirt, with a shock of hair almost covering his eyes. He spoke without really looking at anyone. But as he eased into his talk, I detected waves of vulnerability in his choked-up voice. He took us into his past, and before we knew it, we were in a classroom in a Dartmouth, Massachusetts, high school in 1993.

It is not an exaggeration to claim that what I heard next changed my life.

Karter's presence at MCI-Shirley was no anomaly; it was entwined in our country's complicated history of dealing with children in conflict with the law. The way our policymakers have imprisoned juveniles stems directly from whether or not we see youth as different from adults, and if we afford all children the same rights whether rich or poor, white, black, or brown.[14]

The early American settlers were influenced by their British legal forebears in policymaking, specifically in determining when youth ended and adulthood began. The eighteenth-century lawyer William Blackstone, who in 1753 explicated English doctrine in his Commentaries on the Law of England, saw the intention of "malice" as defining the age of youth culpability.[15] Blackstone and his peers attributed some children, no matter their age, as having "vicious will."[16] Blackstone wrote: "One lad of eleven years old may have as much cunning as another of fourteen. . . . Under seven years of age indeed an infant cannot be guilty of felony; for then a felonious discretion is almost an impossibility in nature: but at eight years old he may be guilty of felony. Also, under fourteen . . . if it appear to the court and jury, that he . . . could discern between good and evil, he may be convicted and suffer death."[17]

Sentencing young people to death didn't sit well with everyone, however. In 1787, Quaker reformers set up the first penitentiaries as a way to deal with "the moral disease" of crime.[18] Boston College law professor Sanford J. Fox wrote that these early prisons in Pennsylvania and New York "reduc[ed] the number of offenses that warranted the death penalty and introduced as an alternative periods of long-term incarceration."[19] Long-term incarceration meant isolation. But there were severe drawbacks to solitary confinement as a way to achieve reflection and penitence.[20] There were other systemic problems as well. In one Philadelphia prison, there were "subterranean dungeons for those under sentence of death," and "in one common herd were kept by day and night prisoners of all ages, colors and sexes. . . . Parents were allowed to have their children with them in jail, and these youthful culprits were exposed to all the corrupting influences of association with confirmed and reckless villains."[21]

Because housing young lawbreakers with adults created a "classroom for crime," chaos resulted in these early prisons.[22] Children of prisoners might seek a life of crime if reformers did not make changes; these reformers wanted to separate neglected and criminal youth from adult prisoners.[23] Their solution in New York, and soon after in other states, was to "rescue" children by forming Houses of Refuge, where pre-delinquents or those not beyond help, so-called "proper objects," could be saved from "pauperism" and "criminal conduct."[24] In 1825, "child savers" opened the New York House of Refuge, initiating what Nell Bernstein called "a mechanism for gaining control over children of the poor . . . a race- and class-driven enterprise intended explicitly for 'other people's children.'"[25] The child-savers could choose to save some children and abandon others, as reform was never intended to be across the board for all children.[26] Dr. Alexander Pisciotta, professor of criminal justice, spelled out how white children (mainly boys) were incarcerated until they were twenty-one, and how reformatories meant schooling, religious instruction, and an apprenticeship by a "racist and sexist" guardian—the state.[27] Such institutions could be profitable. Oliver Warner, Secretary for the Commonwealth of Massachusetts, reported in 1865 that the income earned by labor from its child charges at the Boston House of Reformation was "considerable."[28]

The concept of *parens patriae*—the doctrine that gave the state power to serve as guardian and allowed courts to intervene in the lives of neglected and criminal children—was first judicially recognized in the US in 1838, though blacks and girls were treated differently by this so-called benevolent baby-sitter.[29] Blacks were trained for menial positions and barred from admission to reformatories until a separate reformatory for them was opened in 1848; girls were trained for their "proper place" in domestic positions or as wives.[30] *Parens patriae* allowed the court to decide the juvenile's "fitness for treatment, and that meant it was at the court's discretion."[31] By the middle of the nineteenth century, some parents protested children being taken from their homes, as it was clear by now to the public that children who were poor were often lumped in with those who were delinquent.[32] A report by the Boston Bar Task Force on Criminal Justice stated that the philosophy shifted from "a religious and educational approach to an emphasis on providing a better family life and vocational training."[33] But localities varied greatly on which kids were sent to adult prisons and which went to a not-so-benign foster home or training school.[34]

The first juvenile court was created in Chicago in 1899, and the movement spread rapidly across the United States.[35] In 1906, Boston's juvenile court was created.[36] Early juvenile courts were known for being non-adversarial and more relaxed than their adult counterparts, though the juvenile judges' wide discretion created problems, as they had the power to order children to group homes or shelters without clear evidence that the child had committed a crime.[37]

Even as the seeds of a juvenile court system were being sown, the fear of youthful lawbreakers and the need to punish them—and in some cases, punish harshly—never disappeared, no matter what rehabilitative models developed.[38] As a result, the adult system was never totally off-limits for children.[39]

To understand Karter Reed's story, we must leave MCI-Shirley, where my students and I sat stunned in a kind of pained wonder. We need to go back down the highway, past the fast-food restaurants that have sprung up along a once-quiet Route 2, and head fifty-four miles south, to a world far from Boston and its renowned universities. Past rural towns, each with sturdy pride in its distance from the bustle, with no-nonsense names like Ashland, Holliston, and the more affluent Dover; we bypass the busy high-tech belt of Route 128 that tightened in the 1990s when the tech market bottomed out. This drive leads to old roads with dim highway lights where cars race to get home or campers veer away from Cape Cod. Route 24 turns into Route 140, angling past the town of Fall River and ending in a narrow strip bordered by water. Here we find New Bedford, the city of ships where Karter Reed was born.

After I met Karter at MCI-Shirley, I visited New Bedford several times between 2008 and 2012 to learn more about the place he came from. Karter once wrote in frustration about his hometown that "there's absolutely nothing [t]here but drugs, guns, and crime." His statement was partially right. The first teen in Massachusetts tried and convicted of murder in an adult court was from New Bedford: Antonio Ferrer, a fourteen-year-old charged in 1992 with shooting a man.[40] Only two years before Karter's crime, in 1991, New Bedford was deemed by the FBI as "the most violent city in New England."[41]

Called "Heroin Heaven" in 2009 by a user on the crowd-sourced *Urban Dictionary,* New Bedford has certainly seen its fortunes change dramatically over the last few hundred years.[42] Back in the 1700s, it was a quiet New England fishing and farming village. Barely a century later, the city had become a top-notch whaling port and manufacturing hub. In his 1851 classic *Moby-Dick*, Herman Melville described New Bedford's "patrician-like houses" and "opulent" parks and gardens as some of the most striking in America.[43] However, even back then you could already see the discrepancy between the haves and the have-nots if you looked closely at Melville's Spouter Inn, which he describes as a "dilapidated little wooden house" that "looked as if it might have been carted here from the ruins of some burnt district."[44] Even "the swinging sign had a poverty-stricken sort of creak to it."[45]

While whaling sagged a few years after New Bedford had formally incorporated in 1847, the textile industry aided the city's economy.[46] The population burgeoned as hopefuls arrived to work in the mills; the Irish, French Canadian, and Portuguese joined the Native Americans, Africans, Azoreans, Cape Verdeans, and Brits who already dotted the city's landscape.[47] Long before federal officials tore into the Michael Bianco textile factory in 2007 and arrested approximately 360 out of 500 workers, separating mostly Central American "illegals" from their children for deportation, we might have heard Karter's words in a 2008 letter without a trace of irony: New Bedford was a place "hospitable to immigrants."[48]

By the late 1880's, New Bedford pulsed with industry. At the height of its prosperity in 1920, there were seventy mills producing high quality goods for twenty-eight cotton companies.[49]

Unfortunately, this was the calm before the storm. In 1928, a labor strike paralyzed the city, as 20,000 workers rose up against the mill owners because the over-production of goods was cutting their wages.[50] The workers were out for six months, and many had to take pay cuts to get their jobs back. Then the Depression hit. Tens of thousands of jobs in the textile and apparel industries disappeared and the exodus out of the city began, and New Bedford's economic health grew weaker. Important manufacturers moved to states where cheap labor was readily available.[51] Fishing commerce provided the one bright light, but it wasn't enough to help New Bedford attract new industry. While other parts of the state began to expand, the city's population declined. That decline and the loss of business destroyed any chance of recovery. Industries in aerospace, electronics, defense, and medical research headed elsewhere.[52]

By 1993, while most of Massachusetts was coming out of the recession that had begun in the late 1980s, economic improvement was still nonexistent in New Bedford.[53] The city had no champion to drag it out of its financial plight, no Senator Paul Tsongas to help secure federal monies to remodel its mills—as did Lowell, another gateway city that had once boomed with textiles and manufacturing. Called "gateways" because immigrants looking for the American Dream had settled in these older industrial areas, the towns of New Bedford, Lowell, Lawrence, Worcester, Springfield, and others were labeled the "tenements" of the state, providing cheap housing to new inhabitants and minorities.[54] For this distinction, these cities were looked down upon and often ignored by those in power. When Governor William Weld formed the Hispanic Advisory Commission in 1993, not one representative from southeastern Massachusetts was appointed, despite the large number of Hispanics residing in the state's southeastern cities.[55]

While New Bedford was struggling for recognition and support to help its citizenry during the twentieth century, the fledgling system for juveniles was undergoing transformation. The idea that children's conduct was strongly influenced by their social and familial environments had gained favor.[56] Proponents of a separate juvenile system expressed concern that because children were not the same as adults in terms of accountability, they did not deserve the same punishment.[57] This stance would later find support in brain development research showing that adolescents are different from adults, but this was still far in the future. Instead, children were seen as more influenced by their surroundings, and some, able to change their ways.[58] All of these notions would be considered and challenged as the century progressed, and teens like Karter would be caught in the crossfire.

In the early part of the twentieth century, a family-like atmosphere was what administrators strived for in juvenile detention facilities.[59] But equitable care for all juveniles continued to be a myth, as children with criminal offenses were seen to have behaved "wickedly."[60] As of 1921, the state of Massachusetts could send those between the ages of fifteen and twenty-one to any facility, including to adult courts if they were accused of a crime punishable by death or life imprisonment.[61] It would take until 1948 to modify this and restrict at what age a child could be sent to adult court; that year, the state would give jurisdiction to a Youth Services Board, forerunner of the Department of Youth Services.[62] The idea that permeated the system was still parens patriae, a sort of father knows best, in spite of charges of racism in foster homes and, at other placements, complaints of "whips, paddles, blackjacks and straps."[63]

Juvenile courts of the period were to emphasize the youthful nature of those who came before them. Across the country, children in these courts were "adjudicated," not tried and sentenced as in an adult court of law. But scholar Sanford J. Fox said that in spite of its goals, "It was clear that juvenile courts were really deciding criminal responsibility."[64] Children had limited civil rights compared to adults. Justine Wise Polier, a New York judge, wrote that "youth charged with offenses sat for hours in airless waiting rooms. Noisy verbal and physical battles had to be broken up by court attendants. The hard benches on which everyone was forced to sit and the atmosphere, like that in lower criminal courts, resembled bullpens more than a court for human beings."[65] In the 1930's and 1940's, legal activists began challenging the powers given to juvenile court judges.[66]

The middle part of the century would see changes in laws regarding juveniles, what rights they should be afforded, and the courts that held jurisdiction over them. In a 1948 decision, Supreme Court Justice William O. Douglas challenged what Massachusetts Judge Jay Blitzman called "the closed world of juvenile court."[67] Douglas said the Fourteenth Amendment meant that no child could be deprived of life, liberty, or property without due process of the law, and "prohibited the use of a coerced statement made by a juvenile in a state court."[68] In 1966, the case *Kent v. United States* gave juveniles the right to a hearing before a judge prior to being transferred to an adult court.[69]

Other due process rights for juveniles were gained—and lost—through cases that came before the Supreme Court. A 1967 case, *In Re Gault* attempted to assure that due process would be followed in the juvenile courts.[70] With Gault, Justice Abraham Fortas said "Neither the Bill of Rights nor the Fourteenth Amendment is for adults alone," and juveniles gained—again, on paper—the right to counsel, the right to confrontation/cross-examination as well as the right against compelled self-incrimination.[71] However, in 1971, the ruling in *McKeiver v.*

Pennsylvania, prohibited youth from having a constitutional right to a jury. It was feared that "such a step would signal the beginning of the end for juvenile courts."[72]

As juvenile crime and homicide rates rose in the 1980s, those who considered children as culpable as adults, i.e. "criminals who happen to be young . . . responded to the realities and perceptions of youth violence by facilitating the prosecution of children accused of violent crime as adults."[73] Karter Reed had no understanding of the charges soon to be levelled at his kind in the 1990s by political scientists such as William J. Bennett, John J. Dilulio, Jr., and John P. Walters: "America is now home to thickening ranks of juvenile 'super-predators'—radically impulsive, brutally remorseless youngsters . . . [t]o these mean-street youngsters, the words 'right' and 'wrong' have no fixed moral meaning."[74] While this ideology would be proven wrong, the policies it inspired would proceed into the twenty-first century.

The concept of criminal court transfer was one of such policies. Transfer—when a juvenile is sent to the adult court system, loses his status as a minor, and becomes legally culpable for his behavior—is still in dispute today.[75] We know now that transferring juveniles to adult courts has not made us safer, as juvenile transfer laws have been proven to be ineffective at deterring crime and reducing recidivism.[76] And yet, legislatures in nearly every state have expanded transfer laws to allow or require the prosecution of juveniles in adult criminal courts.[77] In 2015, forensic psychologist Robert Kinscherff, who testified for Karter at his trial, pointed out that our current policies have "criminalized" children.[78]

The house on Hillman Street where Karter spent his teenage years was gray-blue with bright blue shutters. There was a Portuguese bodega across the street, a common sight in this part of town called the West End. Although there were some single-family homes, most everybody lived in what Karter called "three-story tenements or projects." The area was known for having the largest share of New Bedford's eighteen federally and state-funded housing developments. While Karter was growing up, Cape Verdeans, Dominicans, and Puerto Ricans intermingled uneasily with the older Irish immigrants—boys cracking jokes while hanging out in doorways of bodegas, looking for something to do instead of going to school. There were language barriers and cultural boundaries.

Karter, born in 1976, lived primarily in the West End, where he wrote in 2008, in one of his first letters to me, that "few had driveways, much less garages." The West End was in the middle of the city, and Karter said families in that area lived "paycheck to paycheck." They were as overwhelmed by drugs and crime as those who lived in the North or South End, which Karter described as "equally poor." But even the well to-do Sassaquin section and some of New Bedford's downtown with its elegant restored old mansions were a far cry from the more affluent areas of Dartmouth, a town barely four miles down the road.

By 1990, of New Bedford's nearly 100,000 residents, over 6,500 were Hispanic, mostly from Puerto Rico but also from the Dominican Republic, Mexico, and Central and South America.[79] About 87 percent were white, including the many Irish, Welsh, German, Polish, French Canadian, Scotch, and Portuguese Americans who had migrated for work, hoping to leave poverty behind in their homelands.[80] About 12 percent were self-described as black, meaning not only African Americans but also Cape Verdeans, Azoreans, and Pacific Islanders. The remainder included a small minority of Asians and Native Americans.[81]

Longtime residents became devoted to the city, as often happens in neighborhoods where associations seek to assist struggling citizens and help police rout out troublemakers. In 2011, a year after my first visit, I met Loretta Bourque, who at age ninety still ran a community group in her neighborhood. She bemoaned how even during the Great Depression, everyone in New Bedford got along better than they did in the 1990s.[82] But like many who were born in the city, she had chosen to stay, believing in New Bedford's potential. So, too, had Helena Marques, a Portuguese immigrant who grew up in the city and ultimately became executive director of the Immigrant Assistance Program, whose goal was to aid immigrants in adjusting to their new country.[83] As a girl, she had once been picked on at Keith Middle School—the same school Karter attended—for being an immigrant.[84] Marques was all too aware of how stereotyping unfolded. The city's mocking nickname, "New Beige," was a play on the way the town's name supposedly sounded to the first Portuguese people who stepped foot in "New Beigeford."

Ken Resendes, another leader of a local neighborhood group, said that in the era of Karter's crime, tension flooded the city more than in later years.[85] I met Resendes in a New Bedford Dunkin' Donuts, and he talked about the historical separation of neighborhoods. He agreed with Karter that poverty was widespread in New Bedford, and that the North End had always been the safest neighborhood, claiming the newest and best-kept houses. In the South End, drugs had infested the streets. He drove me around that part of the city and pointed out old mills, restaurants, and churches that looked weathered and desolate. Suspicious fires at a small company had left several grass lots burned black, and boarded-up storefronts stood next door to falling-down businesses with names like Squeaky Clean Laundry. In infamous Weld Square, before an attempt at a cleanup, prostitutes mingled among the many elderly residents while kids played in the street.

The revitalization of New Bedford's waterfront had begun in the years I visited, and a spring day meant the smell of the sea and the sound of seagulls overhead. The downtown wharf area would soon pulse with restaurants and nightlife. The city worked hard to preserve its historic buildings and advertised its actively growing seaport and shipping industry. But in 1993, the Whaling City's renowned fishing industry had been decimated by drug use.[86] According to Hans Schatte, a local journalist, part of the problem after the recession of the late 1980s was that the city government failed to develop a recovery plan.[87] *The Standard-Times* ran Schatte's long exposé calling for the need to educate the city's residents and train them for a new job market. In the year of Karter's crime, fewer than half the adults aged twenty-five years or older over had a high school diploma. Fewer than 9 percent had earned a bachelor's degree, and most college graduates moved away. Fall River's Bristol Community College would not develop a satellite campus in New Bedford until 2001, and for many residents the newly established Dartmouth campus of the University of Massachusetts was too expensive. According to Schatte's article, New Bedford's historical dependence on low-skilled jobs had "shredded" residents' "ticket to the middle class."[88]

This economic dead end showed up in the exodus of businesses from the area. Between 1985 and 1993, twenty major employers moved away: Goodyear Tires, Stride Rite Shoes, and Morse Cutting Tools, many having been offered tax incentives in other states or choosing to ship jobs overseas, where labor was cheaper.[89] While Boston had developed over 445,000 jobs after the recession, in New Bedford the unemployment rate was more than twice what it was in state capital[90]—the tenth-highest in the nation.[91] Without work and accessible educational opportunities, local populations suffered; poverty always lurked around the corner and crime was not far behind. Community members, barely scraping by, experienced rising levels of petty theft and aggravated assault, both attributed to the economy.[92]

From Karter's letters and his parents, Sharon and Derek Reed, I learned about how he and his family fit into this picture.[93] Sharon was a blend of Irish and Polish, while Derek was of Irish, Portuguese, and Native American descent. Karter's father's family had made its way to the "city of ships" from Tennessee, while his mother was born and raised in New Bedford. The couple first met in 1975, at a party. At nineteen, Derek, with his charismatic smile and lanky athleticism, was an obvious bad-boy type. He already had two children with one woman and a third on the way with another. He had done time for armed robbery, but he was not yet on hard drugs—that would happen after one of his best friends died suddenly by drowning, followed by the death of his mother.

Sharon, whose surname was coincidentally also Reed, grew up a few blocks from the Hillman Street house. She said that although she was just seventeen years old and knew that Derek was living with another woman in the projects, she ignored all the warning signs. He complimented everything about her, from her gazelle-like body to her long hair that fell in a sheet across her back. They began dating and, not long after, moved in together. Months later, on June 6, 1976, when Derek was twenty years old and Sharon seventeen, Karter was born. He was premature, weighing only 3.7 pounds. Both Sharon and Derek told me they adored their child. But Sharon had essentially grown up without a mother, and Derek without a father. Karter would later say that "although [his] mother and father did the best they could, they had no idea how to be parents."

Despite the difficulties and the poverty, early on they were a happy family. Derek said Sharon was the best thing that ever happened to him, and Sharon believed her new husband would finally settle down. After Karter was born, their daughters Katie and Karla came along in 1979 and 1985. Derek found steady employment working the second shift for a rope company. He took Karter four-wheeling, advised troubled neighborhood kids who were motherless or fatherless, coached Little League, and took the family on occasional vacations. Karter said that everyone loved his parents: "If they knew you needed school clothes, they'd get them for you."

Sadly, the good times wouldn't last; by 1993, Derek was in prison, having been sentenced to eighteen to twenty years. He'd been busted near Cape Cod in 1991 after selling ten ounces of uncut cocaine to an undercover agent for $6,000. Sharon had thrown him out for the third and final time just before the arrest, determined to forget how he had once attacked and choked her, then beat the neighbor who responded to her cries for help. She was drinking a lot and had a new boyfriend, whom Karter hated. Aside from babysitting other people's children, Sharon wasn't working, and without Derek's income—some of it coming from drugs—the family was on the edge of being evicted. Karter's world was falling apart.

Then came April 12, 1993.

2. THE DAY BEFORE

At 3:30 p.m. on Easter Sunday 1993, Gator Collet pulled up in his gray Hyundai and told Karter that their friend Nigel Thomas was going to fight Shawn Pina. Karter had known Gator since they were five, and the two had grown particularly close at Greater New Bedford Regional Vocational Technical High School (known as the "Voke"), which they had both attended until recently. Before moving a few miles away to Dartmouth, Gator had lived right around the corner from Karter. The two were often mistaken for cousins, a fact that annoyed Karter when publicity about his crime later hit the newspapers.

Outwardly, the boys seemed fairly ordinary. With a few other neighborhood friends, they played street games and climbed trees. They first named themselves the "Bloodhounds" until they realized that bloodhounds were floppy-eared dogs and in no way ferocious. So they became "The Wrecking Crue," after a Nintendo video game, and their mischief escalated to include dumping people's trash on the sidewalk, egging cars, and stealing video games from the mall. One summer, they accidentally set fire to an abandoned boat in the woods. They were not caught, the woods did not go up in flames, and no one was hurt.

Such antics could be considered typical of many adolescents trying to impress one another with macho cool. However, a 2012 report by the Sentencing Project which surveyed the lives of more than 1500 juvenile lifers found that frequent exposure to violence both at home and in the community, problems in school, familial incarceration, and relationships with delinquent peers were common in their formative years.[1]

From an early age, Karter went along with Gator's schemes: "He was content to take the blame; I was content to let him," he later wrote. Studies show that antisocial boys are often drawn to those who are aggressive and can negotiate challenging situations or provide protection;[2] becoming friends with Gator may have made Karter feel more visible and accepted.[3] Psychologists at his trial would later posit that Karter's "absent" and "idealized" father might have led to his being influenced by Gator.[4] Without a father present, children are more likely to follow the lead of what law professor Solangel Maldanado calls "their anti-social peers."[5]

Gator had always been more outlandish than Karter. With sunken eyes and a shaved head, he courted the image of the tough guy. Some claimed he delighted in the skinhead look and called him "racist";[6] Karter thought his friend mainly enjoyed having a reputation, whether positive or negative. Gator hated his given name, "Jeremy," and took his nickname from his skateboarding hero, Mark Rogowski, who reinvented himself through skating as Mark ("Gator") Anthony. (Forget that Rogowski had raped and murdered a woman or that he was diagnosed with bipolar disorder upon entering prison—to boys like Gator, he was a rock star.[7])

Gator was the kind of student who infuriated most teachers, as he loved to buck authority. Some of his fellow students believed he idolized the mass murderer Charles Manson.[8] School administrators said he was a bad influence on his friends.[9] Karter wrote in 2008 that Gator once joked to the school psychiatrist about hearing voices, a prank that resulted in a not-so-funny stay at Pembroke Hospital, the local psychiatric facility. Although he had once been a straight-A student, by high school, Gator refused to obey fundamental school rules, such as reciting the Pledge of Allegiance. When Gator said that he was a Nazi who didn't recognize the US flag, his instructor, a war veteran, wanted him to be suspended. After a string of similar antics, Gator was asked to withdraw from the Voke in late 1992, before being officially expelled.

In January 1993, Gator, then sixteen, transferred to Dartmouth High School, where he continued to push buttons. It was there he met fifteen-year-old Nigel Thomas, a freshman, who he introduced to Karter. A friendship eventually formed among the three youths, cemented by similar backgrounds and troubled childhoods, The three boys were called the "skateboarders" by other students, and many at the school viewed them as a gang.[10] After Karter's crime, some of the more incendiary press added to this incorrect notion, calling Karter a member of "the skaters," youths who supposedly wore low-riding pants, baggy T-shirts, and hoodies and who favored a mixture of rap and heavy metal music. "Many of them crop their hair or have their heads shaven," wrote the *Boston Globe*.[11] The 1991 cult film *Video Days* had reinforced this stereotype by portraying skaters as rebellious nonconformists.

In fact, skateboarding for Karter and his friends was a way to be unique; with skating, they could be free outside while inside their worlds were crashing around them. Karter had started skateboarding in junior high, in part because he loved the thrill and the challenge. He also felt there was not a lot to do in New Bedford but skip school, smoke cigarettes or weed, drink alcohol, and commit petty crimes (mostly breaking and entering), none of which really interested him. Also, Karter had no car, and skateboarding allowed him to explore the city. On boards as well as on bikes and on foot, he and his friends ventured everywhere: east to downtown's "Mickey D's," a building arranged like the deck of a ship whose bathrooms were labeled "Gulls" and "Buoys"; to the North End; and even into neighboring Freetown, south to the beach, and west to the mall.

Like Karter and Gator, Nigel had also faced his share of minefields growing up. Before he was ten, his parents divorced, after which his mother remarried a man with two sons. When she died of cancer in 1988, Nigel's biological father moved to Denmark, leaving Nigel in the care of his stepfather. A month or so before the murder, Nigel, who never recovered from his mother's death, told Gator that his stepfather was physically hurting him and that he had filed an abuse complaint against him under the federal Child Abuse Prevention and Treatment Act.[12] The accusation was especially serious, considering that there were no corroborating abuse charges from his half-brothers, and that Nigel's biological father lived abroad and had not been active in his son's life since the divorce. Without a caretaker, Nigel might end up in foster care. Gator thought of Nigel in some ways as a younger brother, and the abuse infuriated him.

After Nigel filed the abuse and neglect complaint, the Department of Social Services became involved.[13] Karter wrote in 2008 that Nigel asked Gator if he could move into his house, as long as DSS agreed. Gator's mother, a bank teller, and his father, a grocer, willingly offered to take Nigel in; word was that the Collets planned to seek custody.[14] Karter felt sorry for Nigel, whom he believed had been devastated by his home life. He wrote that Nigel "often went to school with bruises and black eyes." One time, he saw the boy being picked on at a convenience store when a so-called friend opened a package of oatmeal cream cookies and stuck one on Nigel's forehead. That image held fast for Karter: Nigel was a scapegoat. For Karter, Nigel's rejection and Karter's own self-professed inability "to tolerate injustice" were a fierce combination.

Also stored in Karter's mind at that time was footage from *The Outsiders*, a 1983 film based on S. E. Hinton's classic teenage novel from 1967. It was Karter's favorite movie. The film, called a "librarian's dream" when it went from being a best seller to the screen, made its way into many US junior and senior high classrooms across the country; for Karter, as for many boys of the era, the story spoke of justice.[15] Karter believed with all his teenage being that Ponyboy and his brothers, whose parents die in a car crash before the film begins, are doing the right thing even while breaking the law: as members of the Greasers, they promise to defend their buddies in street fights and from abusive adults no matter the cost. They stand up to a rival gang; they struggle against jealousy and social status. Ultimately, even the law sees their well-meaning ways. About *The Outsiders*, Karter wrote, "I wanted to be the hero, standing up to the bad guys and saving my friends."

So, Karter felt no qualms when, a few weeks before Easter Sunday 1993, the Collets sat down with him and Gator and told them they needed to keep watch over a fragile Nigel. Even though Nigel wasn't one of Karter's closest buddies, he, too, deserved protection. Just as in *The Outsiders*, Gator and Karter clung to the idea that loyalty was key to friendship. At sixteen, Karter needed a creed. He yearned desperately for something to believe in.

The desperation Karter was feeling in the spring of 1993 had begun some years before, as highlighted in this line from one of his letters in 2007: "My earliest memory is being abandoned by my father." This recollection was of the first time Derek left the house for work and did not come home, a pattern that would repeat itself many times and add to Karter's insecurities. When I asked Derek about this in 2011, he wept, thinking about how he had hurt his son. But in the early 1990s, Derek Reed was in the clutches of cocaine. "I wish I could take it all back," Derek said, and speaking about his son: "He always got the short end of the stick."[16]

It wasn't just Karter: no one in the family had an easy time of it, even before Derek was arrested in 1991 and sentenced to eighteen to twenty years in jail, His drug use had been out of control for months before his arrest, and he blew thousands of dollars on cars, jewelry, and furs—extravagances that Sharon admitted she liked in spite of herself. She and Derek fought continually, their fights usually involving kicking and screaming, often sparked either by Derek's drug use or his affairs with other women. For her part, Sharon retaliated by having an affair with another man and abusing alcohol. There was never enough money for the household. Sharon wished she could have protected her son from the clawing anger between her and Derek, a man she truly loved but never married. Karter hated their fights. He remembered times when he and his sisters stayed with friends or relatives until the situation calmed between his parents. Yet amid all the chaos, Karter went to school as if nothing was happening.

A 2010 study by scholars Bruce Western and Becky Petit showed that 2.7 million US children under the age of eighteen were forced to face a parent's incarceration; that's one in every twenty-eight, an increase from one in 125 in 1995.[17] (For black children, the stats are even grimmer: one in nine loses a parent to prison or jail. [18])This loss has been compared to death in the eyes of a malleable child.[19] Those youngsters have a wide variety of traumatic responses: they are more likely to do poorly in school, turn to drugs, develop mental health issues, have a pervasive sense of apathy, lose trust, are susceptible to risky behavior, and experience shame and social stigma.[20] In many cases, kids of the imprisoned try to hide the trauma of parental arrests, convictions, and incarceration. While some act out, or end up suspended or dropping out of school, others, like Karter, mask the pain.[21] It wasn't until years later that Karter discovered the wisdom of sociologist Jackson Katz, whose groundbreaking documentary

Tough Guise showed how many broken boys learn at a young age to put up a guise to protect themselves from their feelings.[22] They succumb to the belief system that equates manhood with invulnerability; they act "tough."[23]

By April 1993, Karter was feeling upset much of the time, and knew his life was a mess. Complicating matters was the anger he felt for continuing to love his father despite being abandoned by him. He was also embarrassed that his family was unable to afford school lunches, so much that he refused a free lunch pass; instead, he borrowed change, went hungry, or stole snacks from the lunch line. Talking about his feelings was out of the question; discussing his emotions was not something Karter knew how to do. So he told everyone he was "fine," and that it didn't bother him that his father was in prison.

Karter had always been taught to tough it out, no matter what happened to him. There was the time when his mother left the five-year old Karter with a babysitter while she and Derek partied at a friend's house. Karter remembered a trip with the babysitter to a nearby convenience store and a pleasant ride in a shopping cart. All of a sudden, the sitter let go of the cart, thinking it would be fun for the toddler, but Karter found himself spinning out of control down a hill. The cart crashed with him still in it; his leg was bent in half, crushed in the middle of his thigh. It hurt—the leg was broken, it was later discovered—but he tried not to cry. There was also the time in seventh grade when he was beat up by a boy who "was looking to pummel some younger victim." Karter wove between parked cars until he was caught, thrown to the ground, punched, and kicked. He yelled for help but nobody came.

Teenagers who experience violence in the home and in their communities often react in extremes. For example, some may do poorly in school, while others feel obliged to always get straight A's.[24] Sometimes, their low self-esteem leads to poor social skills, and they may feel responsible for siblings and/or an abused parent. But children are also resilient, and when violence frequently erupted around Karter and wove its way through his memories, he always managed to keep the hurt inside and stay out of major trouble.

It is not surprising then, to learn that children with incarcerated parents frequently have trouble with attachments.[25] Although they cannot acknowledge it without shame, they experience their parent's incarceration as a rejection of them, and are often afraid to let themselves get close to anyone else.[26] This may be, in part, because many incarcerated parents are very involved in the lives of their children before their imprisonment.[27] With a parent behind bars, families are split apart, and the child begins to feel like he or she is also doing time.[28] Caretakers left behind often do not have enough time for the family, or sufficient finances to manage the home.[29]

After his father left, Karter started to create elaborate fantasies as he walked through dangerous neighborhoods. He imagined both attacking and being attacked, but always with the same goal, as he wrote in 2008: "to end up a hero." Sociologist Jackson Katz writes about how "We live in a culture that connects manhood to . . . a willingness to use violence at the deepest levels of men's identity, telling young men that is the first, and preferred, method of proving you're a man."[30]

A Cape Verdean, Shawn Pina attended Dartmouth High. A teacher would later tell me that in a school that was 90 percent white, Shawn struggled to fit in.[31] About a week before that fateful April day, Shawn had verbally insulted Nigel's mother, and while this was not reported in the media, Karter wrote that

Shawn called her a "whore" and said that he had "fucked her." Nigel warned Shawn to stop saying such things—his mother was dead—but Shawn continued, daring him to do something about it.

While Karter had been a victim of bullying himself, he did not shy away from bullying others. After one boy in his junior high all-white clique was ambushed by a group of African American kids in a neighborhood lot, Karter's group rounded up a random black boy to exact revenge, despite knowing that he was not among those who had done the beating. As they pushed the terrified boy around, Karter yelled along with the crowd: "We know you were one of them. You think you're tough with all your boys, jumpin' white boys?" Finally, Karter realized how scared the child was and, without losing face, said, "Forget it, he's not one of them." The clique walked away, but Karter thought at the time, that maybe he had been too "chicken" or too "soft." He wrote in 2011 that it would be years before he realized that he had been driven by "anger, frustration, resentment and powerlessness." By senior high, the code was clear: Karter and his friends could not be "weak" in any situation. Show courage for your men. Be strong. Don't back down.

By 4 p.m. on Easter Sunday 1993, Karter was piled into the backseat of Gator's car, along with Shad Sacremento and his girlfriend, Beth Streck. Shad was nineteen; by age twenty-one, he would join the military.[32] He was also a skateboarder. Karter looked up to Shad and was glad to have him along—he was wiry and a good fighter. Karter knew that Shad had been in trouble a few times, that his mother, a police officer, had recently thrown him out, and that he was staying across the harbor in nearby Fairhaven with Beth. Hard-hitting and pretty, Beth loved all the Boston sports teams and attended Fairhaven High.[33] The group drove off to do what they believed was the honorable thing: to give Nigel a chance to fight with the boy who had picked on him one too many times.

Upon arriving at Shawn's house, the group discovered a couple of Shawn's friends outside. They told them that Nigel wanted to fight one-on-one to settle the score. "One-on-one" was important to these boys. It meant that each person was pulling his own weight and could stand up to provocation by boys as tough or tougher than they were. It was part of a code of fair fighting, by which you took on your own battles, individually. With a one-on-one fight, people could cheer from the sidelines, but no one could participate except the fighters.

Shawn's crew crowded around the car, harassing Beth verbally, which angered Shad.[34] He jumped out of the Hyundai. Some witnesses said he picked up Gator's metal baseball bat, and, wielding it, chased the guys down the street.[35] But Shawn never mentioned the bat in his testimony at the trial. He said Shad chased them until Shawn's friends ducked inside his house.[36] There was yelling, an attempt to get them to come back outside by the boys in the car, but no one budged.

Finally, the five drove off. Shad and Beth decided to opt out, and after Gator drove them back to Fairhaven, the remaining trio sped back toward Shawn's. When they turned down Shawn's street, they saw a bunch of boys waving sticks or bats—Shawn Pina said there were five, while Karter said twelve or fifteen—daring them to get out of the car.[37] That's when Karter realized they were in too deep. They just kept driving; to get out of the car would have risked too much.

Later that night, Karter, Gator, and Nigel agreed that they had royally screwed up and were in big trouble. They had wanted it to be over, but instead they had angered Shawn and his buddies and failed to finish the fight. The next day, Shawn and his crew would surely be waiting for them at Dartmouth High. The boys prized loyalty above what some might say was rational thought: what happened to their friends happened to them. That night, they made a deal. Although they were supposed to be in school on that snowy Monday, April 12, 1993, they agreed to go to Dartmouth High so that Nigel could find Shawn Pina and have a fair fight, one-on-one, without all of Shawn's buddies involved.

Karter assured his friends that he had their backs.

3. HOW IT HAPPENED

By their very nature, news headlines are designed to do little more than skim the surface of the truth. But, in their few words, they also can construct a perspective or nudge us towards a particular position.

Take, for example, how Trayvon Martin was represented in 2012. Martin was the unarmed black Florida teen killed in a high-profile case that led to the acquittal of white neighborhood watchman George Zimmerman, in the process adding to the firestorm about racial profiling in the US.[1] NBC News chose the following headline to run during its coverage of the case: "Trayvon Martin Was Suspended Three Times from School."[2] Not only have studies shown that black crime suspects are presented in more threatening contexts than white ones, but also that "news coverage can endorse the invisibility of certain groups and can enhance the visibility of other groups."[3] Headlines have the power to shape our thoughts before we even dig into the text of the article.

The first mention of Karter Reed's crime that I came across during my research touched on how infrequently violent crime visited the town of Dartmouth, Massachusetts. The headline from the April 21, 1993, issue of the *New York Times*, "Model School Tries to Cope with Killing in a Classroom," set up Dartmouth as a world away from urban violence, and Karter as far as possible from being a "model" student.[4]

In 1993, suburban schools were just beginning to face the challenges well known to schools in urban areas such as New

Bedford, where many residents lived on incomes well below the poverty line, were part of single parent-households, and relied on social services to provide healthcare, childcare, and other necessities.[5] Dartmouth was only a ten-minute drive from New Bedford, but the residents in the former thought of themselves as far, far away. According to one-time Dartmouth high school teacher Tom Cadieux, "There was an elitist element to the town."[6] Back then, Dartmouth was home to approximately 27,000 people—97 percent of them Caucasian—with a median income of $45,000, which in 1990 dollars was higher than the Massachusetts state average and almost twice that of New Bedford.[7] In 1989, 5.7 percent of Dartmouth residents lived below the poverty level; by 1999, it was 4.6 percent.[8] The town boasted four golf courses, three country clubs, one yacht club, and the exclusive enclave of Nonquitt, where oceanfront homes are still passed down from generation to generation. Dartmouth's neighborhoods, with names such as Smith Mills, Apponagansett, and Bliss Corner, replete with old clapboard houses, sprawling landscaped yards, and pristine beaches, had always defined traditional New England charm. While the town had its share of middle-class and blue-collar residents, crime was not part of the picture typically painted of Dartmouth.[9]

The town had always prided itself on its famous marching band, sports teams (several professional baseball and football players were among Dartmouth High alumni), and the quality of its schools.[10] Not everything was as it was portrayed to be, however. Although Dartmouth High was considered the best school in the area, it ranked in the middle of the state's public high school schools in terms of achievement scores.[11] The school's graduation rate was only 66.9 percent, compared to the state average of 88 percent.[12] The school had recently enrolled more children of fishermen and construction workers from some of Dartmouth's less affluent areas.[13] Some residents feared that these new arrivals, including a few who had moved from New Bedford, might lower the quality of the school and deter its aim of sending more students to college.[14] Approximately 95 percent of Dartmouth High's students were white in 1993—not surprising, given the population of the town.[15] Although it was not spoken publicly, there were fears that welcoming students who did not fit the typical Dartmouth profile—i.e. "inner-city students," (code for poor kids and children of color)—into the town's schools was a mistake.[16]

Although the attitude in Dartmouth was that "violence doesn't happen here," the years 1992 and 1993 had seen a spike in violent crimes committed by students nationwide.[17] Between 1980 and 1993, the number of teens killed in schools grew, and the juvenile arrest rate for murder more than doubled.[18] Between 1989 and 1993, the number of adolescents sent to criminal court increased 41 percent; and if those juveniles were convicted of violent crimes, they were sent to adult prisons.[19] More boys than girls, more blacks than whites, and more adolescents sixteen or older faced adult courts.[20] This was the era in which William J. Bennett, John J. Dilulio, and John P. Walters would promote their theory of the coming of superpredators, warning that teenage boys from "morally impoverished families," were bound to "murder, assault, rape, rob, burglarize, deal deadly drugs, join gun-toting gangs, and create serious communal disorders."[21] "Kids who kill" would be all over the news in the mid 1990's, terrifying the country into believing that a "tidal wave of crime" was on the horizon."[22] While this horrifying and racially coded message would ultimately be proven wrong, it would cause forty-four states, including Massachusetts and the District of Columbia, to change their laws, making it easier to try juveniles as adults.[23] As Dilulio himself would say years later, while the superpredator theory never came to fruition, it affected the climate of the country: "It was out there."[24]

Despite this environment of fear, trouble still rarely visited Dartmouth, a place that attracted those who wanted to escape urban problems.[25] Many in the town likely believed that violence only stalked schools in "bad" areas like New Bedford, or its sister city, Fall River.[26] And so it was not surprising that on April 12, 1993, the doors to Dartmouth High were unlocked and unsecured. The long, two-story building was unburdened by metal detectors or surveillance cameras. Recent cutbacks in funding had eliminated hallway monitors, and no resource officer patrolled the property or hovered at bus pickups.[27] Such measures seemed unnecessary—crime was low and the town police station usually received only a few calls a day.[28] It was thought that a simple "No Trespassing" sign near the school's front door would be enough to keep out those who had no business there.[29]

At 7:15 that morning, Gator, Nigel, and Karter were in Gator's Hyundai on their way to Dartmouth High School. Snow was falling outside, and Karter was wearing a maroon and yellow hat, the one Nigel had worn the night before and disposed of after two girls teased him about it, saying it didn't match his clothes. Karter also had on a blue shirt and jeans. His open knife was in his right pants pocket. He also had a piece of a wrench in his left pants pocket—a rod, similar to a metal pipe. He thought that if the other boys had weapons, these would protect him.

Gator cursed the cracked distributor cap on his car as snow pelted the windshield. Moisture from the rain and snow kept causing the car to stall, and the Hyundai hiccupped down Route 6 into Dartmouth. Karter later told me he was praying that one of them would say, "Let's forget it." But no one said anything as they turned onto Slocum Road, the street that led to Dartmouth

High, and parked in a no-parking zone not far from a sign that read, "Buckle Up—It's the Law."

Inside Dartmouth High, the day had begun like any other normal Monday. Teachers were in their classrooms, getting ready for their students. Principal Donald King, who had been in charge for seven years, had not yet begun his affable daily stroll through the building, talking to teachers and students. Before rising to the top position, King had been a student, football coach, biology teacher, and director of guidance at the school, and he was in his office early that morning, before the homeroom bell rang at 7:30 a.m., preparing to meet with the vice principal, Albert Porter, and the chairman of the guidance department, Frederick Sylvia.[30]

There were undoubtedly mixed aspirations for the 1,140 students who headed into the school building that day, gathering around lockers and gossiping with friends.[31] Some were probably hoping to score A's on tests or preparing to give presentations; some were likely worrying about their SATs. Others were possibly thinking of whom they might ask to the prom. Still others probably imagined getting out of school early, hurrying down the spotless hallways and past the glass cases packed with marching band trophies, piling into their cars and high-tailing it to the mall. A few were undoubtedly chatting up their exploits of the night before. No one imagined what would happen over the next few hours.

Karter, Nigel, and Gator entered the school building about 7:30 a.m. Karter said the three of them went in through the main corridor, looked around, and saw Shawn and his friends at the other end of the hallway, who did not notice them. Nigel led the way as he, Karter, and Gator headed upstairs to find their friends in the school; they wanted to find out what was churning in the rumor mill about a possible fight. Karter passed a couple of students who knew him; he took out his metal rod and brandished it, bragging about what he would do if anyone tried to jump his boy. At this point, Karter felt a kind of energy from showing off, acting as if he was accustomed to flaunting a weapon.

It was Karter who saw them first, coming down the hall, heading straight for Nigel. He recognized three faces: Shawn Pina, Duane Silva, and Jason Robinson. Duane was black, and over six feet tall; Karter wrote in 2008 that "he hadn't been there the night before but he was Shawn's boy and we knew he'd be coming." He had seen Duane a few weeks earlier, when he was at the Stop and Shop in New Bedford's South End where Gator worked. After Gator finished his shift, they gave Duane a ride home, along with Shawn. Duane joked about wanting to steal Gator's car stereo. Jason, a thin, white, gangly basketball player, was a friend of Shawn's and had, for a short time, been a student at the Voke. Karter felt that Jason was probably tagging along to watch Nigel get a beating.

There was a lot of commotion in the hallway as the two groups headed toward one another. Diane Tretton, an English teacher at the school, saw Duane and Jason walk purposefully past her classroom.[32] They did not say hello, which was unusual, considering they had been her students. She attempted to follow the boys, but she could not manage to stay behind them as students began to fill the hallway to see what was going on.

Karter had promised himself that if it wasn't a fair, one-on-one fight, he would jump in. But when Duane and Shawn passed in front of him and he realized they were heading for Nigel, he—and Gator—froze. They watched, paralyzed, as Duane made a few nasty comments and threw a punch, knocking Nigel to the floor. Karter said that Shawn then started kicking Nigel. Nigel tried to get up, but Shawn threw him against a locker while Jason cheered him on.

At this point, about twenty-five to thirty students had

crowded into the hallway.[33] Diane Tretton, trying to stop the fight, ran up to Duane and put her hands against his chest, yelling, "Duane, you have to stop! You have to stop!"[34] He pushed her aside and she ducked into the teachers' lunchroom to call for help on the intercom. Lisa DeCuna, another teacher, hearing her colleague's voice, rushed into the hall. She saw that Nigel was bleeding and tried to grab Shawn, who was kicking Nigel repeatedly, by the shirt.[35] Gator then ran over, pulled Nigel up, and yelled at Karter to do something. But Karter could do nothing. More teachers appeared and tried to stop the fight. Shawn and Duane darted one way down the hall, while Gator, Nigel, and Karter went in another direction. The principal appeared, and teachers told him about the fight; he quickly rounded up Shawn and Duane and sent them to his office.[36]

Karter was pushing and shoving people, furious and ashamed for not standing up for Nigel, as he and the other two boys ran out of the building. Nigel's nose and lip were bleeding, and Karter thought Nigel had broken his elbow. Karter belted a mailbox as they headed for the car;[37] he heard Gator yell at the crossing guard to get out of his "fucking" way or he would run her down. In a whirlwind, the three boys sped away.[38] They headed to Fairhaven to get Shad, whom they felt would know what to do. For Karter, it was all about defending a friend, and he had failed.

At Shad's house, Nigel went inside to wash off the blood. Shad quickly went to the car and said he could not believe they had allowed this to happen, meaning that they had let Shawn and his friends beat up Nigel without even taking a swing. Karter and Gator sat sheepishly. Neither could explain why they had been so afraid. They begged Shad to go back to the school with them to help make things right, but Shad refused. He had plans; the fight was theirs to finish. He told them to wait until after school.

The boys decided not to wait until the end of the school day—they would return to Dartmouth immediately. But a one-on-one, "fair" fight was no longer possible. Instead, Nigel and Gator would beat down Shawn and Duane, and Karter would keep anyone from interfering, and make certain they could all escape. They would bring Gator's baseball bat and billy club, just to be sure. And, of course, Karter had his knife.

The first classes of the day were about to begin at Dartmouth High. James "Woody" Murphy, or Mr. Murphy to his freshmen American government class, was discussing the recent tragedies in Bosnia.[39] Murphy was a combat veteran of the Vietnam War and a former US Marine who had taught and coached sports for twenty-five years; he had been at Dartmouth for seven.[40] He loved to teach and had a reputation for investing himself in the classroom with the kind of humor and grit kids respond to.[41] He had already heard about the early-morning fight and noticed that two of his students were missing from S57, his social studies room: Shawn Pina and Nigel Thomas.

Shortly after 8:15 a.m., Shawn sat waiting outside the principal's office.[42] Minutes before, he and Duane had been suspended for three days. Duane had already left the school grounds, but Shawn was still waiting to be picked up when from the window he saw two boys running toward the school. He recognized Gator and Nigel, and immediately told one of Principal King's secretaries.[43] She told King that "intruders" had entered the school.[44]

Exactly what was said over the next fifteen minutes was disputed during the public hearings and in the press; there is an element of "he said, she said" to all of it. Karter's sentence was ultimately based not only on the facts of the case, but also on these stories, told in a time of shock by a community in crisis and by media outlets looking for news in a year of escalating school violence. His resulting punishment hardly makes sense unless seen in this context.

The three boys came through the same front entrance as they had earlier and walked down the same main corridor. Karter's knife was open in his pocket; he still had the pipe as well. Nigel had the billy club, while Gator carried his metal bat and a double-edged knife; he was full of bravado, clanging the metal against the floor as he walked.

Jane Carreiro, a foreign-language teacher, had just come out of a classroom and was heading to the main office with her attendance sheet when she saw the trio and hurried behind them, thinking they were late for school.[45] Then she heard the clanging of the bat and called out, "Boys, what are you doing here? State your business." They turned to face her, and Gator thumped the bat on the floor and said, "Go to hell."[46] The three boys then charged up the stairs. Carreiro turned and ran to the main office.

In Karter's recollection, the boys quickly made their way down the white-walled corridor and up the stairs, Nigel in the lead. They were heading to Nigel's American government classroom, where they thought Shawn would be. When they reached room S57, Karter said he felt sick and was sure he would throw up. They had planned to go into the room in mid-lesson, but now they all realized their plan was ridiculous. They were unsure what to do. Karter said that Nigel suggested he jump Shawn when he came out of class. Suddenly, at the end of the hallway, Vice Principal Porter appeared. Gator said he couldn't wait and asked Nigel and Karter if they were ready. Karter replied with some version of "Gator, I don't want to do this, but I won't leave you alone."[47] Gator announced he was going in. As if on autopilot, Karter watched from the doorway as his friend walked into the classroom.

Things moved so quickly that it was hard for anyone to comprehend the sequence of events. The following details spilled out at the trial and from Karter's letters:

Gator, bat in hand, looked around the room and asked aloud, "Where's Shawn Pina?"[48]

Mr. Murphy saw the bat and began unraveling with a "Whoa, whoa, whoa, what's with the bat?"[49] He immediately went after Gator.

Nigel, almost tucked inside his black cap, backed away from the action and moved behind Karter, who was standing at the threshold of the room, watching as Jason Robinson, sitting in the back, loudly responded to Gator's question with "Why?" Karter had always seen Jason as part of Shawn's crew, a boy whom Gator had disliked ever since Jason had gotten into a fight with another friend of his a few years back. Karter did not know that Jason played football, soccer, and basketball, had a sister and a brother, and had just bought a Chevy with money he made as a busboy at the University of Massachusetts resident dining hall.[50] He did not know that Jason was the son of Elaine and Burt, stepson of Cherylann, all lifelong residents of Dartmouth.[51]

Gator started down the row of seats toward Jason, wielding the bat in the air, reportedly saying, "Oh, Robinson, you messed with my boy; you're dead."[52] As Mr. Murphy told Gator to get out, Jason bolted from his seat. Suddenly, Karter felt someone come up behind him, and he held up his hands, then surrendered the pipe he had been holding to Vice Principal Porter, who had come running into the room.

By now, Gator was chasing Jason around the room, the two knocking against desks as if in a pinball game. Jason ran toward the windows, and Karter heard him yell back at Gator: "Fuck you. I didn't touch your boy. I didn't touch him."

Vice Principal Porter pushed Karter aside, shoving him into

an alcove in the room.[53] Believing that Karter was being restrained by others, Porter started after Gator. The class erupted. Students were out of their seats chasing Gator, yelling, making threats that Gator was about to be hurt, "wrecked," "fucked up."[54] Karter said he considered trying to leave the room through a different exit, but when he looked around, he saw that it was blocked by students. He just stood there and watched Jason's pink shirt flash by. Mr. Murphy finally grabbed Gator, and the bat went flying into a corner. Along with his colleagues, Mr. Murphy wrestled Gator to the floor.

By now the tumult was intense. More teachers and students had entered the hallways. Karter began to panic. He said he felt that things were spinning out of control. He was again standing inert, desperately wanting to do something but desperately unable to. He felt an obligation to his friends. He had to act. He headed toward Jason, who was a few feet away.

As the blur of the past built up inside him, and as the shoulder of Jason Robinson pressed against his, Karter reached in his pocket for the knife. He never looked at Jason's face. He did not think about seeking revenge. All he knew was that he must not back down. In one fell swoop, he pulled out the weapon and, as cleanly and swiftly as his sixteen-year-old hand could manage, stabbed Jason Robinson in the stomach.

Karter said he didn't remember how the knife got back inside his pocket. In 2008 he wrote that in the next moment: "I was pinned against the wall with teachers kicking me, screaming, 'Drop the knife,' until they realized I didn't have anything in my hands. I knew I was in trouble but I wasn't thinking about courts or jail. . . . I was thinking that I'd be a hero to my friends."

II

Though justice be thy plea, consider this—
That in the course of justice none of us
Should see salvation.

William Shakespeare, *The Merchant of Venice*

4. JUVENILE JUSTICE

Because he could not fit into the back of the squad car with his wrists cuffed behind him, Karter had to ride from the high school to the police station face down on the seat. At that point, he was unsure what he had been arrested for. He reported this exchange with a police officer to Armand Fernandes, his court-appointed attorney, who unsuccessfully challenged it at the trial.

Karter asked the officer if he could use the bathroom.

"Why? Did you shit yourself?"

"Yes. . . . What do you think the charge will be?"

"Attempted murder."

"That's ridiculous. I didn't try to kill Jason. If you want to kill someone, you stab them in the chest or head."

"What do you think you will be charged with?"

"Assault with a deadly weapon."

"Well, it could be dropped to that."

At the Dartmouth police station, a two-story brick building not far from the high school, Karter was booked for trespassing and placed in a solitary cell. He felt humiliated that his pants were soiled—he had lost control of his bowels the moment he stabbed Jason Robinson—and he washed them out as best he could by flushing them in the toilet. All he could think about was if he would get locked up and have to stay back a year in school. He also worried about what his mother would say. After a few hours, an officer came to his cell to tell him that Jason Robinson was dead. Karter collapsed onto the floor. At the trial, a medical examiner said that Jason had died from a deep puncture wound in the center of his abdomen, two inches above his belly button.[1]

When Sharon Reed came home that morning to her slate-colored house on Hillman Street after helping a friend move, she discovered two messages on her answering machine. The details were fuzzy but she understood that her son was in custody, and it had something to do with Dartmouth High School. Frantically, Sharon dialed the number left by a police officer several times, each time getting a busy signal. She knew the message was from that morning because her machine told her the date and time, but that made no sense, since Karter should have been in school at the Voke. Not owning a car, she called Rosie, Karter's godmother, and was relieved to find her at home. Rosie agreed to give her a ride to the station.

Rosie, her husband, and Sharon drove down the narrow streets, passing shuttered homes and others that looked as if they had been ravaged by fire. Paint was peeling off buildings as it was in many neighborhoods throughout New Bedford. As they drove down Route 6, passing gas stations, tire stores, the old Bristol city jail, and a Dunkin' Donuts, the crowded streets gave way to open spaces. They entered Dartmouth with its sprawling houses, lawns checkered with evaporating snow, and frosted trees. When they reached the police station at 12:45 p.m., Sharon was told that Karter had been arrested for trespassing.[2] Hearing the news of this relatively minor infraction relaxed her a little, and she remembered thinking to herself, *I'm kicking his ass for skipping school.*[3] She asked to see her son and was told it would be awhile. Nearly two hours later, Sharon was led from the reception area to another room at the station and informed that her son was now being charged with murder.

That Monday afternoon, Derek Reed was stretched out on a

bunk watching his cellmate's TV at MCI-Norfolk, a state prison just south of Boston. A "Breaking News in Dartmouth" banner blasted across the screen, showing Karter, Gator, and Nigel in custody while an announcer claimed the boys had been accused of killing Jason Robinson in a school stabbing. Derek stared at the TV, thinking, *No way. I'm the one who gets in fights, not Karter.* He bolted out of the room to the hallway phone to call Sharon.[4]

Of course,Sharon was not at home. She and Karter had been brought separately to a smaller room at the police station, one that looked like a library, with bookshelves lining the walls. "Why, Karter?" she said when she saw her son. "Why would you do something like this?" They both cried, then sat in disbelief while they listened to the charges. Along with trespassing, Karter was being charged with two counts of carrying a dangerous weapon, disturbing the peace while armed, conspiracy to commit a crime, and murder.[5] He could not stop shaking.

When I wrote to Karter in 2008 to ask why, at age sixteen, he gave a statement to the police without a lawyer present, he responded that he had been told by the police that things would go better for him if he cooperated, and he believed that telling the truth would win out. Not only did he know nothing about the juvenile system, he'd had minimal dealings with the police. He had no idea that anything he said could be used against him. He was so naive that, after the stabbing, he asked the police officer who drove him to the station if she thought he would end up on the TV show *Cops*. He had no idea how to proceed, and so, before even seeing his mother, he agreed to give a statement.

This situation is not atypical; teens in custody routinely waive their Miranda rights.[6] Fear of the unknown, or of something bad happening to them, as well as the fact that many are not yet capable of understanding the full implication of the law—all seem to play a part in young people renouncing their Miranda rights.[7]

Some believe they can think through the questions from the police without any guidance, or are worried because a member of their family is involved in the crime. In addition, it is not uncommon for police officers to distrust the word of adolescents, believing they are being deliberately dishonest.[8] According to researchers such as Dr. Allison D. Redlich, police departments are taught to interrogate under an assumption of guilt,[9] and young people are especially prone to manipulation and the pressure to confess.[10]

The consequences in Karter's case were so dire that it would have been better for him to wait for a lawyer before giving a statement. A lawyer has the training to look closely at three components of the juvenile justice system when weighing how much a child should be held criminally responsible: competence, culpability, and change.[11] In other words, as juvenile expert Laurence Steinberg puts it, does an adolescent differ from an adult in their ability to understand all parts of the legal process, from waiving their rights to assisting lawyers in their defense?[12] How are they blameworthy, and how should their psychological and intellectual development play into the determination of their culpability? And, importantly, what is the child's "likelihood of changing his or her behavior, or the odds that he or she will respond to treatment?"[13]

Karter could have also waited for his mother to arrive before giving a statement. However, that may not have made much of a difference, as parents often have little say over their child when they are in custody. While states such as Colorado, Connecticut, and North Carolina require a parent or guardian present during custodial questioning, police can question juveniles in other states without parental presence or notification.[14] A thirteen-year-old in Massachusetts must have a parent in the room, but teens fourteen to seventeen only need a "genuine opportunity to consult" with a parent or guardian.[15] Massachusetts law does not require that the police inform the teen or parent that they can talk in private.[16] In Indiana, a child can give up the right to consult privately with their parent or guardian if they are informed of that right and refuse it in their parent's presence.[17]

Parents may also not fully understand Miranda rights themselves.[18] Some parents fall under the power and pressure of the interrogators, or give incorrect legal advice.[19] A distraught mom or dad might demand answers on the spot and inadvertently subvert the rights of their child.[20] Parents are also not necessarily afforded the opportunity to ask meaningful questions of the police.[21] They are sometimes treated as impediments. If an interrogator decides a parent is overprotective, he or she may be asked to be an observer and refrain from talking.[22] Since kids rely on their parents for guidance, it is unsettling for them when their parents are silenced and the police take over.[23]

The Collets, Gator's parents, hired Edward F. Harrington, who at that time was one of the state's most successful defense lawyers. But Sharon Reed did not know a lawyer to ask—not that she had the money to hire an attorney anyway. Like the approximately 80 percent of criminal defendants who are underprivileged and unable to afford counsel, she elected to have a lawyer assigned to Karter.[24] In Massachusetts, that process occurs through the Committee for Public Counsel Services, where approximately three-fourths of the cases involving indigent defendants are handled by private attorneys paid by the hour, and the rest by full-time public defenders.[25] In some situations, a defendant is found "indigent but able to contribute," and assessed a $150 one-time "attorney fee," which the defendant (or parent) then pays to the court.[26]

In 1963, the US Supreme Court made the right to an attorney possible for indigent clients. *Gideon v. Wainwright* spelled out that anyone accused of a serious crime, no matter how poor, had a constitutional right to a lawyer.[27] But in recent years, that right has deteriorated, most notably in the South, where too large a caseload for underpaid public defenders has led to insufficient, or in some cases, no representation for poor clients.[28] While the right to counsel has not changed, financial realities across the country have burdened those who work for the poor, and burdened the poor who desperately need counsel.

Sharon listened while Karter told the police what had happened. She heard how the three boys barged into the classroom, boys who had slept at her house, skateboarded on her street, eaten dinners she had prepared. She cried on and off for almost two hours, realizing, as she heard Karter say he had pulled out a knife, that it was that knife, the one he carried to school. She listened, but could not comprehend how or why her son had killed a boy.

The following day, after being held without bail overnight in a holding cell at the Dartmouth police station, a dazed Karter was brought into the crowded Third District New Bedford Juvenile Court for arraignment. A youth's arraignment—a formal proceeding before a judge where the accused is charged with a crime—is held in juvenile court. Typically, in a serious crime, the police refer the case to the court, and a prosecutor files charges.[29] This can create problems. Massachusetts Citizens for Juvenile Justice, an advocacy and research non-profit, clarified in a 2011 report the loss of confidentiality for youths who are indicted in juvenile court for a serious offense. According to the report, the child loses the "protections otherwise available in the court: the court's file and the courtroom are open to the public, including the media."[30]

Two years before Karter was arraigned, in 1991, approximately 19,000 arraignments of juveniles took place in Massachusetts.[31] By 1993, the national crime rate began to fall due to reasons that no one could agree on (ranging from a stronger economy to a drop in crack cocaine use).[32] As it declined by half from 1993 to 2014, Massachusetts experienced a concurrent drop in juvenile crime.[33] In 2012, only 6,000 youth were arraigned in courts across the Commonwealth.[34] In spite of fewer crimes, there were still racial disparities: Among those who were arraigned in Massachusetts, black and Latino youth were 1.6 times more likely to be detained than whites.[35]

Historically, the juvenile court in Massachusetts had looked upon teens who broke the law as youth needing direction and guidance, rather than as full-blown criminals.[36] Reform, as well as punishment, were its hallmarks. The system's premise was that those who committed crimes at ages younger than seventeen (eighteen, after September 2013[37]) did not act with the same amount of responsibility as adults, and therefore should be treated differently. But these views altered over time, particularly in the 1990s, when several brutal crimes committed by youth in Massachusetts and elsewhere, as well as fear of a coming juvenile crime explosion, created a spate of harsher laws based on punishment, rather than rehabilitation.

The fear of increased youth crime was promoted by experts like Northeastern University professor and criminologist James A. Fox, who warned in 1990 that "a blood bath of violence" was imminent.[38] Fear was fueled with headlines like these on the front page of the July 18, 1990, *New York Times:* "Number of Killings Soars in Big Cities Across US"[39] In Boston, Philadelphia, Milwaukee, New York City, and nearly twenty other cities, murder rates were expected to keep rising.[40] In hindsight, we now know that murders committed by children ages ten to seventeen actually fell by two-thirds from 1994 to 2011.[41] Looking back, Fox and many others have admitted their errors.[42] But at the time, the refrain by law enforcement officials and district attorneys was that "Our homicide rate is going through the roof."[43] Ronald D. Castille, the Philadelphia District Attorney, said, "It's just raining a hail of bullets out there on the streets."[44]

Politicians and policymakers vowed to stop the violence. Newt Gingrich announced, "There are no violent offenses that are juvenile."[45] The idea in the wind was, "If you do an adult crime, you should do adult time." Lawmakers were calling for punishment to take priority over prevention, treatment, and rehabilitation. In response, many states crafted bills that made it easier to try youth in adult courts. Between 1991 and 1998, 38 percent more juveniles were sent to adult jails.[46] In addition, between 1992 and 1999, every state except Nebraska passed laws requiring adult trials for children as young as fourteen who were charged with murder; in 1997, Kansas and Vermont passed laws that allowed ten-year-olds to be tried as adults.[47] By 1996, Massachusetts would go the way of other states, and fourteen became the age that juveniles accused of murder could be tried as adults. If found guilty, the sentencing to an adult correctional institution was automatic. The United States was on its way to incarcerating more of its young people than any other country.[48]

Many of these harsh laws are still in play today in Massachusetts and throughout the country. In spite of a reduction in youth being held in prisons and jails (a 2006 study found that the number of youth in adult prisons fell 45 percent between 1995 and 2005[49]) the US is still the world's larger jailer of juveniles.[50] On an average day there are approximately 10,000 youth in adult prisons or jails.[51] Because of the Prison Rape Elimination Act, passed in 2003 and fully put into place in 2012, a youth must be protected from sexual violence and not housed within sight or sound of adult prisoners.[52] In some states, this has meant solitary confinement for youth; in others, time in a juvenile jail before completing a sentence in an adult prison.[53] According to

Jason Ziedenberg of the Justice Policy Institute, "the rules around management of juveniles who might end up in jail do not extend to youth who may be transferred to the adult court, and tried in the adult justice system."[54] In other words, for many youth, it has been sink or swim in the prison's general population.[55]

There have been some positive changes in recent years. As of 2015, only two states—New York and North Carolina—prosecute sixteen year-olds as juveniles.[56] Massachusetts, along with Illinois, New Hampshire, Mississippi, Rhode Island, and Connecticut, have raised the age of adulthood to eighteen.[57] The US Supreme Court's landmark 2012 ruling, *Miller v. Alabama,* stated that lawbreakers seventeen or under had "diminished culpability and heightened capacity for change," and that sentencing judges could take the youth's age into consideration even in cases where heinous crimes had been committed.[58] The Court importantly struck down all statutes that required a child under the age of eighteen convicted of first-degree murder to be sentenced to life in prison without ever having the possibility of parole.[59] In Massachusetts, a groundbreaking 2013 decision, *Diatchenko v. District Attorney,* went further, nullifying all sentences of juvenile life without parole.[60] Despite these positive steps, fourteen states still set no minimum age in their bylaws for trying and sentencing children as adults.[61] This flies in the face of studies that have consistently concluded that sending juveniles to adult court is ineffective in deterring crime and reducing recidivism. [62]

At his arraignment, Karter wore a striped shirt, a kind of long-sleeved polo, and pants that were baggy at the knees. He stared at the floor or straight ahead, anywhere but at his mother, who sat nearby. On the other side of Karter, and handcuffed to him, sat Gator.[63] His head was still shaven, although a bit of hair had grown in, and he wore jeans. Nigel was not present; Karter would soon discover that he would be arraigned separately a week later, after his biological father arrived from Denmark.

Karter was in shock. He had been in that state from the moment he arrived at the courthouse. "I was shocked to find the parking lot of the police station crowded with news crews from around the country;" he wrote, "shocked that there were even more waiting at the courthouse; shocked during arraignment to hear the D.A.'s account of what happened; shocked to hear and read the news accounts about the murderous hate-filled, violent teenagers who committed such a heinous atrocity. . . ."

Karter's lawyer, Armand Fernandes, stood by his client's side. Fernandes, a Portuguese-American who grew up in New Bedford, would later become an associate justice in the Bristol County Probate and Family Court.[64] Fernandes was one of the attorneys on the lawyer-labeled "Murder List," those willing to work for little money to defend indigent men and women charged in murder cases.[65] Contrary to common belief, being court-appointed does not mean that an attorney will fail to do a good job. In Massachusetts, assigned lawyers may be among the best private criminal defense attorneys in the area, especially for murder cases, where the stakes are so high.[66]

In 1993, Massachusetts judges still had to decide whether to order juvenile murder cases to be heard in adult proceedings. If Karter had been tried and convicted of first- or second-degree murder in the juvenile system, he could have gone to a juvenile lockup and then, to an adult prison. He could have been sentenced to serve up to twenty years.[67] But that was not what the Commonwealth sought.[68] Assistant District Attorney Thomas M. Quinn argued for Karter to be transferred for trial in the adult system where, if convicted of first-degree murder, he could be sentenced to life without parole, essentially condemned to die in an adult prison.

Quinn was no newcomer to the practice of law. His family included two former judges and a brother who was a state representative. He described the prosecution's version of what had happened to the hundreds of southeastern Massachusetts residents who packed the courthouse, painting "a picture of a methodical crime" executed by violent boys, carried out "without remorse."[69] Quinn's strategy was to set up his description of the crime to ensure that the two-part transfer hearing would lead to a trial in the adult system.

Judge Ronald D. Harper was on the bench. Married with children and grandchildren, Harper had been an attorney in private practice for twenty years before being appointed judge in 1974—in Massachusetts, judges are appointed by the governor and approved by the Governor's Council—and was the second African-American juvenile court judge in the Commonwealth, specializing in adoption cases.[70] He ordered Karter and Gator held without bail in the maximum-security facilities of the Department of Youth Services while they awaited the transfer hearing. Perhaps that wasn't a bad move, considering the threats already swirling around Dartmouth and New Bedford. Police reported an anonymous death threat made to a student, and twenty or so of Karter's and Gator's friends feared retaliation and avoided school on April 13, 1993. The Reeds' house had been stoned the night before the arraignment, and Sharon and the girls were forced to move to Parkdale Housing, a temporary solution.

Harper also ordered psychiatric evaluations for Karter and Gator; later, he would order the same for Nigel, contingent on permission being granted by his biological father. The psych evaluations were extremely important, as they could establish whether the boys were "amenable to rehabilitation." This could play a major part in determining whether or not to adjudicate them as teens or try them as adults. Today, a fair punishment for an adult might be considered unfair when applied to an adolescent because juveniles are presumed capable of change, and a child's level of development colors culpability.[71] Studies have shown that teens are less mature than adults: they are more impulsive, have less judgment, underestimate risks, and are vulnerable to peer pressure. All of that renders them less blameworthy under the law.[72] But at the time of Karter's hearing, Massachusetts law presumed a youth accused of murder was dangerous and not amenable to rehabilitation, so his attorney would need the psych evaluations to convince the judge otherwise.[73]

As more and more stories about the killing appeared in the press, locally and nationally, a narrative began to take shape. Much has been written on the idea of "trial by media," that is, the sometimes disastrous effect that news, TV, radio, and now the Internet have on our justice system. There's often a precarious balance between the public's need to dissect a crime and the accused's need for a fair trial. But because words can quickly shape prejudices and predilections in our minds, Karter Reed became a public figure long before his trial—and "heartlessness" became part of the myth.

The boys evidently had no emotion because during the arraignment they showed no emotion. According to an article in the *Standard-Times,* they "stared straight ahead."[74] The paper also claimed that Karter told Principal King, "I stabbed him, and *I hope he dies,*" (emphasis mine). District Attorney Quinn also reported Gator as saying he was "satisfied with what happened and *he hoped the victim died,*" (emphasis mine). About Gator, whose shaved head surely added to the portrait of the boys as stone-cold killers, the paper quoted Jason Robinson's godfather as saying, "He's got no remorse."[75] Articles emphasized the waywardness of the boys through such headlines as "Moral Compass Goes off Course."[76] A *Boston Globe* article reported that the three boys "stormed" into the classroom, "within a few feet of a poster advising: 'Violence—put a dead stop to it,'" and that "a trail of 27 blood stains on the corridor floor marked the path students took as they carried the dying Robinson up the hallway."[77] Yet another headline from the *Globe* read, "Witness Says Boys Joyful after Murder."[78]

At the time, Karter had not yet been convicted of murder in a court of law. As for his emotional state, Karter told me that he was hardly joyful; indeed, his distressed emotional state clearly showed when he lost control of his bowels immediately after the stabbing.[79] Gator did indeed laugh, but according to a letter from Karter in 2009, his reaction was caused by hysteria, not joy. After being called "Mr. Collet," by an officer, Gator said, "Please address me correctly"; when the officer asked his name, Gator responded with "Jesus Fuckin' Christ." Then he laughed hysterically. Such behavior may be called many things—crazed, certainly, or even horrific—but it was not an expression of joy. Yet this account would be repeated in many different forms, often misinterpreted, but always adding fuel to the flames.

After his arraignment, Karter, handcuffed, rode in a police cruiser to the Judge John J. Connelly Youth Center in the Boston neighborhood of Roslindale, known as "Rozzi Secure." Gator was hauled off to a separate youth detention center, also managed by the Department of Youth Services. In 1993, 1128 youths were awaiting trial in such centers in Massachusetts, a 15-percent increase from the year before.[80] Only a small percentage had been, like Karter and Gator, accused of violent crimes.[81] Overall, the population of juveniles committed to various jails in the Massachusetts Department of Youth Services increased by more than 50 percent between 1992 and 2000.[82] By 2003, Massachusetts committed more kids to secure facilities than thirty-two states.[83]

These locked facilities offer some sorely needed services for juveniles compared to adult prisons, but they have the reputation of being overcrowded and short-staffed.[84] When Karter arrived at Rozzi, youth centers in Massachusetts were so overcrowded that DYS workers had difficulty managing the 50 percent increase in their cases, and an escape attempt made the news in Westborough.[85] Sadly, things haven't changed much in the past two decades. According to a 2011 report by the Annie E. Casey Foundation, "the largest share of committed youth—40 percent of the total—[were] held in long term youth correctional facilities;" these facilities were dangerous, too large, and ineffective, they said, among other criticisms.[86] In Nashville, Tennessee, a history of clashes between juveniles and security guards led to assaults, solitary confinement, a riot, and thirty-two kids breaking out of a youth detention center in 2014.[87]

According to experts, these kinds of incidents happen because locked detention in youth centers is often too similar to the environment in adult prison, facilitating crime, mental illness, and self-harm.[88] Detention is also traumatic for young people, as it disconnects them from their families, interrupts their education, and takes them out of their communities.[89] A number of youth facilities are jail-like, surrounded by barbed wire. Windows and doors are barred just like in an adult prison, and it is not uncommon for jailers to wear uniforms.[90] Nell Bernstein also explains how the "we–them" mentality in many of these facilities harms kids: "If there's no relationship except a punitive and controlling one, there's no room to make any progress."[91] (The Annie E. Casey Foundation launched a nationwide attempt to improve how kids are jailed, and in 2014, the group hailed the Missouri model as one of the most promising, highlighted for promoting safety through relationships, not "correctional coercion."[92])

At the time of Karter's imprisonment, Rozzi offered some education—although not individualized—a little bit of counseling, and a number of recreational activities.[93] The place housed primarily adolescents from inner-city Boston, meaning that a disproportionate number were young black males. Today, across the country, a black child is almost five times more likely to be locked up in a juvenile detention center than a white child who commits the same crime.[94] Girls suffer in particular, because the detention system was designed with boys in mind; this is a particular hardship for girls' mental health, since 90 percent have experienced abuse, be it emotional, physical or sexual.[95] Isolation rooms, shackles, loss of privacy, strip searches, bright-colored jumpsuits, or rules that prohibit makeup can be particularly traumatic for girls.[96]

As Karter exited the Rozzi intake area—horrified at having to undergo the strip search—he entered the institution's red brick building with barred windows and barbed-wire fences and thought, "A day and a half ago, I was a high school student. Now I've stabbed someone, and he's dead." He was stricken, starving, and too tired to say anything to the other twenty or so detainees. No one said anything to him, either. Later he learned that the boys had not been allowed to watch TV that evening; therefore, they figured Karter's crime was serious, most likely all over the media. He was "a news story" at Rozzi as soon as he walked through the door.

Karter described himself at this time as "mentally catatonic." He had no conception of what would happen next, nor did he realize, as a detective had said in the interview room, "the world of shit" he was in.[97] He could not know that on April 16, back in Dartmouth, a thousand people would file past Jason Robinson's body at his wake.[98] Hundreds would attend his Mass at St.

Mary's, a white-steepled Catholic church in town. Dartmouth High staff and students would wear blue armbands to the funeral as a reminder that "violence hurts." Jason's brother Chad would be one of the pallbearers. Seated in the front pews would be Jason's sister Shauna, his mother, Elaine Brum, her fiancé, and Jason's father, Burt Robinson. Flags in the town would fly at half-mast, and local kids would soon hold a candlelight vigil to call for an end to violence in the area.[99]

5. THE TRIAL

Karter spent the next year at the Department of Youth Services in Roslindale while shuttling back and forth to court. Sharon spoke to her son on the phone every day and visited him three times a week. Only eight visitors were allowed on Karter's visiting list at one time; his father, Derek, who would not get out of prison until 1997, was not among them. During one visit, Karter told his mother how much he wanted to talk to Jason's parents and express his remorse, but Sharon said it wasn't the right time yet

Visitors are a lifeline to children in prison, connecting them with life outside. Studies have shown that prisoners who receive visits are less likely to receive disciplinary reports (D-reports), and less likely to commit crimes after they're released.[1] Even one visit can have a positive effect, particularly if it's from a parent.[2] States vary on visiting policies; a few allow only one per week, such as North Carolina, while others like New York permit daily visits even for their maximum security prisoners.[3] Some prisons have instituted the practice of visitation by video in addition to or instead of in-person visits, which they charge families for—the average in 2015 was $20 for twenty minutes.[4] However, this practice is controversial: after a jail in Austin adopted a video-visitation-only policy in 2015, prisoner-on-prisoner assaults rose 20 percent, and prisoner-on-staff assaults doubled.[5]

Rozzi operated on a system of behavior modification. The idea was to offer points for good behavior; the more points a prisoner achieved, the more privileges he received. Getting a higher allowance, being allowed to do paid work on the unit or having a TV in one's room were some of the rewards for good behavior. This system was also a method of control. If a charge screwed up, he received an "alcove" from a staff member, meaning a writing assignment, done alone in his room with the door open.[6] Nell Bernstein, in *Burning Down the House,* wrote that this system of reward and punishment, still so common in juvenile facilities today, bears a "striking resemblance" to the level systems of the 1860 New York House of Refuge, where kids were kept in line through fear of corporal punishment, and offered badges for good behavior.[7]

During his time at Rozzi, Karter progressed to the highest level of privileges. While he mostly avoided punishment, he was definitely not easy to handle for group workers or teachers. While he followed the rules, he often made it clear that he didn't agree with them; he argued with staff when he felt they were being unfair; he often played Nintendo instead of being social.[8] Karter's negative behaviors—he once spit in a water cooler, tried to overhear staff conversations, winked at a female caseworker, and supposedly fashioned a weapon out of a TV antenna, an allegation he denied—would ultimately be brought up by prosecutor Thomas Quinn at Karter's hearing. Quinn pounced on these incidents and coupled them with problematic behaviors from Karter's time at the Greater New Bedford vocational school. Quinn would say at the trial that Karter was a teen who "took justice into [his] own hands."[9]

One bright spot at Rozzi was that Karter became a voracious reader, a habit that would become a passion and ultimately help him to educate himself behind bars. He started with books that were assignments for class, such as Harper Lee's *To Kill a Mockingbird* and the Arthur Miller play *The Crucible*. One day, a teacher assigned him a chapter from *The Firm* by John Grisham.

Karter skimmed the story of the lawyer who fights for justice when he discovers that his firm is fronting for the Mafia. Karter said to the teacher, "This is stupid. I will never read it." However, when he was on room restriction one day, locked in with no TV or radio, Karter found a copy of Grisham's *Pelican Brief* on his shelf. Having nothing else to do, Karter began reading the book. He read nonstop, transfixed by the tale of the assassinations of two Supreme Court justices. From a fellow resident he later borrowed Grisham's *A Time to Kill*, another story of justice, this one about a young white lawyer defending a black Vietnam vet who murders two white men after they rape his daughter. Karter was hooked on Grisham's stories of good triumphing over evil; eventually, he sheepishly asked the teacher if he could again borrow *The Firm*.

It is ironic that in the movie based on *A Time to Kill*, the defense attorney says that the psychological evaluation will be all-important to setting his client free, as psychological evaluations would be crucial to Karter's own case, serving as the linchpin on which hinged his amenability to change.[10]

That teens are developing physically, cognitively, socially, and emotionally sets their psychological evaluations apart from those of adults.[11] Psychologist Laurence Steinberg would say in 2015 that the adolescent brain's plasticity, coupled with their unformed character, is in large part what makes youth amenable or good candidates for rehabilitation.[12] Despite having the neuroscience to back up behavioral research on teen development, many attorneys today still have to prove that their young clients are not beyond redemption.[13] Back in the early 1990s, however, Massachusetts law had a "rebuttable presumption" that any youth accused of murder was dangerous, i.e. a risk to the community, and not likely to be rehabilitated in the juvenile system.[14] Karter's defense attorney, Armand Fernandes, was faced with the burden of proof, or else Karter would be tried as an adult.

A forensic psychologist who evaluates a child is not the same as a therapist who aims to establish a bond in order to treat a patient.[15] There is no confidentiality in this relationship, since the court seeks an evaluation specifically to make decisions about the case.[16] For a young person that can be disconcerting, as they might not fully understand why the stranger is there and needs detailed explanations from them. Trust is not implicit; and the situation is hardly relaxed. Psychological evaluators need to determine the truth, and sometimes read between the lines, not an easy task when their clients have much to fear.[17] In addition to conducting interviews, evaluators must sift through psychiatric and school records, administer tests, come up with psychological conclusions, and make predictions about the future.[18]

Dr. Robert Kinscherff, the forensic psychologist who testified on Karter's behalf during his transfer hearing, could not have been better qualified. He worked with the Law and Psychiatry Service at Massachusetts General Hospital, as well as for the Boston Juvenile Court Clinic, wrote extensively on juvenile justice, and had served as an expert witness in the Massachusetts court system. On the stand, when asked his opinion of Karter's actions on April 12, 1993, Kinscherff replied that the teen had made a series of bad decisions in the hours leading up to the confrontation, and then panicked once in the classroom. The doctor had come to this conclusion after reading juvenile records, studying psychological tests and police documents, and conducting interviews with Karter—for more than eight hours—and Sharon Reed, the Rozzi high school principal, and three Department of Youth Services workers. He said: "What's remarkable to me in reading the witness accounts, police reports, and Karter's own report is how extraordinarily impaired his judgment was at that particular moment. He initiated an assault at that time when he is most certainly going to be identified visually and certainly going to get caught. This doesn't suggest that he was acting as some sort of predatory reptile sizing up the situation. That's bad judgment."[19]

Kinscherff believed that Karter was definitely amenable to change at a Department of Youth Services facility, a significant determination in that the doctor had testified in six other murder cases involving juveniles, and Karter was only one of two defendants he found amenable to treatment. Kinscherff believed that Karter would respond to education and therapy and an individualized treatment plan, something certainly not possible in the adult criminal system. If Karter went to a secure DYS setting, he would be able to receive these services until the age of twenty-one.[20]

In terms of the other determining factor that could send Karter's case to an adult court—whether he was currently a danger to the community—Kinscherff stated that Karter could be dangerous, under certain circumstances. He added, however, that Karter most likely would never again be in a similar situation as he had been on April 12, 1993, because he was not a "socialized violent delinquent."[21] In other words, his values were not driven by a gang, and he was not interested in using violence to achieve his goals. According to Kinscherff, school and DYS records showed that Karter had not been a major discipline problem. Therefore, he did not consider Karter to be a risk for continued incidences of violence.

In his cross-examination, ADA Quinn clung to the idea of "dangerousness," a concept in the criminal justice system that is coupled with future behavior and therefore, often with punishment.[22] The more dangerous one is deemed, and the more risk of harm their behavior imposes, the harsher the punishment they might receive.[23] Quinn tried to unspool the doctor, asking him if he might think Karter more consistently dangerous if he found out that Karter had premeditated the stabbing of Jason Robinson. While Kinscherff held his ground, he did report that Karter had described carrying a knife for protection, something the doctor believed problematic because "having ready access to a potentially lethal weapon places one at higher risk for a situation where violence may ensue or injury can occur."[24] But the doctor also said that Karter usually relied on running away from confrontation, rather than pulling out his knife. Thus he saw little risk for recidivism and gave several reasons to support his opinion. Karter's intelligence and good verbal skills were two factors. Although Karter had a tendency to be grandiose, the doctor believed the teen knew the crime was no one's responsibility but his own, and did not try to blame his actions on someone else, which many kids do when caught. Kinscherff concluded that Karter would be amenable to rehabilitation in the juvenile system in one to three years.

Dr. Ronald S. Ebert, who was called by the prosecution, also had a long list of qualifications, including positions as the senior forensic specialist at Boston's McLean Hospital and a faculty appointment at Harvard University Medical School. He had testified more than five hundred times in courts throughout Massachusetts, many times on the very question of dangerousness. Ebert examined the same evidence Kinscherff had, and conducted interviews with Karter as well, but only spent about three hours with him, compared to Kinscherff's eight. Ebert's first conclusion was that Karter suffered from mild depression; his second was that Karter's description of the crime did not agree with what he had read in the incident reports filed by police, students, and teachers. Ebert cited the "jovial nature" of the boys after the crime and said that Karter had not fully acknowledged his actions to police. In other words, Karter was manipulative. Ebert also relied on information from his interviews with the teachers and staff at Rozzi. He said they saw a "two-sided quality to Karter," adding, "He was bright. He was engageable. He had a good sense of humor; he was also a handful according to these two teachers. So, that was one bit of information. The staff . . . felt that Karter was a young man that they could not trust. . . . He had absolutely no remorse nor would he develop remorse."[25] It was a damning indictment of the now seventeen-year-old sitting before him.

Ebert was also very convincing in his analysis of one of Karter's writings from his time at DYS. Karter wrote: "I'm past the point of no return. My wrongs cannot be unrighted. But my punishment is unjust. Two wrongs don't make a right but how about three? I wronged another but now I have been wronged by the system. They took everything from me, except my thoughts and memories."[26] According to Ebert, if Karter felt that his pretrial punishment was unjust, then his idea of punishment was totally off-kilter. Ebert did not expressly say that being held in a DYS facility was hardly a tragedy compared to the killing of Jason Robinson, but that sentiment underscored his remarks. Ebert concluded that Karter was not amenable to change in the juvenile system and posed a danger to the public.[27]

Karter's attorney, Armand Fernandes, tried to undermine the effect of the doctor's opinions. He pointed out that Ebert had never talked to Karter's mother to get her impression of her son. He also tried to establish how many of Karter's testing-the-limits and sometimes oppositional behaviors were typical of just being a kid. "Have you got any children, Doctor?" Fernandes asked at one point.[28] There is also a body of research on how traumatic stress can cause detachment or disassociation from one's physical or psychological being, and Fernandes pointed out that possibility during the crime.[29] He got Ebert to agree that in such a state "things seem surreal. They're going on around them like they're watching it on television. They're not there."[30] Research suggests that the incidence of dissociation increases the more severe the crime.[31]

Fernandes also criticized the doctor for having "psychoanalyzed" Karter's writings and his so-called joviality without spending nearly enough time with the teen to come to an accurate conclusion.[32] He tried to discredit the doctor's idea that Karter would not be ready for treatment until he fully accepted responsibility for the crime. But Ebert held to his position: Karter was a danger to the community.[33] And, importantly, he said he believed Karter would not "gain insight into his problems" or "deal with his anger" at a DYS facility by the time he was twenty-one.[34] Ebert was raising the possibility that treatment might never work for Karter.[35]

Fernandes also called to the stand a forensic psychologist from Bridgewater State Hospital, Dr. Frank DiCataldo, who had testified in more than fifteen juvenile transfer cases. DiCataldo's main thrust was that Karter's family background—notably an absent father whom he "idealized"—might have led to his being influenced by Gator,[36] a relationship that "boost[ed] his self-image."[37] It took DiCataldo nineteen hours of interviews and three hours of psychological testing—a bit of one-upsmanship on Fernandes's part of Ebert's three hours—to come to the conclusion that Karter was amenable to change. In spite of Quinn's attempts to get him to say otherwise, DiCataldo held that any writings about death or suicidal feelings did not mean that Karter could not respond to treatment in the juvenile system. In fact, he saw Karter's expression of such feelings, particularly in his writings, as signs that he would be a good candidate for treatment. He called them "self-absorbed adolescent acts," explorations of themes about the "loss of innocence," "disgust with hypocrisy in the adult world," and "self-pity."[38]

• • •

When Judge Harper returned with his ruling on May 3, 1994, more than a year after the crime, and a month before Karter's eighteenth birthday, he did not cite that juveniles were worth treating and educating in our best juvenile systems. He did not stand against the rising tide in the United States that wanted youth lawbreakers punished more than it wanted them rehabilitated. Instead, the judge—who found Nigel Thomas "not dangerous" and "amendable" meaning that he could grow, improve, and correct his behavior—decided that Gator Collet and Karter Reed were "dangerous" and "non-amendable" in the juvenile system.[39] The two teens were immediately bound over to the adult correctional system and ordered to be tried as adults. Before he was even legally old enough to vote, buy cigarettes, or serve on the jury he would appear before, Karter Reed could be sent to prison for the rest of his life.[40]

Waist-chained and handcuffed, Karter rode in a van to the Dartmouth House of Correction.[41] He reported being met by prisoners threatening to kill him—he later learned he had been mistaken for someone else, a child killer—and was immediately placed in a protective custody unit called "Max," short for maximum security, where prisoners were locked up for at least twenty-two hours of the day. Luckily, Karter was there only for one day; keeping youth in solitary confinement has been shown to harm them in ways that are more profound than for adults. Even a short time in a barren box with no windows, where sound reverberates off the walls and a steel door isolates the prisoner, can cause serious pain and suffering.[42] Adolescents are known to cut themselves with staples or razors, have hallucinations, and lose touch with reality while isolated.[43] The reason solitary is harder on kids is because they are developmentally different from adults, yearning for touch, particularly from their parents, and often have untreated mental illnesses, and thus are at a greater risk for suicide.[44] The American Civil Liberties Union reported that "50 percent of all youth suicides in juvenile facilities occurred while young people were isolated alone in their rooms, and . . . more than 60 percent of young people who committed suicide in custody had a history of being held in isolation."[45] The United Nations has deemed it nothing less than torture, and in 2011 called on all countries to prohibit solitary for juveniles.[46]

The rationale for solitary is that it is for the youth's own protection. The Prison Rape Elimination Act requires that juveniles behind bars not come into contact with adult prisoners, but because many jails lack the space or staff to separate teens from adults in a humane way, kids can still end up in what they call "the hole."[47] In a 2011 study, the Department of Justice reported that 61,423 minors were being held in 2047 juvenile facilities, and one in five used isolation; additionally, there were 95,000 more juveniles in adult prisons and jails, many subject to solitary.[48]

In recent years, prison activists have pushed to ban the practice of solitary confinement altogether, with limited success. By 2014, ten states had adopted measures to cut back on the use of solitary, but it was abolished for juveniles only in West Virginia.[49] In 2015, children could still be punished with indefinite solitary confinement in ten states—Alabama, Georgia, Kansas, Kentucky, Louisiana, Michigan, Oregon, Tennessee, Texas, and Wyoming.[50] There are racial disparities here as well. In one New York prison where 70 percent of the segregation unit in 2015 was disproportionately packed with young people, 57 percent were black, 25 percent Latino and 14 percent white.[51] (New York City's Board of Correction voted to end solitary for prisoners under the age of twenty-one, beginning in 2016.[52])

• • •

After one night, Karter was shipped out of Dartmouth. Without knowing why (such entrances and exits are usually not explained to prisoners), he was taken to the Barnstable House of Correction (BHC). Built in 1933, BHC was known for the clang of its door, peeling paint on its walls, and antiquated locks on its cells. It was located next to a railroad track whose trains shook the building every time they passed. When Karter walked into BHC, he said that "some loser" who had apparently seen too many prison movies yelled "New fish!" Karter was placed in a small dorm-like room with ten bunks. He was the youngest person at the facility (although a couple of seventeen-year-olds would come and go during the year he spent there), and was housed with an embezzler, a deadbeat dad, and what Karter labeled as "other unremarkable types."

The men on Karter's tier played cards, watched TV, and worked out in the gym until Barnstable staff closed it due to overcapacity, turning the space into a makeshift housing unit. Karter wrote in 2009 that "all the windows were smashed out in the summer to relieve the oppressive heat." In winter, they taped them with trash bags. Karter occasionally engaged in shenanigans with others close to his age, "being loud," playing football with a roll of toilet paper, and wrestling, but mostly he kept to himself. The unit was constructed exclusively of bars, so when a person wanted privacy, he hung up a "shit sheet" across his bunk. After one cellmate left, Karter was able to move from the top bunk to the bottom, and for a while he kept the sheet up whenever he read. The electricity was on all night, so the guys would find light bulbs and wire, plug their homemade fixtures into sockets, and read and write.

• • •

Three days after his eighteenth birthday, on June 9, 1994, a grand jury indicted Karter Reed on the charge of murder in the first degree. The prosecution intended to prove premeditation. The automatic punishment for first-degree murder was a life sentence without parole. Karter entered a plea of not guilty. The trial loomed.

Armand Fernandes did all he could to get Karter's case sent back to juvenile court. In September 1994, he filed a motion arguing that Judge Harper's findings had gone against the evidence and that Karter should remain in the juvenile system. The motion failed. In November, Fernandes filed another motion, aiming to suppress before the trial began a long list of statements attributed to Gator, many of which were supposedly said just after the crime had occurred. Since the boys would be tried separately, Fernandes felt that such "hearsay" could compromise Karter's case. Fernandes lost this motion, too, and the statements were admitted, along with mention of the "high-five" that supposedly occurred between Karter and Gator minutes after the stabbing, and Karter's hotly denied comments "I hope he dies" and "Now I can be with my father in jail."

Gator, in custody but not yet convicted, would not weigh in on Karter's case. He would eventually plead guilty to manslaughter and receive a sentence of seventeen to twenty years. He was released after spending ten years and three months in jail. When he talked to school children about his mistakes, he would say that Karter "was there because I asked for his help. He followed me into the classroom, into the police station, the courtroom, and prison. . . . I always remember his saying he didn't want to go in. He didn't make his own decision, I made it for him."[53] At the trial, however, Karter heard no words from Gator, except those that damned him.

Fernandes also fought hard to get Nigel sent back to the United States to testify on Karter's behalf, but his efforts were blocked by lawyers and therapists who said the experience would be damaging for Nigel.[54] Years later, when Karter talked to students in Project Youth, he would say that Nigel showed the most courage—by walking away.

On February 3, 1995, Karter was told that he was being transferred back to Dartmouth for a trial that would begin on February 6. Fernandes went to visit him and said that they were in real trouble because they had drawn Judge Charles Hely. A longtime prosecutor—he had been an assistant district attorney for thirteen years—Hely called himself "restrained," and believed that what prevented crime was "strong families and strong schools." Fernandes called him a "tough judge."[55] Karter worried that Hely might not see that he had intended to harm, but not kill, Jason Robinson. He realized for the first time that he could be convicted of murder rather than manslaughter. But when Fernandes discussed the idea of taking a plea bargain and mentioned trying to settle on a sentence of fifteen or twenty years, Karter was stunned: he could not conceive of serving more years than he had lived in this world. He refused the plea.

Karter's reaction was not uncommon; juveniles refuse plea bargains at a higher rate than adults.[56] A Michigan study showed that juveniles are "at a serious disadvantage in negotiating and understanding plea offers because of their very youthfulness, immaturity, inexperience, and failure to realize the consequences."[57] Teens also have much less ability to evaluate the risk of going to trial. They don't imagine the future in the same way as adults do, and ten or fifteen years behind bars is inconceivable to them, even if it is less than a life sentence.[58] With little understanding of the judicial system, they often go to trial because they believe that people will see that they didn't intend to kill anyone.[59] Lack of parent-child privilege, or the fact that parents cannot be a part of the lawyer-youth conference, can be particularly challenging.[60] In all but nine states, a parent can be compelled to testify against his or her minor child.[61] Additionally, teens might mistakenly take the well-meaning but untrained advice of a family member.[62] Even with an attorney asking them to consider a plea and explaining the consequences in great detail, kids like Karter have no experience in making such a decision.

On February 6, Karter was taken from jail to the old Taunton superior courthouse, a massive stone structure built in 1894 and topped with a copper dome that covered a magnificent ceiling. To Karter it seemed like a medieval dungeon, complete with steel bars, wooden benches, and rats in the catwalk. To enter the courtroom, he was led from a small cell up a narrow wooden stairway, where court officers furnished those on trial with a choice of two neckties, recommending the one worn by the most recently acquitted defendant. Karter, in clothes furnished by his mother, walked past a thick wooden door and vaulted doorway into the courtroom, where Judge Hely sat behind a huge wooden bench. The jury was selected. After a recess and jury instructions, opening statements began.

Thomas Quinn repeated his three-part mantra: "classroom," "school," "room full of students."[63] With images of the sanctity of the place firmly drawn, he described Karter's intentions to kill. Karter "plunged" a knife into Jason Robinson. He "committed a deliberate premeditated murder of Jason Robinson; that is, he thought about killing him, he decided to kill him, and, in fact, he did kill him."[64]

Even as Armand Fernandes tried to change the tone in the courtroom, calling this a "case about chaos"—thirty people seeing and hearing different things while involved in the same event, a scared kid who acted rashly and without premeditation—he admitted there was no way to deny that one of the most sacred of childhood spaces had been violated.[65] Fernandes tried to move beyond the irrefutable, asking the jury to keep their eyes and ears open as they heard the witnesses, to be ready to decipher where bias might be detected in each person's testimony. He told them that in this case, there was no motive, malice, or premeditation: "Whatever [Karter] did that was wrong, it wasn't murder."[66]

Five witnesses took the stand that first afternoon, and Karter became furious because he believed they were "coached with a nice cohesive story that differed from their original statement." He was disturbed to hear a state trooper say he had appeared "calm" when being interrogated at the police station, after Karter had said he had been sobbing hysterically and repeating, "I didn't mean it. I'm sorry." At some point during the proceedings, ADA Quinn asked Karter if he expected the jury to believe that everyone had lied except him. Karter testified, "No," but he would later tell me that he believed many witnesses were not telling the truth.

Fernandes tried to point out flaws in each person's testimony, objecting to the lack of training of a police officer in juvenile inquiry, and insisting there was conflicting evidence at every point: "What confusion. What chaos enveloped these children and enveloped the faculty and maybe even the police," he said about the verbal inconsistencies during Karter's arrest at the school.[67] He insinuated that Karter should have been videotaped while giving his statement to the police.

When Karter took the stand, he went through the beginning of his testimony easily, answering the perfunctory questions that Fernandes asked: where he was, with whom, and on what day. He was composed. Fernandes gave him a pointer and asked him to indicate on a diagram exactly where the boys entered the school and which hallway they walked down. Karter described how he followed Nigel through the corridor and indicated where the three stopped just outside classroom S57. But before he could say what happened next, Karter broke down, overcome with emotion. He wrote in 2009: "I was reliving what happened and knew what was going to happen next. It wasn't about me or my family or going to prison. It was like watching a movie of myself and I was about to stab someone."

In his cross examination, Quinn attempted to get Karter to reveal things he did not think, say, or do, which of course is fair game. He asked Karter questions such as: "Did you consider Gator Collet a 'tough guy?'" "You wanted to 'retaliate' for what was done to Nigel, right?" "Did you and Gator have a little celebration after you bumped into Jason?" and "Did you say 'I'm scared but it felt good?'" To all these questions, Karter vehemently responded *No*. Quinn then tried to show the jury the "heartless" image of Karter that had been painted in the press. He did this by faulting Karter for not asking any of the officers at the police station about Jason Robinson's condition after the stabbing. When Karter said he thought Jason was "all right," Quinn again emphasized: "And you never asked any of those men how he was doing?"[68] Quinn was ignoring what today we would describe as a feature of Karter's adolescent thinking—total absorption with himself at a moment of crisis.[69]

In his closing statement on February 14, Fernandes pointed out that there was no way Karter "had looked into the blackness of his heart and developed some kind of malice, some wicked or corrupt motive" that moved him to deliberately kill Jason Robinson. He reminded the jury that all the "players" in that classroom were children, and that this fact explained a lot of the inconsistencies in the case. Karter Reed's desire to carry a knife was, he said, because the boy wanted to "be somebody." He added: "Karter Reed should not have been in that school. Karter Reed should not have taken that pipe. Karter Reed should not have decided to go in there, whatever Nigel's memory of his mother was. Whatever he wanted to do was wrong, but he didn't want to kill Jason."[70] Fernandes asked the jury to find Karter not guilty of murder but, rather, guilty of involuntary manslaughter, or of what he called "accident, the unintentional act as [Karter] described which is clearly negligence."[71]

While Fernandes's closing statement was convincing in many ways, the one thing he couldn't do was take away the reality that Karter had stabbed and killed Jason Robinson. ADA Quinn's remarks reflected this: "He did it powerfully; he did it purposefully; he did it fatally," he said of the crime. Quinn's final words closed the proverbial coffin: "The last question that Trooper Pierce asked the defendant, 'Did Jason deserve it?' Karter Reed said, 'Yeah, he deserved it.' Well, based on the evidence in this case, the defendant deserves to be convicted of murder in the first degree. Nothing more, nothing less."[72]

Following the closing statements, Judge Hely defined terms before the jury left the courtroom. First-Degree murder required, among other elements, that Karter Reed premeditated the crime, intending to cause death. Second-Degree murder would mean that he caused Jason's death with "malice aforethought" (i.e., the intention to kill or to cause grievous bodily harm). Karter could also be found guilty of two lesser charges: involuntary manslaughter, meaning that he had caused Jason's death by "wanton or reckless behavior"; or assault and battery by means of a dangerous weapon. Lastly, the stabbing could be called an accident, and Karter would be found not guilty.[73] Fernandes had wanted the judge to include the instruction of "voluntary manslaughter," stating that Karter perceived imminent danger before resorting to violence as an issue of self-defense, but Hely refused the request.

The jury left for its deliberations at 12:22 p.m. At 2:43 p.m. they came back with a question, asking for further definitions of malice aforethought and grievous bodily harm. In terms of the first, the judge gave the same definition he had previously given, adding that the jury could consider "permissible inference from intentional use of a dangerous weapon if there is a plain and strong likelihood that death will follow the contemplated act."[74] In terms of the second request, Judge Hely told the jury that he was essentially quoting the Merriam-Webster dictionary, and that he equated grievous with severe. A long discussion with the attorneys ensued. Fernandes wanted the judge to further clarify, saying that grievous implied a much more serious act than severe, since grievous carried with it a likelihood of death. Hely listened, discussed how to proceed, and ultimately stood by his definition.[75]

At 3:30 p.m., the jury again came back, and this time asked for a dictionary. Both attorneys agreed with Judge Hely that speculation on definitions outside the purview of the court might be a problem, and the judge said no to the jury's request for a dictionary. Fernandes repeated his earlier request for Hely to help the jury understand that they needed to decide the degree of risk of physical harm, that is, "grievous bodily harm" (second-degree murder) or "substantial harm" (manslaughter). Hely respectfully declined.[76]

That night, Karter called his mother from jail and told her that he was sure he was going to be found guilty of second-degree murder. She insisted he was wrong; Sharon said that she knew her job was to tell Karter that everything would be okay. The following day, February 15, she headed to the courthouse amid whispers of "That's Karter's mother."[77] She walked by the reporters, refusing interviews, and sat a few rows behind her son, who sat with his attorneys, his back to her.

Karter's incarcerated father did not watch the news from Taunton to hear that his son was found guilty of second-degree murder. The document reporting the sentence stated that Karter Reed would be punished by confinement to MCI-Cedar Junction for and during the term of his "natural life." Karter would be given credit for time served, permitted to appeal the findings for up to thirty days, and would be eligible for parole in fifteen years. Judge Hely ordered Karter to pay a fee of $50 to the Victim Witness Assistance Fund. Fernandes asked the judge to waive the fee, saying that because Karter had been a juvenile at the time of his arrest, he should pay less than an adult. Judge Hely's response to Fernandes's request: "Denied."[78]

Sharon Reed collapsed as she heard the verdict; she had to be removed from the courtroom. She could not bear to watch as her son was cuffed and hauled off to the courthouse jail cell. There, Karter would wait for the prison van to take him to MCI-Cedar Junction, once called one of the "circles of hell," where he would begin serving his life sentence.[79]

6. GROWING UP IN PRISON

Upon Karter's arrival at MCI-Cedar Junction (previously known as the infamous Walpole State Prison), a corrections officer handed him a note from a guy named Spiffy. Karter would later describe Spiffy as six feet four inches tall, weighing 260 pounds, covered in tattoos, with long hair and a handlebar moustache. According to Karter, "Spiffy had just been returned to Walpole from the Feds," meaning he had done "a bid" in a federal prison. The note seemed straight out of a bad prison movie: "Bash the first motherfucker who even looks at you the wrong way with a mop wringer, and don't stop till the cops pull you off. You'll go to the hole for six months or so but people will respect you."

Karter initially had no idea who this person was, or why he was writing him such a note, but he soon learned that Spiffy was considered the most dangerous man at MCI-Cedar Junction. Not until much later did Karter discover that it was his father, Derek, incarcerated at MCI-Norfolk, who had contacted Spiffy through an intermediary in order to "school" his son and make sure he received proper protection. Ironically, the man who had abandoned Karter on the outside was now the one looking out for him inside. Shortly thereafter, Karter received a letter from his father, what prisoners call "a kite," telling him that to survive behind bars meant never looking in other people's cells, carrying himself with respect, and minding his own business.

Unfortunately, minding one's own business can be impossible for youth in adult prison, who are often traumatized by the horrific things they see—not on TV, but right in front of them.[1] Instead of focusing on things like education, they're worrying about burly officers pushing into their cells for searches.[2] From the conflicts they witness, these youth learn several painful lessons: that self-preservation at all costs is the path they must follow in prison; that there is no shame in employing violence to resolve conflicts; and that domination and retaliation are the way of the prison yard. They forget that these "skills," writes R. Daniel Okonkwo, executive director of D.C. Lawyers for Youth, are "the polar opposite of the skills necessary to survive in society on the outside."[3] Most young people fervently hope to avoid becoming what prison seems to demand, and if they do give in, crime behind bars becomes acceptable. The shock wears off as they see more and more beatings, brutality, and rapes.[4]

Youths in adult prisons are often directly impacted by the violence around them. Compared to youth in juvenile detention facilities, those in adult prisons are nearly twice as likely to be attacked by other prisoners or by staff.[5] They are also five times more likely to be sexually assaulted than those in detention facilities—not only by other prisoners, but by officers as well.[6] Many of these assaults result in physical injury as well as deep emotional scarring.[7] Young female prisoners are particularly susceptible, often forced to engage in sex for such prison privileges as phone calls and medical care; they rarely receive treatment behind bars for the resulting trauma.[8] Girls who enter the prison system have often been victimized beforehand, sexual abuse being one of the primary predictors of girls' entry into crime, and they report higher rates of abuse than boys.[9] The coercive power that a guard can exert puts young female prisoners in an incredibly vulnerable situation, and women are most often guarded by men—more than 75 percent in New York State, for example.[10] The rate of sexual abuse for youth is also higher among lesbian, gay, bisexual, and transgender prisoners.[11] A male corrections officer in Washington D.C. was convicted of sexually assaulting a young transgender prisoner, forcing her into a restroom.[12] Such incidents resulted in an outcry from activists, and in 2015, the San Francisco county jail became the first facility in the United States to jail people based on each individual's gender preference.[13]

It is too soon to determine the impact of The Prison Rape Elimination Act, introduced in 2003, which requires those under eighteen to be separated from older prisoners. States were fined if they weren't in compliance by 2014, and audits had begun to occur, but some states have refused to cooperate.[14] Allegations of rape have continued even since the Act was introduced, and lawsuits have continued to be filed. In Michigan seven teens sued the state for sexual assaults by prisoners and harassment by officers between 2010 and 2013, saying they were never protected in prison.[15] (The suit was thrown out.[16])

The risk of suicide following sexual assault behind bars compounds the horror of sentencing kids to adult prisons.[17] One seventeen-year-old who set a trash bin on fire was repeatedly raped, and eventually hung himself.[18] These tragedies are not uncommon with juveniles, who are eight times more likely to commit suicide behind bars than those who are physically mature.[19] Young prisoners have also reported how shocking it is to find that a cellmate committed suicide: "I came in as a child. You want to be blind to it, but then you see people . . . killing themselves," said one Massachusetts boy.[20] Guards have been known to tell young prisoners to "grow up" when they express fear of taking a shower or going to sleep.[21] When juveniles are bullied by older prisoners and attacked with weapons, depression as well as fear can set in.[22] Juveniles are susceptible to "immature and irresponsible behavior" wrote Supreme Court Justice Anthony Kennedy in *Roper v. Simmons* in 2005.[23]

In Karter's case, he protected himself by holding in his feelings and keeping his distance from the other prisoners. Nevertheless, while in prison he was exposed to conversations he likely would not have overheard on the outside. In one, a prisoner gave a "clinic" on how to dismantle door locks to a rapt listener who wanted to change "careers" when he got out. In another, a man complained about double-bunking in cells: "You know what needs to happen, motherfuckers need to kill a few hundred of these swine [COs] . . . and that'll teach them. Every time they put you in a cell with someone, kill him or try to kill him." Certainly, such comments were not uttered by every prisoner, nor were they indicative of the many men who tried to keep away from the dark side. But, as we have seen, violent intimidations were sometimes not just idle threats.

After two weeks at MCI-Cedar Junction, on March 2, 1995, Karter was shuffled into yet another van, this one headed to MCI-Concord. Karter had been to Concord, a medium-security state prison, once before, to visit his father. But after he and his family had driven the two hours from New Bedford, a paperwork snafu prohibited Karter from visiting with Derek; he had to wait in the car with his uncle while the others went inside. By the time Karter arrived for intake in 1995, MCI-Concord was the Department of Correction Reception and Diagnostic Center for all men newly sentenced to prison. Upon arrival, the prisoners were screened, evaluated, and classified to the appropriate security level. It was supposed to take six months for a prisoner to be classified and then, usually, sent to another prison.

Karter was immediately confined to a bunk in a makeshift building that had once contained an auto shop and a laundry, on a tier known as L6. Overcrowding at Concord had forced him and others out of the J tiers, which were located in the building for newbie orientation and screening. This situation was supposed to be temporary, but the men housed there—almost as if they were in prison limbo—were without a schedule, lacking caseworkers and important privileges such as a gym, yard, rec room, haircuts, movies, phone, and canteen. Karter said that a group of guys had been in the Ls for weeks. He fell in with this disgruntled bunch, which was led by a twenty-six-year-old man named Gino.[24]

For a young prisoner, learning to be tough and getting a "crew" for protection can become a necessity. Some kids feel they must rely on weapons or gangs.[25] Others are just tired of being picked on and know officials don't "have their backs;" a gang might promise respect or power.[26] In many ways, gangs are surrogate families for these kids: they offer approval, protection, reinforcement, and a sense of belonging.[27] Gangs also can take on the role of teaching young prisoners the ropes. David Skarbeck, a senior lecturer in political economy, wrote how about some of the unwritten rules of prison, which include not ratting out other prisoners, keeping one's word, remaining loyal to fellow cons, and never being a "sucker."[28]

Gino immediately hatched a plan to get them all out of the Ls. Step one involved shaving their heads with state-issued razors to protest not being given haircuts. Since Karter was expecting a visit from his mother, he declined this, but the rest of the fifteen or so men agreed, including one they called "Rain Man." Rain Man was a particularly troubled soul who had gone a bit 'round the bend, and continuously asked for his own radio.

The presence of prisoners with mental health issues is yet another shock for youth who are sentenced to adult facilities. Today, many prisons across the country are being nicknamed "the new asylums." Since numerous psych hospitals have closed in the last several years, the punishment system has stepped in and criminalized many of those with mental illness; the United States incarcerates ten times more people with psychological issues in prisons than in mental hospitals."[29] In 2015, reports spelled out that as many as two-thirds of males and three-quarters of females behind bars were diagnosed with psychiatric illnesses.[30] Among state prisoners diagnosed, 49 percent were incarcerated for violent crimes.[31] Sociologist Susan Sered wrote that across the country "incarcerated men and women have higher rates of hypertension, anxiety, myocardial infarction, psychotic episodes, asthma, arthritis, major depression, cervical cancer, urinary tract infections, chronic headaches, tuberculosis and hepatitis, than Americans in the general population."[32] In Massachusetts alone, 24 out of 100 prisoners deemed to have mental-health issues were on medication, which Sered called "chemical restraints" for prisons where talk therapy was not readily available.[33]

Gino's plan also involved the men putting on their coats and hats, packing up their belongings in pillowcases, and surrounding one of the correctional officers, a man who liked to sleep on the job, and hitting him over the head with a mop bucket and then demanding to be moved. Gino figured that the "hole"—the disciplinary unit—was big enough for only ten men, so they wouldn't be able to put all of them in there. Gino suggested that Karter be the one to "hit the cop," since he had a life sentence. Karter was appalled but didn't show it. Although he realized what a not-so-bright idea it was to be involved with Gino, he did not want to take a stand against him. Instead, he said coolly, "It's your plan, you do it!" Gino likely had no intention of taking the fall, so he found someone even younger than Karter to do his bidding. Manuel, aged seventeen, was serving three to five years for armed robbery and had arrived at Concord only hours earlier. The guys all agreed, and Manuel maybe to show off or maybe because he was ready for a fight, went along. This is not uncommon. If a teen goes against an older prisoner, he could ultimately be the one to get punished—locked in his cell or even sent to solitary.[34] Quick violence is everywhere, and as a prison guard once told me, "I don't care at all about the circumstances, if a guy on my watch fights, he's locked."[35]

Gino's motley crew threw on their coats, and with pillowcases on their backs—a bunch of "denim-clad Santa clones," Karter later wrote—they formed a circle around the officer. He was asleep, his hat over his face, his body leaning against the chain-link of the CO's cage, a small enclosure that contained his desk. Manuel grabbed the bucket and slammed it against the cage, rattling the officer awake. At this point, half the crew deserted, leaving six or so, including Karter, to issue their demands to be moved. The officer said he had nothing to do with this. A captain and a lieutenant were summoned. They told the men to step into the hall. The captain wrote down all of their names, and then, to Karter's surprise, asked them to voice their grievances. They told him about the horrendous conditions in L6 and that they wanted to be moved. The captain said he would look into it. Later that day, the men were all moved to the Js.

At the time, Karter was pleased, but a part of him began to realize that although their complaints were justified, prison authorities were rewarding bad behavior, something he would later write was a not-uncommon practice in a world of seemingly random decisions. Guards have been known to allow some to break rules for which they discipline others.[36] When staff apply inconsistent rewards and punishment, prisoners more often than not feel that their decisions are unjust.[37]

In those first weeks at Concord, Karter felt anger at every perceived injustice, and was not interested in changing the thinking that fueled his hate and resentment. At this point in his life, he welcomed a whipping boy. Newly incarcerated youth are not good at coping with the daily stresses that confront them,[38] and when they see a predator-prey mentality all around them, they feel compelled to choose sides.[39]

Right after being released from L6, Karter was on his way to the Js when he passed by Protective Custody, the unit that housed prisoners at risk of being harmed in the general population. There he spotted Mack, a known pedophile who had raped two little girls in Barnstable, Massachusetts, or so Karter believed. Researchers have shown that "sex offenders are the most feared and despised group in this country."[40] Behind bars, such predators are often the easiest target for those who, themselves, feel targeted. It is not uncommon for prisoners to gang up on a pedophile with the backing of others on their floor, or unofficially, even the prison staff. The child molester and former Roman Catholic priest John Geoghan was killed in his cell in 2003 by another prisoner, although some thought it was a setup by guards.[41] In the 1974 play *Short Eyes* by Miguel Pinero, himself a former prisoner, jailed men gang up and murder an accused pedophile, an act that is sanctioned by officers. More than forty years later, in 2015, older prisoners instigated a culture of violence by manipulating younger prisoners to go after convicted child molesters in an Australian prison.[42]

Karter walked right up to the small square window of Mack's cell and threatened him, saying, "That's right you fucking skinner, I know who you are, and when that door opens, I'm gonna kill you." When he got to his new bunk, Karter began yelling to others that there was a "skinner" on the floor and that they should get him. An officer overheard this and contacted Internal Perimeter Security (IPS), the officers who investigate alleged security abuses inside the prison. IPS officers arrived, warning Karter that he was an instigator, and if he didn't watch out, someday a sex offender who wasn't small or scared would beat him up. Then Karter would try to exact revenge, and would end up buried in Concord. Not surprisingly, Karter paid little attention to the officers' warnings; he wanted to prove himself.

Later, when Karter was moved to another unit, he saw Mack walking around freely on his floor. He was livid. At the time, Karter had a protector named Eddie, an older Latino man whose wife's niece was going out with a friend of Karter's from New Bedford. Eddie heard that Karter wanted someone to beat up Mack and take the punishment. He told him that he had just the guy, a man who knew how to take care of these things better than anybody. Eddie introduced Karter to Carlos, a Cape Verdean, also from New Bedford.

According to Karter, he and Carlos went to Mack's cell.

"Step out," Carlos said. He leaned into the cell ominously. "You know my boy?" He pointed at Karter.

Mack said nothing.

Carlos pressed on. "He tells me you're a skinner."

Mack burst out, "I didn't rape anyone, I swear." He cowered, his words trying to divert Carlos's glare. "It was statutory; she was my girlfriend. I'll show you the letters. I was seventeen; she was sixteen. Her parents pressed charges, but it's bullshit."

Carlos laughed and told Mack he was "coppin' pleas."

Karter's conscience then began to kick in. He worried that maybe the guy was not really a sex offender after all. Maybe he had made a mistake. However, he could not let himself feel these emotions—worry, anxiety, guilt—because he still needed a front to fend off the pain, grief, and remorse. So, he stood there and said nothing. Carlos warned Mack that he had twenty-four hours to get off the block.

The next day, as Karter was returning to his cell from the shower, he saw Mack rushing out, his face bloodied, and his belongings in a pillowcase. Mack screamed at the officer on duty,

"Somebody beat me up. I need to get out of here!" The officers tried to pry out of him the name of his attacker, but Mack refused to say another word. Ratting could get him killed.

Internal Perimeter Security arrived, and the officers flipped through what is known as the "bed book," a record of where prisoners are at different moments; they found out that Carlos had been in the area. When asked directly, Mack finally relented and fingered Carlos, whose hand was swollen. Mack was immediately transferred to another unit, and Carlos was sent to the hole—Department 9, as it was euphemistically called at Concord.

Karter may not have felt directly responsible, but nonetheless, because of him, a human who had done him no personal harm had been hurt. Karter's prejudice had been bolstered by other inmates, but as the prison activist Angela Davis has noted, bigotry is reinforced by the punishment system itself, as "prisons are havens for backwards ideologies."[43]

After the incident with Mack, Karter felt that his punishment, albeit less explicit than Carlos's, was to be assigned cellmates whom he could not tolerate. The first was a man Karter called a "chicken hawk," or a known sexual predator who preyed on young kids. He tried to lure Karter with comments such as, "Gee, it must be real lonely for a young guy to have to do so much time without women, no?" His next cellmate was a disturbed man who Karter said tried to kill himself by drinking a bottle of floor stripper.

It seems bizarre that a prison would allow men like these to bunk with a teenager, but that is exactly the problem with sending juveniles to adult prisons. Journalist Dana Liebelson reported in 2015 that the United States is an outlier in this practice: "China, Afghanistan, the Democratic Republic of Congo and Haiti have banned . . . trying kids as adults. Some Western countries, like the United Kingdom and Germany, do allow youth to be sentenced as adults, but they don't put them in prison."[44] In England and Wales, the closest to a prison for juveniles would be what they call "youth offender institutions" for those fifteen to twenty-one years of age.[45] These places still have fights, gangs, and the kind of tension that comes from being locked up without family and friends, but they also have education, sports, yoga, the arts, and programming such as anger management courses.[46] Suicides in these kinds of institutions are rare, and juveniles get shorter sentences than adults, and only those convicted of the most dangerous crimes go on to adult prisons after they're twenty-one.[47]

Organizations such as the Children's Law Center in Massachusetts recommended in a 2009 report that convicted juveniles stay in DYS facilities until they turned twenty-one.[48] The Annie E. Casey Foundation suggests small, community-based treatment-oriented secure facilities for most teens, to keep kids close to home and families engaged.[49] Their Juvenile Detention Alternative Initiative (JDAI) which is now operating in 150 jurisdictions in thirty-five states, has reduced by 34 percent the number of youth who get committed to state facilities where they are housed with adults.

The one site begun by JDAI that seems most promising in terms of treatment and cost savings is the Missouri Model, which stresses therapy instead of punishment. It intentionally welcomes kids with carpeted dorm-like rooms, no iron bars, and the chance to wear their own clothes instead of uniforms.[50] There are also treatment teams, individualized case management, dedicated staff mentors, family involvement, job readiness programs, and an emphasis on life skills—all which add up to care along with custody.[51] Because units are small—no more than fifty beds—and in the most secure facilities treatment lasts at most until the teen turns twenty-one, there is incentive for kids to do well.[52] While anyone over seventeen is considered an adult in Missouri, and judges have the option to transfer those who commit serious crimes to the adult system, they also have the option of a "dual jurisdiction" program: if the charge does well in the juvenile system, the judge can suspend the teen's sentence to an adult prison.[53] De-institutionalization models keep kids from returning to crime, stop brutality, and prevent many youth from taking their lives while behind bars.[54] They also save money. According to the Missouri team, "Steering one high-risk delinquent teen away from a life of crime saves society $3 million to $6 million in reduced victim costs and criminal justice expenses, plus increased wages and tax payments over the young person's lifetime."[55]

Following the attempted suicide of his cellmate, Karter's cell stayed empty for four days. Karter was convinced that IPS wanted to stick him with the worst of the worst to get him to explode. Why else? he wondered, were men were sleeping on the gym floor and in the hallways while the other bed in his cell remained unoccupied. Karter believed they were just waiting for the right guy to come along.

And they finally found him. As Karter described him in 2009: "Tim is 27. He looks 47. Thinning reddish / brown hair, an emaciated sickly Woody Allen doppelganger with no teeth and a heart condition. He claims to be married with several children and to be related to one of the kids in the Pam Smart case . . . but all of it . . . is a lie. His 'kids' are little boys he's cut out of magazines and taped to the wall; his 'wife' is his mother. One of the things he tacks to the wall is a letter to his 'son.'" Karter eventually managed to get Tim to agree to request a transfer. But IPS told Tim to stay put. Karter stewed, certain that he was being set up.

On his tier, Karter wrote, was a prisoner who ran a "store," an illicit canteen that provided a lucrative side business. The understanding was that you had to pay back double for whatever you bought: if you got $15 worth of food, you owed $30. Tim had recently gone to the store, but had no money to pay. The prisoner who ran the store showed up at Karter's cell, looking for Tim, who was hiding in his bed under the covers. The prisoner began yelling when he didn't see Tim. Karter sat on his bunk and tried to ignore the whole scene. The prisoner then decided to see what he could take from Tim's possessions and settled on his sneakers.

After the man left the cell, Tim screamed that Karter had given away his sneakers. When the officers arrived on the scene, they took Tim into the hallway. The next thing Karter knew, he was being dragged to the isolation unit—the hole—and written up for stealing Tim's sneakers. This incident would result in one of the few disciplinary reports Karter received in his years behind bars, and it would fuel his paranoia. Karter was learning to trust no one.

In June of 1995, Karter was transferred yet again, this time to MCI-Norfolk. The largest medium-security prison in Massachusetts, MCI-Norfolk has a stone wall five thousand feet long and nineteen feet high, enclosing thirty-five acres.[56] It's most famous prisoner was Malcolm X, who in 1948 took advantage of the prison's library to educate himself behind bars.[57] This was a coveted move for Karter, as here, he had some "protection," because his father was also at Norfolk.

Karter wrote that after arriving, he spent two days in what was called "Receiving," a place essentially no different from the hole. He was then released into the general population, where he encountered his father. It was the first time they had seen each other in three years. Derek took one look at his son's "goofy attempt at a wispy goatee" and his "pale curveball"—Karter said he couldn't finagle a haircut so shaved his head before leaving Concord—and said, "What the fuck did you do to your head?"

Then he hugged his son and said, "And shave that stupid shit off your chin." Derek then told Karter to wait while he went to his cell. He came back with a laundry bag full of stuff—sneakers, shirts, pants, and a hat (these were the days before uniforms were instituted in US prisons) that he put on Karter's head and told him to wear until his hair grew back. The two of them then took to the hallways, walking and talking, with Derek showing Karter off to his buddies.

At Norfolk, Karter had a single cell and a job as a janitor, earning $33.75 a week. That was good money for prison labor, and enough for him to support himself without help from his family. He also worked out, played handball, watched TV, and read. Karter also spent a lot of time with his father, who was close to parole and a transfer to a lower-security facility. Karter wrote that one of the happiest times in his life was when he turned twenty years old in prison with his dad. The June day didn't start out so happily, however, as Derek said nothing about his son's birthday. When he stepped into his cell that night, ready to go to bed, however, Karter saw a letter from his father on top of his TV. "In two pages," Karter wrote, "he talked about how proud he was of who I was becoming and how sad he was that I had to go through what I was going through. He lamented his mistakes and failures in life, and his regret at not having set a better example. But he also talked about how much he believed in me and how he had known since I was born how special I was. He told me how he pushed me as a kid because he wanted me to succeed, wanted to give me the encouragement that was missing from his own childhood." In his twenty years, Karter realized that this letter was the most meaningful gift he had ever received.

I would relate this account to Derek years later when we sat together in the food court of a mall where he had agreed to talk to me about his son. He shook his head almost disbelievingly, sighing at the half-eaten sandwich on the lunch table in front of him, and then broke down in tears. It was not the first time he cried over what he had put Karter through.

It was at Norfolk that Karter began his process of transformation. It started with the program in which I had first seen him participating at MCI-Shirley: Project Youth, where prisoners take full accountability for their crimes and tell their stories to kids. Initiated by Hank Powell Arsenault Jr., Project Youth began in 1964 at what was then Walpole State Prison.[58] Arsenault, the last Massachusetts prisoner sentenced to the electric chair, robbed a home along with two other men in 1955, killing the young lawyer who owned it. The other two accused won commutations, but not the shooter, Arsenault. In November 1957, Arsenault sat in the death chamber, sixteen minutes away from execution. All too aware of his own mistakes, he sought to strike a bargain with God. If he received mercy, he promised that he would spend the rest of his life talking to kids and helping them stay out of crime. At 11 p.m., a call came from Lt. Gov. Robert Murphy, a known opponent of capital punishment, "who was running the state while the governor was down with the flu, phon[ing] to commute the death sentence to life imprisonment."[59] Arsenault spent the next seven years trying to convince prison officials to let him create Project Youth. He finally succeeded, and began talking to kids in 1964, and by the time he was fifty-one, had talked to more than 130,000 of them, from drug addicts to runaways, always using his own life as an example.[60] By age seventy, still behind bars, Arsenault had helped spread the program across the United States and abroad.[61] Today, Project Youth boasts that its participants have talked to more than half a million students.[62]

Karter flung himself into the program, talking to as many groups as possible. As he told his story to students, something new began to open up inside of him. He began to grapple with the idea that maybe he had gone too far that day in Dartmouth. At first, he tried on the feeling like a new shirt. Gradually, he began to see that, as he put it, "many people had been dealt far more No's" than he had but had not killed another human being. Karter remembered how, when he was sixteen years old, his grandfather offered him his car—that is, if he got a job. He applied for only one job, and when he did not get it, he complained that the world was against him. He now realized that if his life was going to improve, he would have to be the one to make it better.

In 1998, at the age of twenty-two, Karter became a Project Youth team leader at Norfolk. He was now responsible helping newcomers to the program tell their stories, and expected to push himself and others to dig deeper as they talked about their lives and what led them to crime. He gave feedback to participants, made sure the group ran smoothly, and led discussions with the young audiences.

Karter's stated goal at this time was to reach out to the groups of students who trooped into the prison to hear the prisoners talk about their experiences. He wanted to encourage the students to resolve conflicts before they escalated to violence. In a 1999 booklet about the program, he wrote: "Sometimes . . . new prisoners will stop me and comment on my young age. Most ask how long I am going to be in here. When I tell them 'Life,' they shake their heads and say that they feel sorry for me. I don't want anyone feeling sorry for me. I'm not the victim. The victim is a sixteen-year-old boy who is lying in a grave and who never got to live his life because of me and the stupid choices I made. There are so many other victims. His mother, family and friends . . . all those other kids who were in that classroom that day? I messed up their lives as well."[63]

For the first time in his young life, Karter began to feel that he was helping other people. Yet, he was helping himself just as much, if not more. He was starting to take stock of what he had done. He was starting to realize that violence was wrong and solved nothing, and he could speak with authority about this to other people. Nevertheless, he had not yet truly comprehended that "no human being has the right to make someone else suffer," something he wrote in 2009 that took him much longer to learn.

One day in 1999, six correction officers came to the door of Karter's cell and told him to "cuff up." He began "freaking out"—he had no idea what was happening. Karter was brought to Norfolk's hole, and no one uttered a word to him about why. Finally, a day and a half later, Sister Ruth, a nun who volunteered inside the prison, came to see him. He was frantic. Sister Ruth tried to calm him down, explaining that she had talked to the coordinator of Project Youth, who had talked to the prison superintendent. The institution had recently hired Mike Sardina, a man who was employed at Roslindale when Karter was being held there. Sardina had testified as a witness for the state at Karter's transfer hearing, and the Norfolk administrators were worried that Karter might try to exact revenge on him, or so the superintendent was told, so they decided to transfer Karter out of Norfolk, not because of anything he had done but because of what they feared he might do. Sending him to the hole had been their way to "protect" their new hire. No one was able to get Karter moved back to general population, and he stayed in the hole for more than a month before being transferred.

Karter was distraught. All the work he had begun through Project Youth, the small amount of good he had started to make out of his tragedy, what had it meant? He had to work hard not to turn back to his old familiar mental tapes. Luckily, he discovered that he had been reclassified to Bay State, the next best medium-security facility. He felt the DOC was throwing him a bone.

After thirty-five days in the hole, Karter climbed into a transport van to leave Norfolk, cuffed and chained. An officer casually mentioned something about the ride to Shirley. Karter's mouth dropped open as he realized he was not going to Bay State after all. He panicked, his heart rate shooting up so high that for a moment he thought he might have to go to the hospital unit. He had heard that MCI-Shirley was the worst medium-security prison in the system. Karter was feeling more alone than ever.

It was September 1999. That year, in the United States, more than 13,500 youths younger than eighteen were admitted to adult prisons.[64] Karter, at age twenty-three, had been incarcerated for more than six years. His world was about to change once again.

III

O! It is excellent
To have a giant's strength, but it is tyrannous
To use it like a giant.

William Shakespeare, *Measure for Measure*

7. PAROLE

By the time Karter arrived at MCI-Shirley in September 1999, he had completed less than half of the fifteen years he was legally required to serve before he would be eligible for parole in 2008. For Karter, the remaining nine years felt like a lifetime ahead of him.

At the time of Karter's sentencing, Massachusetts had set fifteen years as the earliest possible parole date for all second-degree lifers, including juveniles convicted in adult courts. By 2013, however, as a result of several important court cases—*Miller v. Alabama*, *Diatchenko v. District Attorney*, and *Commonwealth v. Brown*—the parole landscape in Massachusetts changed for juveniles with homicide sentences.[1] Legislators battled it out but ultimately set parole eligibility for anyone convicted of second-degree murder to a range of fifteen to twenty-five years.[2]

After Miller, many states were forced to grapple with what their new minimum sentence would be for youth convicted of homicide.[3] Statutes passed, as of 2014, set the minimum sentence between twenty-five and forty years throughout the country.[4] That meant that a young person who went to prison at sixteen might not see parole until age forty or fifty, depending on where he or she lived. Many activists argued that these long sentences went against allowing a meaningful opportunity for release, a concept outlined in *Graham v. Florida*—which cited juveniles' ability to change—and underscored in *Miller*.[5] Even more egregious, if a judge deems it necessary, most states allow juveniles to be sentenced to life without parole, as long as it isn't mandatory.[6] This is contrary to international standards, according to a 2015 United Nations report on torture.[7]

Parole offers an opportunity for prisoners, but it is not a get-out-of-jail-free card. Instead, it allows a prisoner to finish their sentence outside of prison. Parole aims to provide freedom under supervision, and ideally, it lends support to prisoners, not just a list of rules. Many young men and women realize that while parole means hope, it also offers them an opportunity that their victims never had. For many prisoners, their crimes and the lives they destroyed are never far from their thoughts.[8] "I know this is a tragedy of my own making," said one Washington state man sentenced at fourteen for murder.[9] A California prisoner wrote, "Three months after my sixteenth birthday I was shamefully involved in a crime that drastically affected the lives of many people. I am truly remorseful for my actions, and I believe my guilt justifies my '45 to life' sentence. However, a small part of me hopes that someone would give me a second chance at life."[10]

Intellectually, Karter understood that he was responsible for Jason's death; emotionally, he was tormented by it. "I have spoken to over 20,000 students in Project Youth," he wrote in 2008, ". . . done every possible thing I can to better myself and to give back; I've been without a television for five years, my room is full of books, and I still feel I'm not doing enough because no matter what I heap onto my side of the scale, the suffering, loss and desolation on the other side is immoveable. The closest word I can tell you to describe that is despair."

Karter tried multiple ways to deal with the pain. He enrolled in as many programs as were offered at Shirley, at one point estimating that he had been involved in more than forty—among them barbering, repairing computers, book groups, therapy, anger management, Bible studies, and academic classes. He took some of the programs just to keep busy; others because he knew they would expand his worldview and help him gain insight into his behavior. He also knew that if he wanted to earn his parole, he had to prove to the parole board that he could turn his life around. Programs were one way to do that.

Prison rehabilitation programs are surprisingly random—availability varies by state and by what is deemed to work in each facility, an opinion sometimes based on hard data and research but often on word of mouth. Many programs come and go quickly. Some grow out of societal trends, such as yoga and aerobics. Theater occasionally finds itself in favor, but in the tough-on-crime eras, it is seen as fluff. Programs considered innovative and immensely successful can be duplicated in other states, which occurred after prisoners in Wyoming trained sixteen hundred wild horses over more than ten years before the project was replicated in Arizona in 2015.[11] But programs can just as likely dry up, as happened when a popular and effective stress reduction and meditation course in Massachusetts was cut, rumor had it, because it was criticized as "too soft" in the press.[12] The quality of the program often depends on the leader as much as the curriculum.

Quite often, waiting lines to get into programs are long, and only a miniscule amount of state prison funds are directed toward programming, along with food, clothing, housing, and medical care—in Massachusetts, that figure is only 2.09 percent—with the rest earmarked for security.[13] A 2012 Sentencing Project survey revealed that 61.9 percent of juvenile lifers were not involved in any rehabilitation programming: 32.7 percent, because their life sentence made them ineligible; 28.9 percent, because either they were housed in prisons with insufficient programs, or they'd already participated in all those available.[14]

One program that had a lasting effect on Karter was the Alternatives to Violence Project. AVP was co-founded in 1975 by Larry Apsey, a Quaker lawyer with a background in peace and prison work, and a group of prisoners at a maximum-security prison in Green Haven, New York.[15] Through skills training and workshops, AVP's goal is to empower people to lead nonviolent lives.[16] Thirty-two states and fifty countries have offered AVP classes both inside and outside prisons over the last four decades; in 2013, a total of 12,607 prisoners across the country were part of the training.[17]

Karter liked the idea of transforming his pain and anger into something positive. AVP calls this "transforming power," and Karter participated in workshops where he and other prisoners practiced productive ways of dealing with violence. This deepened his understanding of himself, as he learned about the relationship of awareness to healing, which helped him feel the opposite of "abandoned," a word he had once associated so completely with his father. Karter became a leader in AVP, and this role, too, pushed him to grow.

Karter's continuing relationship with Gator Collet while behind bars illustrates how his understanding of violence evolved. When he was at Norfolk, during the early stages of his Project Youth work, Karter reconnected with Gator, who was also housed at Norfolk. One day, Karter was walking the quad with Gator and two of his friends, whom Karter described as "wannabe skinheads with their swastika tattoos and white supremacy rhetoric." Gator kept making comments about "dirty" this and "filthy" that. Karter put up with the racial epithets for a while, but he eventually reached a breaking point. "I've had enough. You are more ignorant than any of those you're degrading," he said to Gator. Standing in the middle of the quad, Karter told Gator that he refused to allow anyone to disrespect his family. "If you speak like that one more time, I'm going to drag you in the alley and beat the shit out of you." He knew he was threatening Gator, but he was too angry to stop himself. Afterward, Karter didn't talk to Gator for five years.

Then, in 2003, Karter heard that Gator was close to being released from prison, and a realization came to him, almost like an epiphany: Gator had been in prison because of something Karter had done. He did not focus on the fact that Gator had encouraged him to go into the classroom all those years ago. Instead, he wrote to Gator saying he felt nothing but sadness and remorse for what he'd cost him and hoped that Gator succeeded when he got out. Gator wrote back, telling Karter that after he left Norfolk, he had decided it was time to take Project Youth seriously and change his thinking. The proof of his success, Karter said, was what Gator did after prison: he found a job, married his high school sweetheart, had a daughter, and dedicated himself to speaking regularly at schools, trying to make a difference in the lives of teens.

Karter desperately wanted to believe that what happened to Gator was a common story for boys who became men in prison. But all too often, this is not the case, as youth are more likely to recommit crimes after serving an adult sentence—and to recommit them more quickly— than if they are adjudicated in juvenile court.[18] One study followed 315 juveniles who were "best matched" for crimes they committed; of those released from adult prisons rather than from juvenile facilities, less than 50 percent stayed out of prison after release, while approximately 66 percent of those judged as juveniles were successful at forging new lives.[19] The Centers for Disease Control and Prevention found that youth in the adult criminal system are 34 percent more likely than youth retained in juvenile court to be re-arrested for violent or other crime.[20]

As Karter matured, his understanding of killing Jason Robinson continued to evolve. Guilt, he wrote, is a "fire that is eternal . .

. the best and absolute worst that has ever happened to me. . . . One day I didn't feel guilty . . . and one day I did." He made friends behind bars who also pushed him along this path, men he would later say he trusted, who were "determined to go against the prevailing moral tide in prison." As young prisoners become determined to make meaning out of the tragedy they have caused, they often seek to change who they associate with, try to heal their family's wounds, consider what justice means, decide to give back to society, and find people they can communicate with about their lives.[21] Certainly there are men and women who cannot get out of the cycle of poverty, addiction and crime, or escape from systemic racism and criminalization in this country. But Karter would tell me, years later, that the men who befriended him in prison never returned to crime.

Karter also began reading the classics. Eager to educate himself and perhaps, seeking more answers, he delved into philosophy, math, psychology, physics, history, and literature. He also began writing more prolifically. Karter considered that he might be able to do something valuable with the remainder of his life. By the time I received my first letter from him in 2007, he was thirty-one-years old and had spent almost half of his life behind bars. In six months, he would be eligible for parole, and at times, could imagine that he was almost home.

Karter's parole hearing was scheduled for March 2008. At first, I intended to just write a support letter for him, an appropriate gesture I thought for someone who had received thirteen letters from a convicted murderer. But after the parole board changed the date and forbade volunteers from attending the hearing or testifying on Karter's behalf, and after it rearranged the schedule three days before the hearing, I could not refuse his request to testify in person. Karter was allowed only three people to speak for him, and no one knew if his father would show up. By now, I believed that Karter had earned a second chance.

Since it is a human system, parole is also an imperfect system. Errors will always be made. However, when parolees commit brutal crimes, society is unable to tolerate error, and insists even more fervently on locking up prisoners forever. But when we look at how many of our citizens are locked up and how much it costs to keep them behind bars, parole becomes a much more appealing and sensible option. And so the pendulum swings.

The concept of parole was first developed in an English penal colony and in Irish prisons as a way to release prisoners into the community by providing them with points for good behavior, and work and program participation.[22] The earliest legislation authorizing parole in the United States was enacted in Massachusetts in 1837.[23] The state's parole officers were charged with assisting released prisoners with jobs, tools, clothing, and transportation.[24] The first parole system which spread across the country was developed by Michigan's Zebulon Brockway.[25] By 1940, parole was used nationwide to determine when prisoners were deemed rehabilitated by a board that supposedly could identify and evaluate their behavior.[26] This process brought with it problems. Some complained that a medical model was unreliable if the judges of parole lacked medical qualifications and training. Others wanted to abolish parole altogether, saying it could only lead to erratic decisions. "Experts" were often political appointees, ensuring that prisoners felt the deck was stacked against them; critics, meanwhile, worried about rampant releases. Over the years, concerns were raised about how voting was done by parole boards and whether panel members tried to unduly influence each other.[27] By the 1960s, several states wanted nothing to do with parole. Many legislators believed that rehabilitation was impossible, and they claimed that releasing prisoners early was too lenient.[28]

But then the country's prison population swelled—by 2008, the United States had more than four times the number of people incarcerated than in 1980—and as a result, there was a renewed emphasis on trying to figure out how to make parole work.[29] Experts pointed to studies that showed that more than 95 percent of incarcerated men and women eventually would be released after serving their sentences, and with supervision and support, parole could reduce recidivism.[30]

Massachusetts currently has a system in place called "discretionary parole," meaning that the parole board is to "exercise discretion" when determining who can be granted parole, when he or she can be released, and under what conditions.[31] The statute insists that a successful applicant must have sufficiently changed as to no longer pose a threat to the community. It reads: "No prisoner shall be granted a parole permit merely as a reward for good conduct but only if the parole board is of the opinion that there is a reasonable probability that, if such prisoner is released, he will live and remain at liberty without violating the law, and that his release is not incompatible with the welfare of society."[32]

In Massachusetts, those serving life sentences for first-degree murder convictions are automatically sent to prison for the remainder of their lives; this was true even for juveniles until 2012, when the Supreme Court ruled in *Miller v. Alabama* that for youthful lawbreakers, mandatory life sentences without parole were unconstitutional. According to a 2012 report by the Sentencing Project, one in every nine individuals incarcerated in US prisons was serving a life sentence, and "in 22 states and in the federal government, at least 35% of the lifer population [was] ineligible for parole."[33] By 2014, after the Miller and Diatchenko decisions, Massachusetts, along with Delaware, Wyoming, North Carolina, Washington, Illinois, Iowa, Mississippi, Nebraska, and Texas, allowed those sentenced to life as juveniles to seek parole—applying Miller retroactively.[34] In January 2016, the U.S. Supreme Court, in a 6-3 decision, allowed all juveniles (some 2500) currently serving life sentences to seek parole, or in some cases, to have their cases retried.[35]

Parole for second-degree life sentences has always been particularly contentious, even though some states have found that persons who commit many of the most serious crimes are statistically among the safest to parole—that is, they reoffend and recidivate the least.[36] In fact, a 2009 Michigan study showed that those who'd been incarcerated for homicide were the least likely to recommit any kind of crime—an 80.1 percent success rate—with a rate of return to prison of under 8 percent, most often for larceny.[37] Research shows that people age out of crime and that most violent crime is committed by those under thirty years of age.[38] In 2011, a California study reported tracking 860 people convicted of homicide and sentenced to life, all of whom were paroled beginning in 1995.[39] Since their release, only five individuals—less than 1 percent—had been returned to prison, and none for life-crimes.[40] This is a particularly stunning figure when compared to California's 2011 overall recommitment rate to state prison for new crimes of 48.7 percent.[41]

Michigan and California are not unique. In a Massachusetts study by the Criminal Justice Policy Coalition of 161 second-degree lifers released between 2000 and 2006, 72 percent were not re-incarcerated and 14.3 percent were returned to prison for technical violations (such as missing an appointment with a parole officer or breaking a parole rule without recommitting a new crime).[42] Notably, in the Commonwealth, it cost $53,040 to house a state prisoner in 2014, compared to $5000 to keep someone on parole.[43] Paroling second-degree lifers helps reduce prison costs, and while it may seem counter-intuitive, it does not endanger public safety.

Parole was a goal Karter had long dreamed about. He spent his waking hours planning for release and feeling terrified that it would never happen. He knew, as did all other prisoners who appear before parole boards, that no matter how much he had changed, his fate was not entirely of his own making.

On March 11, 2008, I drove to Natick and was escorted down a long hallway to the second floor to discover that the parole hearings were held in a surprisingly small room. This space had none of the feel of a courtroom; it seemed more like a converted warehouse, with a couple of shaded windows in the wall behind a long table. Rows of chairs were set up to face the table, with an aisle between the two sections. All twenty-three of Karter's supporters were on one side, and three members of Jason's family—his father, sister, and brother—and the trial prosecutor, Thomas Quinn, were on the other. A journalist from the *Boston Herald* sat behind them, furiously scribbling on a notepad. A thinner, paler version of the Karter I had met at Project Youth was in the front row. He was seated and shackled near the corner, his breathing audible even from the back, where I took a seat on his side of the aisle.

Slowly, from behind closed doors, six of the seven parole board members made their way into the room and sat at the table, each focused on some object they could touch—the table, a pitcher of water, eyeglasses in a free hand. One chair was unfilled, a common practice when state money is tight or the governor has not yet gotten around to reappointing a vacant seat. But that day, the member was merely absent; he would need to listen to tapes of the hearing before casting his vote. Legs were crossed. Pleasantries were exchanged. Water was poured.

The chair of the board sat in the middle of the panel. She began to speak, citing statute: they were there to determine Karter's risk to reoffend and to decide if he would be a suitable candidate for release. I scanned my row. At the end, I saw a soulful-eyed woman next to the wall. She seemed ten years younger than I, and she was smiling slightly and held her head up. Her chin was set; her expression fixed. She was much prettier than I expected. Years later, when I met Sharon Reed, and saw the animated version chain-smoking and filled with words, I would remember how deeply scarred she seemed at this moment.

A man in front of me was nuzzling up to a young woman who, I guessed, was perhaps eighteen years old and looked up at her paramour as if they were on a date. His hair was sandy and familiarly buzz cut, and he had a lean build from the back. Then, as he turned sideways, I saw that boyish face and pieces of a sizzling smile, the face that had always been Derek Reed's calling card. The young woman pressing against his shoulder was, no doubt, Karter's father's newest girlfriend.

The chair of the board took us back to April 12, 1993. "Why did it happen?" and "What were you like then?" she asked Karter. In a tear-filled voice, Karter told his story: of his father going to prison, his family being on welfare, his non-communicativeness, his poor grades in school. The only surprise came when he related an antic he and Gator had been arrested for, at age fourteen: larceny and breaking and entering. I remembered how Karter once wrote that "B&E's" were not unusual for many of the boys he knew; the haul always turned out to be "stuff nobody would want." The victim of his larceny was there testifying on his behalf, Karter said. At that moment, the woman next to me smiled and nodded.

A parole board is charged with figuring out how much a prisoner has changed, and in so doing, they are not supposed to retry the case. However, each panel must determine how important the facts of a case are to public safety, and how much weight to give the prisoner's record behind bars. In addition, they must consider letters from program staff inside the prison, friends, counselors, teachers, and family—that is, how much the petitioner has transformed in attitude and behavior. The board also must decide if a prisoner has a workable reentry plan, with good prospects for work, housing, and all the other necessities that, for the most part, are difficult to have in place before release. In Massachusetts at the time, the parole board could either grant release, or it could deny with a "setback", anywhere from one to five yerars, meaning that the prisoner would have to wait that amount of time before reappearing before the board. The rationale for a setback was to help the person gain release by providing guidance about what he or she should focus on before the next board appearance, although this direction did not always occur.

The panel continued to probe Karter about the day of the killing for twenty or so minutes until the chair asked some important questions that challenged Karter to assess his experience in prison: "What did you need to change about yourself? . . . What insight did you need to undergo to show the board that you are not a risk to reoffend?"

Karter was articulate as he talked about learning to take responsibility for the crime, using phrases like "understand the consequences of my actions."

"Looking back, is there anything that could've saved Mr. Robinson?" a board member asked.

"Perhaps if I'd been confronted a little more forcefully, shaken, taken a look at myself. . . . Maybe I was trying to prove something to my father."

"How do we predict that you wouldn't turn back into an impulsive, hard-headed man?"

To this question, Karter replied that these days he had many outlets for positively expressing himself.

The board went on to discuss Karter's exemplary prison

record. He had only two disciplinary reports and had participated in almost every program the Department of Correction offered. Karter impressed some members of the board with his detailed plan for reentry: he wanted to go to a long-term program that would allow him to transition more slowly and gain experience in the workforce. He had written to several programs that offered counseling and the chance to continue his education. He hoped to work with computers, get a degree in sociology, and eventually start a program like Project Youth on the outside.

A board member asked Karter what his strengths were. He replied: "Compassionate, caring, honest, dedicated, and committed to family and society and to the process of atonement. I can never give back what I took."

Jason Robinson's sister turned sharply when she heard these words, while her brother sat impassive, forlorn. Jason's father, alone without his wife, who he said later was too distraught to attend, was bent over and staring at his hands; he said nothing. Their pain was palpable.

The panel had its turn to react to Karter with questions and comments; everyone in the room watched intently, most likely trying to gauge how each member would vote.

One member asked: "What have you given to kids?" Karter replied with "Project Youth" and continued: "I think every day about my victim and my victim's family. It tears at my heart." Again, he was wracked with sobs. The member's cool stare didn't give much away.

Another board member commented on Karter's behavior, saying he was "giving excuses."

I wrote them both down as *no*'s.

Two other members, however, looked pleased when Karter explained in detail his ability to earn a living as a barber while working toward a degree. Two yesses. Another member commended

Karter for doing a lot of soul-searching. He then compared the effect that Karter's crime had on the Dartmouth community with what happened to him at one of Boston's best high schools, where a stabbing also took place. According to the board member, Karter "clearly didn't get it yet." He compared Karter's stabbing of Jason Robinson with the shooting at Columbine High School. A definite no.

By far the most sympathetic regard came from the chair of the board. She wanted Karter to realize it wasn't disrespectful to be both remorseful and to claim change. When he said, "If I am granted parole, or even if not, it would be a disgrace for me to harm others," she replied, "I think you understand the nature of the crime and have been transformed by it."

If there were three yesses and three no's, it would be left to the absent board member, a former parole officer, to cast the deciding vote.

The room seemed to take a collective deep breath when the family of Jason Robinson began to speak. I found it distressing to listen to the pain inflicted on the Robinsons, even if I believed that Karter deserved a second chance. Thomas Quinn went through some of the evidence again, saying that Karter's current behavior—his tears—showed that he was "apologizing" for asking for parole. Jason's father, in a raspy voice, said "Karter still has his life . . . he still breathes . . . Jason is stuck in time . . . fifteen years is not enough." Jason's sister said she dreaded every day her daughter went to school, and that her family had been "shattered." It "sicken[ed]" her that Gator and Karter could communicate when she could no longer speak to her brother. She added, "There should be no second chance for this killer." Jason's brother read a letter from one of Jason's best friends who said the memories of that day still haunted him. He then talked about how he could not yet forgive Karter and wished he would stay behind bars, but he also hoped, whether or not Karter received parole, that "he meant the things he'd said here today."

The Robinsons' testimony was followed by uncomfortable rustling. Papers shuffled. Heads bent toward each other. The room seemed to exhale. Finally, it was announced that the board would hear those who had come to speak for Karter. Of the three people including myself who offered testimony, Sharon Reed was the last. Her friend who sat next to me discussed Karter as a child, what turned out to be a harmless robbery of her house, and how he had helped his family, and I testified that the best way to make restitution was through a well-lived life. Sharon faced the most daunting task. Parents who testify at parole hearings—those who have lost a child and those whose child has killed another—have the kind of courage Karter did not yet know.

Sharon walked by her son to sit in a chair facing the panel. She was wearing a simple outfit on her thin frame, and her hair settled in a sheen of black on the back of her jacket. She pulled out notes and identified herself. I watched Karter's back—that is all I could see—and she began to speak as if her life depended on it: clear, precise, direct. She said that Karter sent her a card every Mother's Day. He once had a check drawn from money earned behind bars to pay for fire victims in the community. She answered the panel's questions about the effect of drugs in the household, and the fighting that surrounded their family. When she said, "I could have been a better mother," I heard Karter's muffled cries.

After she praised Karter for not wanting to return to New Bedford and for wanting to live in a residential program and attend college, Sharon's eyes looked from one board member's face to the next. "It's an Olympian effort," she said. "One in five parolees fail, but Karter won't be one of them." She paused. "Give him an opportunity to carry that torch." And with that, she stopped talking. The board thanked her. The room emptied.

It would take six to eight weeks before the board would notify Karter and his victim's family whether he had earned parole. Because of a moment in time Karter could never take back, a boy was dead. There were many who hoped Karter would live the rest of his days behind bars.

8. VIOLATION

In 2008, there were 868 prisoners serving second-degree life sentences in Massachusetts, and those seeking parole were required to serve twelve to eighteen months in minimum or prerelease status before their release.[1] However, there was a catch to this: potential parolees were prevented from being transferred to lower security facilities if their crime was connected with taking a life.[2] This made it much more difficult for them to take the kinds of programs that helped them to adjust back into the community, such as job readiness and other life skills offered only in lower security settings. In essence, Karter had to earn his parole before he could move out of the medium-security unit at MCI-Shirley.

This catch was due to classification regulations in Massachusetts. Classification is a system that determines the level of custody and programmatic needs of prisoners.[3] The security level decides, in part, the facility where a prisoner will be housed, and lower levels of security afford more privileges. The Department of Correction can decide to alter a prisoner's classification status based on "pending disciplinary reports, immigration status, 'institutional negative adjustment' and prior criminal history."[4]

Karter had protested aspects of this rule in 2004, after being told he was being denied classification to a minimum-security prison because of his crime. He spent the next two years unsuccessfully challenging the Department of Correction's classification policies, which had come under fire for two reasons. First, prisoners were serving out their full sentence—in many cases, refusing to go through the lengthy and difficult parole process—and being discharged to the street without supervision, services, or support.[5] Unsurprisingly, such prisoners are more likely to return to jail.[6] (In 2012, Massachusetts was ranked two times more likely to directly discharge prisoners to the street than the national average—more than all other states except South Carolina, Ohio, Oklahoma, North Carolina, Maine, and Florida.[7])

Secondly, the Massachusetts' policy to move those it considered more violent into higher security units had backfired. After defrocked Catholic priest John Goeghan was transferred from a medium to a maximum security prison, he was strangled by another prisoner.[8] Activists said that while his crimes against children might be horrific, the classification system was nevertheless "corrupt," as it shifted more prisoners to higher security than was necessary.

While he understood the serious nature of his offense, as a model prisoner with only two disciplinary reports on his record, Karter claimed that it made no sense not to transfer him to minimum security. In 2008, he wrote to the associate commissioner of correction: "Now that I am within 15 months of possible release, I am no longer eligible because of new guidelines. What happens if I am released? Where is my reintegration? I have been in prison since I was sixteen years old. I have never had a job. I have never paid taxes, never had health or car insurance. I was just a kid. Why am I not being prepared for my possible release?" Karter also wrote to then governor-elect Deval Patrick, referring in his letter to a 2004 report by the Governor's Commission on Correction Reform, established under Governor Mitt Romney, which said that 75 percent of prisoners were being released to the street from maximum or medium security facilities, versus only 21 percent from minimum security—"a serious impediment to reentry."[9]

Karter's complaints received no response, but despite losing these battles, he continued fighting the war. However, in terms of the parole board's decision, he had no choice but to wait it out. While biding his time, Karter spent many hours in his eight-by-ten-foot cell, with its sink, toilet, desk, footlocker, trash barrel, and shelf. He had filled the shelf with books, a hotpot, a Walkman, and old clothes. In the two-by-three-foot wall space designed for pictures, he had hung a map of the world. His room was overflowing with paperwork, personal documents, and letters destined for the Department of Correction. Life outside his cell included cutting hair, his only job at Shirley. He also lifted weights and participated in programs every day and, often, at night. While his mind told him that parole might not be granted, he kept hope alive in his heart.

On Wednesday May 14, 2008, Karter was on his way to his barbershop program to take a shaving test when he was diverted to the Programs Office, where a female officer called him in to talk.

"I have the decision," she said. "You got your vote."

Nothing registered with Karter.

"And it's a good vote; it's not a bad vote."

Karter thought to himself, Okay, one or two years . . .

She went on. "It's not like you're going home tomorrow. . . . You have to go to a prerelease."

And then it hit him. He was going home! An unstoppable smile spread across his face, and next thing he knew, he was crying. Karter's head was spinning as the officer explained the decision—words he would need to hear again and again to believe them.

Karter had won parole in a 4–3 decision. The minority felt he was still a danger to society and wanted a five-year setback; the majority ruled that Karter's program involvement, positive prison record, strong community support, and personal growth proved that he warranted a second chance. He would ultimately be released after stepping down to minimum and then serving six months in a prerelease facility.[10]

Karter returned to his unit, having been mercifully released from work, and told and retold the story to his fellow prisoners. Everyone in the unit was slapping Karter on the back with a sincere "You deserve this, man." Karter, however, felt an ambivalence. "I'm not sure if this is the happiest or saddest moment of my life—sometimes both simultaneously."

When Sharon Reed got home that day, she turned on the computer and saw "Breaking News: Karter Reed Granted Parole, 4-3." She started screaming with joy and began calling everyone she knew. When Sharon reached Karter's father, she discovered that he already knew. "How the hell do you know?" she asked Derek. He told her that it was through the prisoner grapevine: one of Karter's released friends had told another who called another who lived in Worcester and knew Karter's father, who called Derek and gave him the good news.

The family of Jason Robinson was "stunned by the decision" to grant Karter parole.[11] Members of the Dartmouth community, such as Thomas E. Kelly, who'd been assistant school superintendent at the time of the crime, said they were disappointed in the decision; Shawn McDonald, who'd been elected chairman of the school committee one week before the stabbing, said, "It was, it still is, and it will always be a sad day in Dartmouth history . . . I only hope Karter does something with his life to prove that he is worthy of being granted parole."[12]

The *Boston Herald* reported the fury in the community over Karter's pending early release: "Outraged family and friends of a sixteen-year-old boy mercilessly slashed to death inside a classroom . . ."[13] WBZ-TV, one of the most followed local news stations in the Boston area, reported incorrect details about the day of the crime: "Reed, who was sixteen at the time, stabbed Robinson to death in a social studies classroom while two of his friends, Nigel Thomas and Gator Collet, held the boy down."[14] On the website of another Boston TV station, accompanying an *Associated Press* story, was a picture of a brutal-looking knife, not the one used by Karter, but a reminder that a similar knife had served as the murder weapon.[15]

The conservative journalist Howie Carr, also of the *Boston Herald*, criticized the Democratic governor's newest parole board for finding in Karter's favor. Carr, known for his assertions that prisons coddled criminals,[16] believed that Karter was and always would be a "monster."[17] Massachusetts was now under "liberal bleeding-heart management," he wrote, and "Killer Karter [was] the first of what will no doubt be a long line of murderers . . . cut loose."[18] In fact, in 2008, thirty-two paroles were approved for prisoners serving second-degree life sentences, compared to forty-seven in 2004, under the Republican governor Mitt Romney.[19]

The responses to Karter's parole were par for the course—the press revving up the ante, protests against the release of a criminal who victims think should stay behind bars, and a lack of understanding of parole conditions by the public. Karter read every piece of damning news. Although he was proud of what he had accomplished in prison, he knew that the outcry against him contained this truth: the agony would never be over for Jason Robinson's family.

It may seem like an anomaly, but being awarded parole does not necessarily mean a prisoner will get out of prison. Three states—Maryland, California, and Oklahoma—require the governor's approval after parole is granted.[20] In Michigan, it is up to the parole board whether or not they want to deliberate on a particular lifer: the board can declare "no interest" in a case.[21] A number of states including Hawaii, Iowa, New Jersey, New Mexico, Oregon, West Virginia, South Carolina, and Wisconsin, offer what is called "presumptive parole," which allows most prisoners, barring extraordinary circumstances, to presume release on the day they become eligible for parole.[22] In Massachusetts, lifer parolees may have to complete programs such as violence prevention, drug rehabilitation, or life skills prior to their exit; often, lower security facilities must be located for the prisoner to go to take these programs before they are released. Sometimes, there are waiting lists for programs that the DOC has mandated, which can delay release even longer.

Karter knew that he would need to serve sixty days of so-called "minimum time" before beginning his six months of pre-release. The total of eight months served could be in the same facility, but he would have different privileges and responsibilities and be housed in different parts of the prison during the stages of release. Everything depended on when beds were free. Eight months could easily turn into more than a year.

Karter turned thirty-two in June 2008. Impatient to start fresh, he used his remaining time at MCI-Shirley to make plans as best he could. He finished his barbershop program, read up on colleges, finances, and driving, and with a rejuvenated sense of humor, wrote: "I have a manual . . . and the good news is, I did Drivers Ed, and had my license in '92, so seventeen years with a spotless record." He read profusely: *Crime and Punishment*, *War and Peace*, several Shakespearean plays, *A Tale of Two Cities*, *Stranger in a Strange Land*, *Light in August*, and *Spanish for Dummies*. He cheered on the Red Sox and began a transition program that was all about preparing for reentry. Finally, on August 28, he learned that he'd been approved for a bed at a facility—the Boston Pre-Release Center, or BPR, in Roslindale—where he could do both his minimum and prerelease time.

The evening before leaving MCI-Shirley, Karter stayed up all night as dozens of guys came to his cell to say goodbye (how this occurred, I never asked him). He also had to decide what to take with him and what to give away. Giving one's possessions to others was technically not allowed, but, according to Karter, everyone did it anyway. Bleary-eyed by dawn, he skipped breakfast. When he got the call for the transport van, he went to a holding cell for six hours before boarding. As the vehicle finally exited onto Harvard Road, Karter said he almost felt dizzy, overcome by images of the friends he left behind, as well as feelings of guilt, remorse, and joy.

His destination, the Boston Pre-Release Center, opened in 1972 and is meant to be a prevention piece of the recidivism puzzle. A photo on its official website emphasizes its positive role: flowers in front of a pleasant brick structure, noticeably missing fences.[23] The goal of BPR is a "gradual transition from prison life to the community" through "work, education, and counseling programs."[24] Along with this notable goal, the recidivism rate is lower when prisoners exit a prerelease center. In 2011, Massachusetts reported a three-year study that showed 27 percent of prisoners went back to crime when exiting from a prerelease, compared to 50 percent who were released from a maximum security prison.[25]

When he arrived at the Boston Pre-Release Center, Karter could not believe he had finally made it to a step-down facility, and he was thrilled to be in the minimum security unit.[26] He was giddy from being outside without locked doors and razor wires, with traffic he could actually see; he was reeling from the taste of freedom in the fresh air, trees, and lawn. "I was outside today," he wrote. "Out. Side." Dazed, he walked without handcuffs through the front door, accompanying an officer to the parking lot. The officer, knowing Karter's background, pointed across the street at the Department of Youth Services facility, and with a smile he asked Karter, "Does that look familiar?" It was the Roslindale DYS detention center where Karter had started his prison journey in 1993. He had come full circle.

That first day, Karter also explored the inside of BPR, ambling from space to space, unhindered by the scrutiny of eyes watching his every movement. Despite finding the library lacking, the weight room off-limits for a couple of days, and the yard small, he wrote that he was in a state of amazement: "I have a wardrobe dresser in my room and a real chair. There is a washer and dryer at the end of the hall. And you get up and go, pretty much whenever. It is incomprehensible. Unfathomable. It is foreign . . . and this is just the beginning."

The next morning, after another night of barely sleeping, Karter was paged at 5:45 a.m. via the intercom system that summoned prisoners to work in the kitchen. As a prep cook, Karter chopped, diced, slivered, and sliced. He also managed to go out on the road that day, accompanying a friend from Shirley who had created a groundskeeper job for himself. Karter couldn't get enough of being on real streets in a real community.

Being outside reintroduced in Karter the urgency of wanting a relationship with a woman. Guys on work crews that picked up trash in the community told him there were "women everywhere and women approaching them." Growing up without an adolescence takes a toll on young men and women, and they use different methods to try and establish romantic relationships while in prison: reaching out to old romantic liaisons by letter; trying to connect with volunteers who come into the prison; asking their friends outside to find them potential partners to write to; and after they turn eighteen, subscribing to prison pen pal services where they pay a fee to have their picture and profile listed. Since state prisoners don't have access to the Internet, they are forced to wait for responses by snail mail. In the age of blogging, prisoners also make connections through creative sites like Between the Bars in Massachusetts, where hundreds of authors from prisons around the country reach out to people on the outside through their letters, essays, art, and profiles.[27]

In his fifteen years behind bars, Karter had managed to have a few girlfriends. However, there was only one young woman whom he called a "real love." After his transformation had begun while at MCI-Shirley, he met Elizabeth.[28] She was between college and graduate school, and as a volunteer at the prison, she slowly got to know Karter. Once she stopped volunteering and the strict no-contact rules no longer applied, she and Karter began corresponding. Karter said they developed feelings for each other, and soon Elizabeth began visiting him. She was all the things Karter imagined he might want in a partner: "smart, funny, beautiful . . . she was pre-med." She came from a family he admired, with professional parents. Karter said that Elizabeth respected his drive, work ethic, and discipline, but not surprisingly, she came to the realization that waiting for a prisoner could feel like forever. Eventually, she stopped writing. Karter carried the hurt for two years but did not stop believing that if he had met her first on the outside, their liaison would have lasted.

Perhaps because he was lonely or perhaps because he was so close to freedom, Karter's judgment flagged at Boston Pre-Release, and his actions toward Elizabeth were the first clue. Although they had been out of contact for years, he decided to call her. Everyone at BPR had contraband cell phones, Karter said, in spite of rules that forbid them. Officers considered them a gateway to crime, but the devices also clearly revealed another problem: the telecommunications system in prison is exorbitantly expensive.[29] In 2013, a fifteen-minute phone call from a prison or jail averaged more than $17.36. Prisoners either had their families prepay by setting up an account with whatever private phone company serviced the prison, or else they called collect; either way, the fees quickly added up.[30] (Beginning in 2016, after a ruling from the Federal Communications Commission, prison phone calls were capped at 11 cents a minute.[31])

Karter had money in an account, and he promised himself he would not jeopardize his future by borrowing a cell phone. A guy he worked with suggested that he use the pay phone; the Sergeant okayed the request, and Karter bit the financial bullet and reached out. As it turned out, Elizabeth had not heard that he had been granted parole, so they spent most of the call talking about his situation in BPR. She asked him to call her back so that she could tell her story. Karter was excited, to say the least. Until he called—and heard that she was engaged. He found himself beset with longing and flooded with a renewed sting of rejection.

In October, Karter began a new job, working on Boston's famed "Emerald Necklace," which comprises half of the city's park acreage. The activity perked his spirits. He learned landscaping and horticultural skills while picking up trash to maintain the beauty of the natural spaces. On some work assignments near the coast, he was able to see and smell the ocean and walk barefoot in the sand. Sometimes he would be admiring the view when a pang of guilt would hit him, and he would remember how he had taken all this away from someone else. He would never be far from such reflection, but he also felt hopeful for his future.

The following month, Karter attended a reception for the Emerald Necklace crews, where he posed in a picture with

Governor Deval Patrick and former governor Michael Dukakis, something that pleased him to no end. Karter soaked up every bit of appreciation and cherished the moment of validation by shaking the politicians' hands. He wrote that Thanksgiving was a blur, a "mash of undecipherable scenes," and attributed the confusion to knowing that this would be his last such holiday behind bars. He yearned for his family and the new memories they would create together, but he also missed the old, and he cherished recollections of how he and his Shirley friends had survived hard times in prison.

In early December, Karter was again classified by the DOC, meaning he was finally eligible for the last part of his prison journey: prerelease. He was relieved that BPR would allow him to transfer from one part of the facility to another, and he hoped to make the move from minimum security to the prerelease section by end of February. Doing so would mean that he would be out by fall 2009 and able to go to school. His head was whirling with images of cars and apartments. Bunker Hill Community College for computers. The University of Massachusetts–Boston for sociology. Karter had also been moved from the Emerald Necklace crew to the statehouse, home of the state legislature and the office of the governor; he was overwhelmed with downtown Boston's smorgasbord of delights. It was not just the beautiful women he saw every day on the street but the mix of neighborhoods, history, and architecture. It was all new. He saw clothes he had never worn, new haircuts, and jewelry that was unfamiliar. He couldn't wait to figure it all out.

During this time, Karter's elbow had started to hurt from an old sports injury he had sustained at Shirley, which had turned into tendonitis. The pain had progressively worsened because of raking, shoveling, and breaking up ice, as well as from his work in the kitchen. At BPR, he had a workout partner, someone he knew from Shirley who also suffered pain, in his case from an accident. The two of them decided they needed the joint supplement glucosamine/chondroitin, which Karter had read could help tendonitis and other types of inflammation. Glucosamine was available at some prison commissaries in the state, but at the time, Karter did not know that; it was not available at Boston Pre-Release. He and his workout partner asked fellow prisoners who spent their days outside to buy glucosamine pills, readily available over the counter at local pharmacies, for them. In addition, since Karter had been between moves and unable to get new underwear, he asked the guys to get that for him as well. These were prohibited activities—a prisoner was not allowed to have more than a certain number of pairs of underwear, and unless the item was sold at the prerelease canteen, he was out of luck. But Karter said these were the kinds of actions often overlooked by correction officers, who were more concerned with prisoners' families and friends smuggling in contraband weapons, drugs, and cell phones.[32] Karter, who had earned only two disciplinary reports in his fifteen years behind bars, had no idea how such seemingly insignificant actions were about to change his life once again.

January 20, 2009 saw the inauguration of the first African American president in the United States. The New England winter weather was crisp, and the mood was abuzz with celebration. I opened a letter from Karter to discover that six days before, in a routine search of his locker, officers had found the underwear and so-called contraband. In the report, officials mislabeled the approximately 140 glucosamine pills as "prescription medication," an obvious infraction if that had been true. Prison officials do not ask "why" when they suspect that a potential rule violation has occurred. Without testing the pills, which had been stored in an empty cereal box, they shipped a distraught Karter out of BPR and back to a higher-security facility, Old Colony Correctional Center (OCCC) in Bridgewater.

Karter's ninth correctional facility, OCCC was a medium-security prison. According to the DOC website, the name "Old Colony dates back to the founding of our Nation, and fosters a sense of hope and 'new beginning.'"[33] Housing units were named after heroes of the Revolutionary War. Karter's first reaction at Old Colony was to "revamp his life." How could he have given someone money for underwear and glucosamine? Was it some shameful self-destructive behavior, or had he forgotten the fragility of his position? How could he do this to the people he loved? In a way, he was right. His family was wildly upset and confused by his series of missteps.

Desperation made Karter vow to never again break any rule, no matter how much he deemed it small and irrelevant. He cleared his cell of books that were over the limit, disposed of extra paper clips and a spare plastic spoon. He removed "the tiny pieces of plastic/rubber" that kept his ear piercings from closing. He knew he couldn't keep up this obsessiveness forever, but such details were all he could control. He wrote, "It means not just understanding but believing there are no exceptions. I was not ready to accept that . . . I can't even comprehend the damage I have done. It's like *The Wizard of Oz* if it were written by Stephen King . . . I hope this is all not too painful for you—I can't bear to write this all to my mother." Now that he had three disciplinary reports on his record, Karter knew he was on the edge of a dangerous precipice. Not only did he have to report to the disciplinary board at the prison, but the parole board could choose to revoke its original decision, i.e. "rescind" his parole.[34]

On January 22, 2009, Karter headed to the disciplinary board hearing that is held whenever a prisoner commits an infraction.

He was being charged with "possession of a contraband, category 4," for the underwear, and "possession of an unauthorized medication, category 3," for the glucosamine / chondroitin. The second charge was submitted because no one knew that glucosamine was not a prescription medication.

Disciplinary hearings at Old Colony were presided over by a supposedly impartial officer. The proceedings included statements, witnesses, and other sorts of seemingly "due process," but the officer was ultimately in charge of all aspects of the hearing. Disciplinary-report hearings were permitted to be tape-recorded, but only if arranged by the prisoner or his or her representative. A written record was kept, which was important to the accused, since the only way a prisoner could protest the finding of a hearing was through the courts. But if the hearing was not recorded, it contained no transcript, so the written record might be inadequate.[35] Unlike in a court of law, the prisoner usually represented him- or herself. Some sought help or studied up on their rights before their hearings, but all were aware that prison justice was decided by the officials who ran the jail.[36] Karter said he'd heard that most prisoners with disciplinary reports received a guilty finding.

Karter was first told that the prison administrators had realized that glucosamine was not a prescribed medication, and immediately the officers dismissed that charge. The less serious charge of "possession of a contraband," for the underwear, was continued without a finding for thirty days. That meant that if Karter was not issued another ticket within that time, the charge could be dropped. However, parole board members had received word from the Old Colony institutional parole officer that Karter had broken a rule deemed worthy of a D-report. Because of this infraction, the parole board could rescind his parole, no matter how small the charge.[37] The board could call the infraction minor, but they also had the option to consider Karter's action equal to "new criminal behavior."[38] Karter thought it wrongheaded that one institution—the Department of Correction—could define an infraction as minor, but that the parole board could deem it significant. He returned to his unit, worrying about what would happen and what this turn of events might do to his mother.

Thirty days later, the Old Colony board found that Karter's category-4 infraction warranted the minor sanction of fourteen days without canteen.[39] His hopes soared. He busied himself with learning Spanish, nursing a herniated disc, and asking every day if someone, anyone, had information on his case. February passed quietly into March. Early that month, the prison reclassified Karter, which meant that he could be returned to Boston Pre-Release just as soon as, but only if, he jumped the parole board hurdle.

Two weeks after the decision was made, Karter learned the news. Apparently, no one at the board had considered that Old Colony deemed Karter's infraction minor. In fact, Karter wondered if the institutional parole officer at Old Colony ever even informed the board that his ticket had been dismissed. The new parole board chairman had voted to rescind Karter's parole.[40] Karter's freedom was now up to the rest of the board.

9. JUSTICE DELAYED

Karter was officially notified that the parole board was to hold what was known as a "rescission hearing panel" at Old Colony Correctional Center;" the panel would then vote to reinstate, modify, or deny his parole.[1] Because he had killed someone, Karter would be on lifetime parole, and he knew a rescission hearing put him on precarious ground. Which members would attend, Karter wondered? Could he persuade them that this situation had been blown out of proportion?

A rescission of parole is different from a revocation in that it occurs before a prisoner has actually exited a facility, if the board deems that something the prisoner has done warrants taking away his or her parole. Most people with no ties to the criminal justice system do not realize that parole can be withdrawn before a prisoner even steps outside the prison walls. Some rescissions are based on new information that arises or severe violations that occur before release, and as controversial as they are, they often can be justified. One example is Pablo Costello, a New Yorker sentenced to twenty-five years to life for taking a hostage and killing a police officer in 1978; he was denied parole five times.[2] At the age of fifty-eight, after earning several college degrees and participating in service organizations, Costello won parole. But then the hostage, the family of the deceased, and a wounded officer testified about the impact of the crime on their lives, and the parole board's decision was overturned based on this new information. Costello stayed behind bars.[3] In contrast, if a parole officer believes a released parolee has violated a condition of his or her parole, that person can be returned to prison, i.e. a revocation.

Karter's hearing was originally scheduled for April 2009. However, he wanted to be thorough since so much was at stake, and he was having a hard time gathering the necessary materials to present his case. So he had the rescission hearing postponed to May. Karter thought by then he would have a slew of documents in hand, including the disciplinary report filed by the institutional parole officer at Boston Pre-Release; the original parole board's "vote sheet," and BPR work reports, evaluations, and support letters from people he had worked for in the community.

To prepare for his case, Karter spent as many hours in the law library as he could. According to the 1996 US Supreme Court decision in *Lewis v. Casey,* prisoners do not have an absolute constitutional right to a law library, but they have a right of access to the courts and a right to seek a redress of grievances.[4] This means they have a legal right to access court documents while they're behind bars.[5] The way this occurs varies from state to state, but by 2013, more than forty states provided access to some form of electronic legal research in their prisons.[6]

Old Colony's law library, like those in many other Massachusetts prisons, was crowded, and Karter had to wait in line to enter. The library had a "No Xeroxing" policy, most likely instituted because of cost, although some state prisons do offer a copy machine in their law libraries.[7] Though Old Colony did offer the LexisNexis database specifically for legal research, the Internet was not accessible to Karter, so he had no way to type "parole rescission" into a search engine and explore. Could he have done so, Karter might have discovered more cases to help him defend himself.

Karter was able to find cases in Massachusetts where a prisoner's parole had not been rescinded despite actions he considered more grievous than his own. Charles Ponticelli, serving a second-degree life sentence, earned parole in 2005. The parole board then provisionally rescinded his parole, stating that he had "delivered inappropriate correspondence to a female staff member," which, according to Karter's information via the prison grapevine, meant that he'd "propositioned a female staff member on his way to prerelease."[8] Ponticelli's parole was ultimately upheld, and he was sent to a long-term residential program in 2008. Ultimately, he committed additional violations after his release, causing a parole revocation.[9]

Karter worked hard to prepare the best case possible, knowing that the odds were against him. Little more than half of the 253 Massachusetts prisoners who had rescission hearings in 2008 had been released, and Karter was aware that his life-sentence status reduced his chances even more.[10] He knew that the Department of Correction was prepared to send him back to prerelease if the parole board agreed.

On May 18, 2009, Karter's rescission hearing was held at Old Colony before two members of the parole board. Appointed by the governor, parole board members serve for five years, or fill the unexpired term of a prior member; they spent a great deal of their time holding hearings in the field, traveling to state and county facilities. For this they are compensated well, earning in 2015 a salary that averaged $100,000 per year.[11]

On reading the transcript of the hearing, what unfolded seems bizarre. First, there was obviously some kind of commotion outside the hearing room, as the person who was transcribing the hearing wrote the words "LOUD CRASH," and "inaudible" in several places.[12] Second, the two board members seemed not to know much about Karter's case, getting dates mixed up, and misunderstanding that Karter had never had prescription medication, and in fact, that the charge had been dismissed by the DOC.[13] The board members also seemed to be unaware that glucosamine was available in some prison canteens, insisting instead that it was prohibited. Even after Karter mentioned that the DOC had dismissed that finding, one board member said it was "a criminal thing you know you break the rules, not do what you're supposed to do, try and I'll work my way round it and let someone buy it. I'll bring it in and I'll find it and I'll violate DOC rules and do what I want. Rather than what I'm supposed to do. . . . These rules are strictly written."[14] The panel ended the hearing by telling Karter that they were tasked to decide if he would be a good candidate for supervision, or if his actions might predict future "criminal behavior."[15]

After the hearing, Karter went back to his cell, too furious to write anything except that the hearing had lasted barely ten minutes. It seemed to him that the rescission panel had put little thought into important parts of the statute. Karter pointed out later in his legal complaint that he believed the parole board did not follow their own rules at the conclusion of the hearing, which state that, "The rescission hearing panel makes its decision in private" and a vote sheet is prepared with reasons for the decision.[16] Regulations also state that "after a decision is made, the rescission hearing panel calls the inmate and representative into the hearing room at which time the presenting member informs the parolee of its decision as to each rescission charge, and whether or not a new parole date is appropriate."[17] There was no immediate decision. Instead, the two members told Karter he had to wait again, this time for the complete board to vote on whether his original parole would be upheld.

Karter celebrated his thirty-third birthday in June 2009. At the end of the month, he finally heard back from the full board: they had voted unanimously to rescind his parole. He was to have yet another parole hearing in August to find out how long his setback would be.

Over the next several weeks, Karter thrashed around in letter after letter to me, screaming on the page that all he had worked for might be lost. Didn't they realize that "No amount of punishment" could "undo Jason's death?" He went back and forth between blaming himself and blaming the board, was prone to distraction, and tried to busy himself with the guitar, playing softball, and rewriting the out-of-date computer class curriculum. But in his "rants," as he called them, he wondered if the board felt that if he hadn't learned to follow the rules in the sixteen years he had spent behind bars already, maybe he would need another sixteen to learn them. In one letter, Karter quoted Robert Frost's famous poem "Fire and Ice": "I think I know enough of hate / To say that for destruction ice / is also great / and would suffice."

That summer, Michael Jackson died and the world was sent into a paroxysm of grief; the esteemed US senator Edward Kennedy also passed away. When I wrote to Karter and told him how sad Massachusetts residents were about Kennedy's death, he responded: "Death is a strange thing in prison. Even more so than on the outside, it is something people maintain a considerable distance from. . . . It's what put them here, so either it's something shameful or painful, or (in the case of those who think it was justified or unavoidable) infuriating. . . . So when your parent or child or best friend dies, there's no one to turn to. . . . And there's no room to grieve."

Karter had seen death firsthand on several occasions while he was in prison: at Old Colony, a prisoner suffering from mental illness had suffocated himself with a plastic bag; before that, when Karter was at Norfolk, a man hung himself; and at Shirley, someone he had known for over ten years attempted suicide. But the pain was so troubling that Karter could not place the years when these incidents occurred. He wrote, "Time is like one of those stretches of Arizona highway that goes on seemingly forever with no distinguishing landmarks or points of reference."

One hot night that summer, Karter lay awake in his cell. He turned over events in his mind, as he often did before sleep mercifully fell on him. He had decided to postpone the August hearing, fearing that the panel would give him a five-year setback, given that three of the current members had voted that way the first time. He had not set a future hearing date; maybe he would wait a few months, maybe a year. Maybe he would wait until some members of the board retired; maybe he would seek legal recourse against the rescission. All these ideas bubbled up inside him, and the heat did not help. He tossed and turned, wondering if he had done what was right for his family.

His thoughts were interrupted by his cellmate, a man whom Karter described as so violent that, after he had beaten a previous cellmate at MCI Concord, it was claimed, "they needed a mop for the blood." The man said, "Do you mind if I ask you something, and I'm not trying to be a wise-ass, but you seem like such a respectful, polite kid, un-aggressive, laid back . . . What made you stab someone, I mean what pushed you that far? Cause you know I grew up that way and have been hurting people my whole life, smashing them with Kahlua bottles, pipes, whatever, it's just how I am, I have a quick temper, fly into a rage, and it's usually bad for the other guy . . . but you're not like that."

Karter lay there, thinking about how to answer the question. Ultimately, he said nothing. He had not felt violent that day in April, just desperate. Knowing what desperation had cost him, however, was too much for words. But something had changed for Karter. He had resolved that, no matter what pain and responsibility he bore for Jason's murder, at this point, keeping him behind bars was a waste—both for himself and for the Massachusetts taxpayers. He would fight the rescission with everything he had.

The first thing he did was to file a formal parole reconsideration with the board, outlining all the reasons his parole should not be rescinded, attaching documents—more than 150 pages worth. He also wrote to the governor criticizing parole policies, and sent letters about his case to lawyers and agencies that helped prisoners. He also sent poems and essays to writing contests, some of which were published, and he wrote a fifteen-page paper on his vision that a humane justice system should not be called the Department of Correction but the "Department of Rehabilitation."[18] He was reaching out on all fronts, desperate to get back his parole opportunity. He wasn't yet sure how, or if he would even schedule another hearing. But he did know one thing: There would be no more mistakes.

In July 2010 Karter was moved to a new unit. At this time, Old Colony was enacting a changeover, moving many prisoners out and many others in while aiming to serve as a destination for mentally ill prisoners within the state. Finally, Karter had been moved away from the cellmate who, he said, had used a bat to beat his girlfriend nearly to death and, out of the blue, would threaten Karter about his guitar, saying, "If you play one more fucking note, I'm going to smash that fucking thing into little pieces." Karter's new cellmate Rich was "quiet, passive, respectful."

That fall, Karter was able to see his family on several occasions, including his father, who was free and sober. Derek had been through several bouts with drugs after prison, and it took him a while to get clearance to visit his son. Karter very much wanted to see his stepbrother Chace, born in 2000, to his father and Josephine, a recovering drug addict whom Derek met when he was at a halfway house after prison. Josephine eventually returned to the streets and died from drug-related causes when Chace was three years old. Karter said that all of his father's relationships after Josephine affected Chace, who was understandably a needy child. Karter planned to help take care of Chace when he finally got out of prison. This goal motivated him even more to win back his parole opportunity. By November, 2010, he had filed his formal request to the Board, asking that they reconsider their decision to rescind his parole.

One evening, before dinner, Karter was talking to his cellmate Rich about school. Karter never finished high school, but had earned his GED while at the Barnstable House of Correction. He had wanted to enroll in college at several points during his incarceration, but the DOC had denied him such programming, he said, "because of the severe nature of his crime." He considered his inaccessibility to higher education a travesty. Recently he'd had some educational opportunities, though. Beginning in January 2010, Karter had participated in the first Inside-Out program piloted in a Massachusetts DOC facility, a college-level course where students from the outside mix with prisoners behind bars.[19] Inside-Out aims to create an educational exchange between prisoners and college students, and all classes take place inside a correctional institution. It had been the first thing at Old Colony that truly excited Karter.

For young prisoners like Karter who have their education interrupted and literally never know if and when they will get out of prison, education is a way for them to stay sane and become less prone to violence,[20] as well as helping them reconnect with the outside world.[21] However, since 1994, higher education behind bars had been a spotty affair in the United States. That was the year Jesse Helms, then US senator from North Carolina, managed to get an amendment forbidding Pell Grants for prisoners tacked on to President Bill Clinton's Omnibus Crime Bill.[22] Less than 1 percent of those receiving Pell Grants were prisoners, or only 25,000 prisoner-students out of the 4.7 million grants dispersed; but without such grants, many higher education programs in prison dried up.[23] After that, college in prison existed only if funded by universities or other outside sources.[24] This despite the fact that research shows that the more education a prisoner can access, the more likely he or she is to avoid a return to crime and be able to find a job upon release.[25]

By 2010, for most US prisons, basic education and GED programs were the norm; college programs were sparse. If no college program was available, and a prisoner had no financial support, he or she had to choose between paying for correspondence courses or for basic necessities like toiletries and in some cases food and clothing.[26] It took until 2015 for the US Department of Education to announce that as part of President Barak Obama's initiative to reduce mass incarceration, the country would reinvest in higher education in prison. With the expressed goals of "helping them get jobs, support their families, and turn their lives around," the Second Chance Pell Pilot Program allows a select number of incarcerated Americans to pursue higher education.[27] Additionally, the REAL Act was introduced in May 2015 by Rep. Donna F. Edwards (D-Maryland) to ensure that all state and federal prisoners would once again be eligible for Pell grants. However, as of this writing, the act had not yet become law.[28]

Charged up from his Inside-Out experience, where his professors had encouraged him not just to go to college but to earn a PhD when he got out of prison, Karter had managed to obtain a coveted place in a community college writing program. Although he thought the class was easy, it still gave him a chance to express his ideas in writing. His cellmate, Rich, commenting on Karter's papers for the class, said, "Do you realize that they're all about prison?"

Karter responded, "No, but what else do I know? I'm thirty-four years old and have been in prison eighteen years. . . . We had an assignment that was to write about an unforgettable moment, good or bad—what was I supposed to write about? I was only on the street for sixteen years. I grew up with a father who was a drug addict, unfaithful, verbally and physically abusive, and went to prison. I didn't do good in school, in sports or at home—where was I supposed to have an unforgettable good moment?"

Rich covered his face and began to weep.

"Rich, what's wrong, are you all right?" Karter worried he had triggered a bad memory in Rich's personal life. Rich had been a highly paid executive before a first-degree murder sentence sent him to prison.

Rich shook his head and finally looked up at Karter. He was silent for a while. Then he said, "You've had this really hard life, and it's sad."

Karter was taken aback and tried to explain that he was not upset; yes, he had had a rough time, but he was trying to make the best of it. He had taken advantage of everything available in prison, he told Rich. And that was what kept him going.

On December 26, 2010, a parolee named Domenic Cinelli shot and killed a police officer during a burglary attempt at a department store in a town on the outskirts of Boston. The response to the crime was outrage, and immediately, conclusions were hastily drawn: an officer shot meant that the parolee should never have been released. But that was not the whole truth. In fact, research later revealed that the Cinelli crime was likely a result of systemic problems in the Massachusetts parole system.[29] Cinelli was shown to have had "inadequate" supervision by parole officers, and a review of the case found there were no risk-assessment tools in place when Cinelli was released to determine his dangerousness, nor had the unit responsible for getting information to the board done a good enough job highlighting the "violence and seriousness of Cinelli's crimes."[30]

Instead of admitting to the public that parole is a fallible system—a human system—and taking steps after the tragedy to fully research what were called, in criminal justice jargon, "evidence-based practices," Governor Deval Patrick instituted a number of knee-jerk reforms, which included forcing the resignation of five parole board members.[31] Much to Karter's dismay, hearings for men and women serving life sentences were put on hold while new board members were appointed and trained.

Critics felt that the governor's move to revamp the parole board was for political gain. It seemed that Patrick had acted unilaterally, choosing to disregard what other states had shown to be effective ways to improve parole in the aftermath of such a tragedy. In nearby Connecticut, for example, the governor and legislature had come together to pass reforms—imperfect perhaps, but at least they made the decision in unison.[32] By contrast, Patrick installed Joshua Wall, a former prosecutor, at the helm of the board and sent a clear message that no more mistakes would be made in parole decisions.[33] In other words, keep people locked up.

This decision set the state backward in terms of a healthy parole policy: in 2010, the board had granted parole to lifers 33.1 percent of the time; by May 2013 that number had plummeted to 14.3 percent.[34] (By the end of 2014, after Wall moved on to become a superior court judge and forensic psychologist Dr. Charlene Bonner took over the board, rates improved to 36 percent.[35]) In his writings, Karter chastised Massachusetts officials for "paint[ing] hundreds, perhaps thousands of genuinely reformed, remorseful, and rehabilitated prisoners and ex-prisoners with the same brush." He also wondered how he could possibly be perceived as a greater risk to society than Cinelli had been.

In 2011, the median annual household income in the United States was approximately $50,000.[36] The country spent nearly as much incarcerating Karter Reed, and many others like him. The state of California was ordered by the Supreme Court to reduce its overcrowded prisons, called examples of "cruel and unusual punishment." Packed US prisons were reaching a crisis level, such that even well-known Republicans like Newt Gingrich began insisting on a reduction in incarceration rates; these voices were, of course, advocating for financial savings rather than against the ethics of over-incarceration.[37] While some said the tide was turning nationwide, and parole was gaining traction as a key to public safety, Massachusetts was still running scared, with prisoners paying the price.[38]

IV

We know what we are, but know not
What we may be.

William Shakespeare, *Hamlet*

10. LAWYER UP

On Richard Neumeier's desk in his downtown Boston office was a small statue of an English barrister, complete with wig, robe, and a law book under one arm, the phrase "Sue the bastards" engraved on the base. Next to the figurine was a thank-you card from an Alabama prisoner, the only death penalty case that Neumeier had ever litigated. When I visited him in December 2013, months after Karter contacted him, the first thing he showed me was this card from a case he had worked on pro bono for eighteen years, getting the man off death row and enabling him to transition into the general prison population. It was quite the victory for an attorney who had spent most of his practice fighting insurance lawsuits.

Neumeier was not the first lawyer Karter had contacted, and he certainly seemed an unlikely choice. But he was the perfect man for the job. He answered his phone with a sturdy "Neumeier" that let you know he was ready to take on the state; he believed pro bono work was the duty of lawyers; and, importantly for Karter, he was the lawyer who had litigated what was the only parole rescission case in Massachusetts, *Lanier v. Fair.*[1]

Albert Lanier had first earned parole in 1984, and was subsequently transferred to a halfway house. One morning at 4 a.m., about a month after his arrival, Lanier was found to be missing during a routine bed check. He later contended that he was in the shower, but authorities discovered his window open and accused him of trying to escape. Whatever the truth, he turned up half an hour after bed check. Lanier was immediately transferred back to higher security and charged with "being out of place."[2] Three weeks later, the charge was dismissed in a disciplinary hearing, but a supervising parole officer recommended that Lanier's parole be rescinded. Eventually, after a circuitous route, the parole board upheld the rescission, and Lanier remained in custody.[3] He alleged that his rights had been violated, sued for damages in state court, and was denied release in 1986.[4]

Enter Richard Neumeier, who appealed Lanier's case to the First Circuit Court of Appeals and lost. Despite this defeat, *Lanier v. Fair* had a great effect on rescission case language, as the three-judge panel wrote in their opinion that prisoners had a "protected liberty interest" in remaining at halfway houses.[5] This meant that a parolee could not lose his or her freedom and be transferred from a halfway house back to prison without good cause. The decision also declared that prisoners were entitled to a full explanation of the judgment in writing.[6] These points would later become important to Karter's petition.

Before Karter found Neumeier in 2012, he had spent nearly three years writing letters to lawyers, seeking representation. Once tried and convicted, and appeals decided, a prisoner doesn't have a right to a lawyer to fight parole decisions, and finding an attorney from inside prison is difficult.[7] The few lawyers in the state of Massachusetts known for defending parolees—Karter said he wrote to ten—were either working on other cases or did not respond. One lawyer wanted a $10,000 retainer, while another told Karter it would cost between $100,000 and $200,000 to defend him. While representatives from Prisoners' Legal Services of Massachusetts litigate on behalf of prisoners, advocate administratively, and counsel clients, they often focus on class-action lawsuits relating to the treatment of prisoners and cannot respond to every prisoner's individual case.[8] This is not uncommon; the relatively few individuals and groups that do advocate for prisoners across the country are hindered by scarce resources, especially when compared to the many needs of the men and women behind bars.

Karter was frustrated as letter after letter came back with a "No," or were not answered. As a result, he got busy learning the law so that he could defend himself. From the moment he heard that his parole was rescinded in June 2009, Karter had poured over the LexisNexis database, trying to uncover the best way to present his case, learning the legal definitions and ideas behind complaints, memoranda, and motions for injunctions, anything he could file pro se, "on his own." However, the numbers were against him. In 1994, more than 97 percent of pro se federal lawsuits were dismissed by judges.[9] Law professor Margo Schlanger wrote that it only got worse for prisoners after the 1996 Prison Litigation Reform Act undermined their ability to "bring, settle, and win lawsuits."[10] In 2015, she reported on data from 1988 to 2012 that found a decline in both filings and victories, concluding that "courts are becoming less and less hospitable for prisoners' claims."[11] In addition, filing fees and an eye untrained for the law makes it difficult to craft a legal argument from behind bars.[12]

Jailhouse lawyering is also a lot of work, and demands a level of literacy that many prisoners do not possess; indeed, the most recent data available, reported in 2010 by researchers Bruce Western and Becky Petit, revealed that "state prisoners average just a tenth grade education, and about 70 percent have no high school diploma."[13] Those prisoners who do persevere in their legal defense risk additional obstacles: one study found that those engaging in litigation faced increased retaliation from prison employees.[14] While Karter could have taken his chances with another parole hearing, he knew that the climate in Massachusetts was against him. Since the Cinelli tragedy, the parole board had issued five-year setbacks in its parole denials for sixty-two out of eighty-eight lifers.[15] If he went up for parole again, Karter felt certain that would be his fate, too. What choice did he have but the courts?

Karter's legal work on his rescission case was striking. Before Richard Neumeier came on the scene, Karter had examined the details of what he believed were mistakes made by the parole board, and searched to find cases that supported this assessment. For example, in the denial of his rescission reconsideration in 2010, the board wrote that Karter had "stipulated" (or agreed) to his rescission. This he knew to be false. He had agreed to the facts—that they found underwear and a dietary supplement in the form of pills in his locker—but that is not what the board decision stated. He made this point in June 2011 when he filed a complaint to the Suffolk County Superior Court saying that the board had unlawfully and unconstitutionally rescinded his parole. He used the Lanier case as one of the examples in making his argument, saying that he had a "protected liberty interest" in his parole release date.[16] However, much to Karter's chagrin, the court upheld the board's decision and his release was ultimately denied in May 2012.

After that, Karter fell into a kind of despair. The stress of Old Colony was wearing on him. Every day it seemed that more and more second-degree lifers were being denied parole, facing inordinate delays in receiving decisions, being treated rudely at hearings, or feeling that little attention was being paid to their successful prison records.[17] A wife of one parolee, who chose to remain anonymous because she feared retaliation against her husband, described a hearing: "They seemed so hostile and like they had already made their decision. . . . Watching how they treated [my husband], I felt horrible. . . . They made [my husband] feel like his sixteen years of success meant nothing."[18] Another parolee was shocked after his revocation hearing: "Going in front of the old Parole Board was terrifying . . . during those hearings, I had some badgering, but they looked like saints in comparison to this board."[19] Karter wondered, in a July 2011 letter to a reporter at the *Boston Globe*, why the parole board, and the press for that matter, paid no attention to "the 141 lifers paroled in the last five years who were law-abiding tax-paying citizens? Or the 340 currently under parole supervision?"[20] It was a good question.

A powerful example of this type of treatment was a prisoner Karter met at Old Colony named Antonio Ferrer, who, in 1992, had been convicted of second-degree murder as a juvenile.[21] Ferrer served fifteen years and earned parole in 2008; he had a narcotics charge while released that was eventually dismissed, but in 2010, all hell broke loose for him. It was then, according to Karter, that a confidential informant told the police that Ferrer had drugs at home. His house was raided. No drugs were found, and Karter wrote that Ferrer's parole officer told him not to worry. A few days later, the officer asked Ferrer to report to the parole office to discuss the raid. And just like that, Ferrer was cuffed and returned to custody. Whether or not this story was true was never made public. Karter claimed that when Ferrer went back before the parole board for his revocation hearing in 2011, a board member said to him: "I don't know how you got out to begin with; you're not rehabilitated; you just weaseled your way out—you're a weasel." The board ordered Ferrer to serve a five-year setback. The decision by the board—posted on the parole board's official website—took nineteen months.[22]

Between 2011 and 2013, these types of delays were not uncommon, whereas prior parole boards had managed decisions in four to eight weeks.[23] In 2014, the average wait time for prisoners in Massachusetts to receive decisions was more than seven months, instead of the two months common when

Karter received his decision in 2008.[24] In 2012, chairman Joshua Wall blamed the backlog of cases on the previous board, what he claimed was a more rigorous scrutiny of potential parolees since the board overhaul, and staff shortages.[25] But advocates said the delays were "inexcusable" both for victims' families and for those seeking parole.[26] In 2015, after forensic psychologist Dr. Charlene Bonner became chair, the decision time returned to sixty days.[27]

One day in 2011, two years after his parole had been officially rescinded, an acquaintance who Karter had been assisting with legal work asked him to type up a letter for his case. At the time, Karter was taking a computer class where he often tutored prisoners who needed help with technology questions. Karter asked the instructor if he could assist this man, named Steven. Steven wasn't in the class, but he wanted to sit with Karter while he typed so he could put things into his own words. The instructor obliged, and Karter and Steven began working together. Karter typed while continuing to field questions from students who visited his desk.

Soon after, a sergeant who saw Steven go into the classroom arrived on the scene and said: "Leave. You're out of place." Steven tried to explain that Karter was helping him and that he had permission from the instructor, but the sergeant said he could not be in the school area unless he was enrolled in a class. He escorted Steven out. An hour later, the sergeant reappeared, this time with a lieutenant, who asked Karter what he was doing. Karter said that he was assisting other prisoners with their assignments as well as working on the letter. One of the officers told Karter, "Pack your bags, you're done for the day."

Karter went back to his unit, a bit disgruntled, but he figured there are always correction officers who will do what they will do. He did not think twice about the encounter. However, the next day, Karter was called into a CO's office and told that he had received a disciplinary report because he had disobeyed a direct order to "put down the legal work." Karter was livid. Not only was this accusation untrue, but he knew that another infraction, the dreaded D-report, was a parole nightmare. He also learned that his tutoring position had been revoked and that he was forbidden to use the computer.

Back in his unit, the only thing going through Karter's mind was how the parole board would say, "See, you never obey rules. You will never obey rules." Even if he protested the disciplinary report, which he planned to do, they would say, "You're trying to wiggle out of that too." He would get the fourth mark on his permanent record. Who knew what would happen, particularly with a parole board seemingly set against releasing lifers?

In August 2012, Massachusetts enacted its version of a three-strike law, another result of the Cinelli furor that had seized the state's criminal justice system. The "habitual offender" law made those convicted three times of specific violent crimes ineligible for parole, diverted resources—possibly $1.25 million a year, according to some estimates—away from prison programs, and moved Massachusetts another step away from the de-incarceration thinking that was spreading to many quarters of the country.[28] Judicial discretion was not a part of this law, thus tying the hands of any judge who might find an exception.[29] Three strikes laws are opposed by the American Civil Liberties Union because they take away judicial discretion, have a disproportionate effect on people of color, and by and large, do not prevent most violent crime.[30]

Karter wrote at this time: "People are tired. Meetings [that in 2008] used to have 35 excited, ambitious hopeful members have 8–10, 12–15 on a good night. One meeting last week was just me and another guy. That's it, in a classroom designed to hold 40. Not even 4 years ago, they were turning people away. It was the 3rd year of Deval's term and 2nd of Commissioner Clarke's—people had a renewed sense of hope. Now you will not find one single prisoner who will think the system will improve . . . . I know the law now and how it works. I know these conditions are illegal. All of them can be changed through the courts. . . . You know the axiom: power concedes nothing without a demand."

For Karter, this was definitely the darkness before the dawn.

Richard Neumeier received Karter's letter in July 2012, and was immediately impressed. (One reason was that Karter had read the Lanier case.) Neumeier wondered if he might have a good claim. "The key thing is that they didn't have good cause," he said that day I visited him in 2013, leaning across his desk and gesticulating with his glasses as if he had just arrived at that conclusion. He paused for a moment, mid-thought, above the "Sue the bastards" statuette. "Excess underwear? Not good cause. They knew they were supposed to write down the cause for the parole rescission, and they didn't," he said.[31]

Neumeier called Karter's mother and asked if he could drive down to New Bedford and look at the papers Karter had filed with the court (she had copies). At the time, Sharon lived with her fiancé Kevin, who had been friends with Derek in their youth. The couple lived in a first-floor apartment on a quiet street near the house Karter had grown up in. Karter was overwhelmed when he later talked about this meeting, saying that Neumeier sat down with Sharon and said, "I want to help your son." Neumeier told her that he would not charge a fee. Sharon and Karter were astounded—his offer of free legal counsel was almost impossible to believe. Karter's excitement was apparent in his letter to me dated July 25: "Quickly: I may have a lawyer! Not just a lawyer, *the* lawyer. Richard L. Neumeier."

Neumeier examined the documents at Sharon's place, and, on first pass, saw that the Department of Correction had dismissed the excessive medication disciplinary report. He then speculated that the parole board would not want to create a public record with this fact: rescission for excessive underwear. In August, Neumeier and Karter met at Old Colony, and began working on their next steps. Neumeier filed papers with the court indicating that he was representing Karter. Then, he decided to take a deposition of whomever the parole board designated to explain why the members had rescinded Karter's parole. A tool for discovery before a trial, a deposition is "a formal statement" made under oath by a person "who has promised to tell the truth" so that the statement can be used in court.[32]

Neumeier wanted to take depositions for several reasons. First, he wanted to hear what the parole board would say about Karter's case; the statements would record the board's story so that it could not be changed later on. He also knew that, after the Cinelli debacle, Governor Patrick had forced the resignation of five parole board members—all of whom had voted on Karter's case—and he wondered who the board would produce to explain why they had rescinded Karter's parole.[33] Which remaining members knew anything about Karter's case? Neumeier also knew that the board had provided no written reason for the rescission, and would have to come up with one during the depositions.[34]

Karter was relieved to finally have legal representation, but in no way did that end his involvement in his case. He now felt more empowered when delving into the law and wanted to examine the legality of the conditions he saw around him, in particular, those affecting juveniles who had been sentenced to life without parole. More than a dozen of these men were housed with him at Old Colony, and from his other prison stints, he'd met many of the others—a total of sixty-three who ultimately became eligible for parole after the Diatchenko decision.[35] Karter's letters to me were now filled with comments about the progress, or lack thereof, that Massachusetts was making in criminal justice.

In October 2012, Richard Neumeier traveled to the parole board's office in Natick to take the deposition of Lynn Ferraris, whom the board had named as its spokesperson. Interestingly, Ferraris, now chief of transitional services for the parole board, had considered Albert Lanier's violations so grievous that she had started the ball rolling for his parole rescission in 1989. Now, she was responsible for, among other things, case preparation for hearings, so she was required to know about parole cases, although she had no direct involvement with Karter's case. Karter was not in attendance.

To the layperson, a deposition feels formal, similar to giving testimony in a trial, but it involves no courtroom, judge, or jury. When asked if she had ever been deposed, Ferraris replied, "A very, very, very, very long time ago."[36] Ferraris was protected by Timothy Dooling, the board's attorney at the time, who objected whenever he felt that Ferraris could not answer or should not be asked certain questions.

The most interesting exchange, as recorded in the deposition transcript, began with Neumeier establishing that Ferraris would not say or did not know who wrote the parole rescission decision. By doing so, he raised the question of board competence. Later in the deposition, Neumeier inferred deliberate misrepresentation on the board's part for saying that Karter had agreed or "stipulated" to the rescission. He also pointed out for the record the absurdity in the case, asking, "Have you come across any other case since you've been here where parole was revoked, rescinded, because somebody has excess underwear?"

Ferraris responded, "There are many cases at the Parole Board. I have not reviewed all cases to be able to respond to that question appropriately."

Neumeier was not deterred, "Was there anything special about the excess underwear that Reed had that indicated that was some kind of a threat to him being on the outside?

Ferraris refused to answer: "That was not a decision for me to make."[37]

The rescission decision looked pretty foolish, although the contention that Karter "stipulated" to his parole was not going away any time soon. When at the end of the deposition Neumeier asked, "Is the decision of the Parole Board supposed to state some reasons for rescinding parole?" Ferraris dug in her heels and held firm to her position, apparently not required to respond to this question at a deposition.

Neumeier pushed on, "But it's obvious to you from reading the transcript that Mr. Reed did not stipulate to rescind his parole?"

"Obvious is your word, not mine," she replied.[38]

Later that month, Neumeier began getting ready to go to trial, filing a joint pretrial memorandum with the court. He received news that the trial would be in six months, on April 29, 2013. The board wanted the case to be decided by a jury rather than a judge, perhaps to focus on Karter's crime rather than on a parole rescission over six pairs of underwear. Dooling informed Neumeier that he was retiring as parole board counsel and that they hoped to have his replacement by December.

Karter was disappointed that the trial was so far away—another Christmas in prison. He wrote to me in December, 2012, "When you wrote about the first snow, it reminded me of something I'm not even sure is real but I wish for in a way that's indescribable: the absolute peace and quietness after a heavy snow when the whole world (as far as the eye can see and the ear can hear) has stopped—it's something you can never have in prison." It was now more than four years since Karter had received his affirmative parole decision in May 2008. He continued to busy himself with myriad activities, especially research in the law library to find potentially relevant cases to help his own. He also assisted others with legal work, helped run Old Colony's Lifers Group, participated in Toastmasters, the public speaking group, went to band rehearsals, gave haircuts, worked out, and read books. He compiled lists of the cases he found on a typewriter because he had lost his computer privileges. He wrote some legal arguments to Neumeier and instructed him where and how the board's responses made no sense—anything to help his case and to feel less powerless. He wrote to me less frequently, feeling suspended between hope and despair.

On April 16, 2013, the day after the tragic Boston Marathon bombing, I entered the Suffolk County Courthouse, an imposing stone building in downtown Boston, to discover that the judge was late to Karter's pretrial conference, stuck at jury selection for another trial. His delay was not particularly troubling to the two attorneys, Neumeier and Janice Noble, the parole board's newly appointed counsel. The two lawyers discussed the case, sitting on pew-like benches in the rectangular courtroom that contained little more than a flag and a few law books beyond the judge's dais. Noble looked to be in her mid-thirties and had worked as a prosecutor in Suffolk County before becoming general counsel to the board. She believed that she had to walk a "delicate line," since it was her view that the public and parolee had "competing interests."[39]

A pretrial conference is mostly managerial for the judge,

and an opportunity to ensure that both attorneys are ready for trial.[40] As soon as Judge Garry V. Inge entered the courtroom, he apologized for being late and called the attorneys to the bench. Inge had been a judge in Suffolk Superior Court since 2009, and Neumeier had heard that he was fair-handed.[41] The judge turned to Neumeier, who explained that the attorneys had agreed not to have a jury trial. "After that, I think we don't agree except that the trial will be short," Neumeier said. No one laughed. They discussed logistics—the trial time would have to be set late enough in the morning for Karter to be brought from Old Colony, more than an hour away. They expected the trial to last only one day.

Next, the attorneys offered their own assessments of the case. Neumeier said that he had given Noble "twenty-two pages of proposed findings of fact and conclusions of law together with a copy of fifty-two proposed exhibits, all on March 13," and she had not responded. He added that she had had plenty of time to respond and knew the material for the case was due in December, and that his client had been incarcerated for four extra years. Police sirens blared outside the courtroom.

"They voted to rescind, and at the end of the day, the Parole Board has good cause to rescind," Noble responded.

"They found it was glucosamine, which is for purchase in the DOC," answered Neumeier. "What it comes down to is six pairs of underwear."

At this point, the judge interrupted. "Underwear?"

Neumeier answered in the affirmative.

Noble then asked for a one month continuance, saying that she needed to get up to speed on the case. Neumeier objected, noting that she had had time to review his proposed findings and write a lengthy motion to dismiss. He added, "My guy has been in prison waiting for this for months."

The judge compromised, postponing the date two-and-a-half weeks. The trial was now set for May 17. Karter would have to wait, again. However, by now he had more perspective than he'd had as a boy. To his little brother Chace, who wondered in every phone call, "When are you getting out of there?" Karter knew the answer. It was something he would tell Chace many times, but something he also told himself: "Your patience will be rewarded very soon."

11. GETTING OUT

When Karter received the signed settlement agreement dated May 1, 2013, he could not believe what he was reading. He reviewed it several times, got up, sat back down, and for five minutes paced in his cell until he could bear it no longer. Then he screamed out the window to a buddy who was in a cell block across from him, because, as he said in a letter, it would not be true until he "spoke it into reality."

The official one page document stated that, despite disagreeing about the case, both parties wished to "settle."[1] What that meant in practical terms was that the lawsuit was over; there would be no trial, and Karter would finally be freed. After six months at a long-term residential treatment program or halfway house, he would be released on lifetime parole. He was the first person in Massachusetts who—as far as anyone knew—had ever won such a case against the parole board.

"You always have to keep in mind your client's objective," Richard Neumeier said in 2014 when speaking about the settlement.[2] He knew that Karter's goal had been to get out of prison, and if Neumeier had tried the case, a decision might not have come for another several months, perhaps even longer. The parole board could then have asked for a stay, which could have kept Karter behind bars until he appealed. Neumeier had to walk a fine line between letting the parole board think they had no case (i.e., the excess underwear charge) while at the same time working to settle.

The agreement was essentially a contract, ensuring enforcement by both sides, and the conditions were in keeping with Karter's parole from 2008. The requirements echoed many such conditions for parolees exiting prisons in Massachusetts, including an approved home plan; substance abuse evaluation and drug/alcohol testing (even though Karter had no history of alcohol or drugs); a check-in with one's parole officer on the day of release; a mental health evaluation; and a waiver of work for two weeks (meaning that the board expected Karter to secure a job after that time).[3]

Karter also was to have no contact with the Robinson family. He had accepted this long ago, though it ruled out processes such as restorative justice. Restorative justice promotes forgiveness, and allow victim and perpetrator to meet—not necessarily with those involved in their specific cases, but with those who have experienced or committed similar crimes.[4] This challenging undertaking requires a delicate balance of making amends and giving voice to the victims, who often feel shut out of the prosecutorial process.[5] While the Robinsons, understandably, may have not wanted to participate in such a dialogue, many families have benefitted from restorative justice.[6] Sujatha Baliga, senior program specialist for the National Council on Crime and Delinquency, said that she once saw the parents of a young man charged with murder talk with the parents of the girl he had killed, a process that she said was "one of the most remarkable things I have ever seen."[7] Over an eight month period, they were able to ask questions and achieve some type of understanding that would not have been possible in court.[8]

Karter had expressed interest in making amends in his letters, and at one point, after he received news of his settlement in 2013, he wrote, "I will constantly have to give back," and "do all I can to honor Jason and his family while not forsaking my own life."

Karter had a long list of things to do before he could officially exit Old Colony. First, he had to find housing. For men and women leaving prison, such options are limited; in fact, a shocking one-tenth become homeless because they cannot find or afford a place to live.[9] The majority end up living with family members or intimate partners.[10] Karter's aunt and uncle had wanted him released to them when he first earned parole, as they had a job for him and lived in what the parole board had considered a neutral neighborhood, far from where he had committed his crime. There he would face much less difficulty in establishing a new life.

However, Karter's new parole requirements made this option impossible. While the parole board was not requiring Karter to return to a prerelease facility—a point that Neumeier had made sure of in the settlement—it did mandate that he find board-sanctioned transitional housing. Rearrests and re-incarceration rates in Massachusetts are lower for former prisoners who enter the community from these types of housing units, rather than directly from prison.[11] Transitional housing include halfway houses, a handful of which operate in Massachusetts; a report by the Urban Institute in 2004 cited that only fifty-five were available for former state prisoners nationwide.[12] The report also said that for federal prisoners, there were 282 halfway houses with 6911 beds for over 18,000 returning men and women.[13] While halfway houses are often a positive temporary solution, aiming to provide a supervised bridge for parolees for a prescribed number of months, they have not been free from criticism.[14] Halfway houses in New Jersey have been riddled with bad management problems and escapes; Florida's halfway houses have been poorly monitored; and in Pennsylvania, staff were not trained properly in "substance abuse treatment, job training and other programs designed to improve [one's] transition back to society."[15]

Karter had heard positive reports about Dismas House, which had been founded in Worcester in 1974 by Reverend Jack Hickey and students from Vanderbilt University who wanted to help former prisoners adjust to society in a supportive community setting.[16] "Dismas," in the Christian tradition, refers to "the good thief" who repented and wanted to be remembered by Jesus in Paradise.[17] The program had offshoots in cities across the country and in Ireland, founded by religious men and women, all with a mission to support reentry for former prisoners.[18]

Worchester is about fifty miles from Boston and about eighty miles from New Bedford. While the city had all the troubles with unemployment that had beset the nation since the recession that began in 2007, that also meant that housing there was affordable.[19] Most important, Karter's father and Chace lived there. Being close to his stepbrother was important to Karter, and he was willing to work through his concerns about being near Derek for a chance to take part in Chace's life. Dismas House also appealed to Karter because it required its residents to get jobs, encouraged enrollment in school, involved participants in family-style dinners, was free of alcohol, drugs, and violence, and cost only $75 a week.[20] The long list of housing agreements included quiet hours, chore sharing, and curfews. Karter applied and was accepted. He then began the all-too-familiar process of waiting for a bed to become available.

Individuals who are exiting prison need to have a life plan in place before they are released. Because a prisoner does not need to worry about medical insurance, Karter registered for MassHealth, the state's free and low-cost health insurance plan.[21] He also planned to get his driver's license, which meant honing up on the rules of the road that had changed since he was sixteen-years-old. He looked into food stamps and other assistance programs. Karter also thought about college, and what courses he would take. While tying up these loose ends, he read several books that had gone unfinished, including one by a former death row prisoner, *Life after Death* by Damien Echols.

The last of the more than one hundred letters I received from Karter was dated August 1, 2013. In it, he told me the news that he would be on his way to Dismas on August 5: "It is still too surreal and somehow unfathomable that I am leaving even with the settlement, acceptance into Dismas House and the certainty that it was just a matter of time until a bed opened up. I have lost (as a result of these twenty-plus years) my capacity to comprehend freedom." The idea of freedom is frightening to many prisoners, and Karter was no exception. He had heard stories of his buddies getting out and having anxiety attacks in the middle of malls. A man who lived in a cell near Karter was about to be released, and was terrified. Unlike Karter, the man had no money, no six-month support system at Dismas, and no family to speak of. Family support, in particular, has been shown to be crucial for the success of released prisoners. According to the Urban Institute's Justice Policy Center, "research has found that strengthening the family network and maintaining supportive family contact can improve outcomes for both family members and prisoners."[22]

Karter spent his last days behind bars getting handshakes, pats on the back, and a "barrage of hugs" from well-wishers. On August 5, he went as early as possible to what Old Colony called "New Man's," the booking area for incoming and outgoing prisoners.[23] He was wearing ragged gray scrubs, an old white T-shirt, and a holey pair of Nikes. Ironically, when Karter had been lugged from prerelease to Old Colony in 2009, he had been wearing a pair of the contraband Perry Ellis underwear, which had never been confiscated, so he had a pair on for his release. Before he saw his family, he planned to put on the suit, tie, and dress shoes that his aunt had brought to the prison two years before, when Karter thought he would need to look presentable in court.[24]

At the desk of the correction officer, Karter deposited his last two bags of belongings to clear for his exit, and received the $50 that Massachusetts gives exiting indigent prisoners. This so-called gate money varies in purpose and amount from state to state, but is usually between $0 and $200.[25] Some states provide bus tickets, too; others provide nothing. With no job and no other source of income, Karter had no money in his prison account; he had used the cash he earned to buy canteen items such as soap and toothpaste. He had recently made a little money "on the side" by selling stamps to other prisoners, but essentially he had nothing except the $50.

The correction officer verified Karter's identity—standard procedure—and then told Karter he could exit through the Visiting Room, a large, drab institutional space painted white, with blue metal chairs around the perimeter and down the center. Aside from the furniture, food and drink machines were the main decor lining the walls. Karter walked through this space, where he had been countless times during the four years he had spent at Old Colony. He passed the corner where men visited with their children. In many ways, he was still the scrubbed schoolboy from 1993. But now, twenty years had passed, and he was leaving behind all the rules he knew by heart—the number of visits he was allowed each week, how he could only hug and kiss his visitors while standing up, and then only when he first saw them and when he said good-bye. He was not yet allowed to put on the suit, so he carried it with him.

The clang of steel doors sliding closed echoed behind Karter as he entered through a doorway into what was called "the trap." There was a short walk from the inside to the outside, and, just like at Shirley, coils of barbed wire swirled overhead. As soon as Karter heard the second door close behind him, he caught a glimpse of his family and asked if he could please change his clothes. He was allowed to put on his suit in the bathroom, and there followed a whirlwind of cutting off tags and dressing as fast as he could.[26]

It was not much after nine in the morning. Karter had told his family to arrive as early as possible—you never knew what might come up at a prison—and he would later discover that they had been waiting since 7:30 a.m. The corrections officer mentioned that he had never seen so many people waiting for a parolee; Karter was unprepared for the crowd. As he walked through the last door to the prison's entryway, dressed in his suit and tie, he saw a sea of family, thirty people including his mother, four sisters and stepsisters, their partners and kids, his aunt and two uncles and their three daughters, his grandfather, and his brother. Chace was the first to hug him, and soon everyone was hugging and kissing and in tears. For the Reeds, it was as if a veil had been lifted. Videotape rolled; cameras flashed. Karter was home.

Karter's first day of freedom was speckled with delight; of his family in the sunshine at his aunt's pool party; idyllic summer weather with green grass and trees he could touch; riding in a car with his grandfather, who said he wished he could have helped Karter more as a boy; his mother laughing after she gave Karter a smartphone, which took him only a few minutes to learn; the emotional first call he made to his father, who was working and unable to attend the festivities; driving around Worcester with his aunt, a city none of them knew yet, while trying to find a store that sold reasonably priced socks—Karter's were wet after he wrestled Chace and both of them got dunked, Karter discovering to his amazement that his friend Jay from prison had set up a computer for him at Dismas House; and, finally, Karter in his own room, shared with another resident, twice the size of anything he had known in prison, with a window looking outside.

The highlight of Karter's second day of freedom was finding out how easy it was to get lost on the Internet. He set up e-mail and Facebook accounts. He began exploring jobs. He went off on sidetracks, realizing thirty minutes later that he had forgotten what he was intending to research. Within a week, Karter had applied for food stamps, had his driving permit, and, thanks to his family, had bought some new clothes. He also submitted an online application to attend the local community college in the fall.

Trouble began two weeks later. It was noontime. Karter had just hopped on his bike to pedal downtown to see his parole officer, which he was required to do at regular intervals, when Artie, an administrator at Dismas, pulled up in his car and told Karter that he had been asked to transport him to the Worcester parole office. Karter tried not to panic as he got in the car.

"What did you do?" Artie asked.

"I didn't do anything," Karter answered. He felt almost dizzy. He had no idea what was happening.

"Were you in touch with your codefendant?" Artie asked as they pulled up to the storefront on Main Street.

"I haven't had contact with anyone," Karter said.

Artie went inside the parole office to see what was going on and told Karter to wait. Karter suddenly had a thought. Gator had requested that Karter "friend" him on Facebook, and he had accepted his request. In Massachusetts, statute says that "if a parole officer believes that a parolee has lapsed or is about to lapse into criminal ways or has associated or is about to associate with criminal company," the officer can take the parolee into custody.[27] But "association" is not well-defined, and has not been updated to include anything about social media. In a panic, Karter immediately took out his phone and deleted his Facebook account.

Artie came out and said the parole officer was claiming that Karter had been in touch with his codefendant. While he had never actually spoken to Gator, Karter knew that since the Cinelli case, people could be sent back to prison for the smallest of infractions. Revocations, as they are called, hit 15 percent of parolees in 2013, and 13 percent of those returns to prison were for activities that had not resulted in arrests.[28] In fact, 31 percent of the 648 revocations that year were for the very vague category of "Irresponsible Conduct."[29] Going back to prison could be a disaster for someone trying to start a new life—a loss of school, job, relationships, and any sense of rehabilitation. On his way into the parole office, Karter managed to leave messages for his father and Richard Neumeier, just in case. He was terrified.

The parole officer sat Karter down, yelled at him for disobeying rules, and threatened to send him back to prison. He became even more enraged when he went to access Karter's Facebook account and realized that Karter had deleted it.

Karter pleaded his case. He said he did not know much about Facebook or that "friending" was "association"—he was still learning about answering friend requests and readily admitted that he had deleted the account out of fear. The parole officer then brought in his superior and neither would hear any of Karter's excuses. They sent Karter to get his photo taken, a sure sign he was going back to prison. Karter said they cursed at him, saying, "Do you really think we are that stupid?"[30]

Both men then left the room. When they returned, they announced that Karter was receiving a formal sanction. He was banned from all social media and told that any future violation whatsoever would mean a return to custody. Karter was too scared to breathe a sigh of relief.

When I asked Karter if he knew how the parole officer had discovered that Gator had connected with him on Facebook, he said he was not sure; he wondered if someone wanted him to fail on the outside. It seemed to go unnoticed that Gator Collet had been out of prison for more than fifteen years, was not and had never been on parole, now had a family and a job, and was living as a productive member of his community. Karter had also found six other men on Facebook, all formerly incarcerated, who had helped him through tough times behind bars and, presumably, could have supported him outside as well. But support from formerly incarcerated people was clearly not allowed.[31] The rules seemed filled with contradictions: Karter could "associate" with his father and other family members who had been in prison, as well as with parolees at Dismas House. But in reality, he could associate only with prisoners in situations deemed exceptions by the parole board. Karter would need much more time to settle into the strict reality of being on parole for life.

One day, about two weeks after his release from prison, Karter went shopping with his father at the Wrentham Outlets, an outdoor mall south of Boston. Derek's girlfriend Maria and her daughter, Lisy, also went along. Lisy was thirty years old, had a master's degree in psychology, and worked as a high school adjustment counselor; she was an athletic Portuguese beauty who loved basketball.

Karter had no clue what clothes to buy; style had certainly changed since he was a sixteen-year-old. Lisy seemed to have an eye for fashion, however, so he asked her for help. Lisy knew very little about Karter, except that he had been incarcerated. They hit it off . . . or at least Karter thought they had.

Lisy told me that, after that afternoon at the mall, she had gone home and Googled "Karter Kane Reed," and found the combination of factual and distorted articles about his crime that live online. She was a little scared, as she had recently broken up with a dominating man and wanted no part of that kind of relationship again. Yet, she thought that Karter seemed sweet.

Two days later, Karter was hauled down to the Worcester Parole Office for the Facebook incident. Later that day, he called Lisy. He asked her to meet him in a nearby park. Before he could open his mouth to tell her about his crushing day, Lisy began grilling him about his past. She asked him questions about his crime and his time in prison, as well as what he hoped for in life. She dug deep; she wanted to know details. In spite of his own pain, Karter tried to answer her. He knew that being a man had nothing to do with carrying a knife or with proving himself at all costs; he wanted a partner and he wanted a family. He told me he had promised himself he would not get involved with anyone for at least six months, but here he was telling Lisy he wanted to be a sociologist, to create meaning out of his life, and to make amends for the life he had taken. Eventually, he told her the entire grueling story of what had happened at the parole office that day. Lisy was sympathetic, but warned Karter to think through everything in the future even more carefully.

Lisy began to join Karter in the open family-style dinners that were held at Dismas House. She also accompanied him to a family party at his aunt's house in late August. The house was pulsing with summer greenery, and the garage was filled with potluck dishes, chips and dip, frosted desserts, and drinks in coolers. Outside, above the double garage door, hung a sign that read, "Welcome to freedom." Karter's family held their collective breath when they saw Lisy; they knew it was much too soon for him to have a girlfriend. But Lisy and Karter held hands like two teenagers.

"Are you going slow?" someone at the party asked Karter.

"No," he answered, with a huge grin.

In September, Karter enrolled in three classes at Quinsigamond Community College in Worcester. Karter looked at community college as a stepping stone and was excited when he drove onto the campus atop a hill, parking his very own car (his aunt and uncle had given him one as a present) in the lot. He had taken the walk across campus before, entering one of the brick buildings to register amidst students handing out leaflets and advisers pointing people this way and that. His credits from prison classes might transfer, he learned, and he managed to dig up the GED he'd earned almost twenty years before.

While Karter was never able to get excited about two of his community college classes—Computers and Introduction to Sociology—he truly connected with the third, Composition and Introduction to Literature. The class had only five students. The writing—literary analysis—was unfamiliar to Karter, and the teacher was demanding. Karter was thrown off his game. He had always thought of himself as a competent writer, but suddenly he was encountering writing formats that included new ways of putting ideas on the page. He earned an 80 on his first assignment, his lowest grade since high school. To his astonishment, this made him work harder. Eventually, his grades improved. He managed the five hours of homework per week, just for this class. He not only wanted to learn what he didn't know, but, perhaps as important, he also wanted to prove himself—this time in a positive way.

That first semester, Karter earned all A's.

While in prison, Karter had had high hopes of finding employment when he got out. In a letter he wrote in 2008 to my Voices behind Bars class after he first won parole, he bragged about his skills; he was a proficient writer and reader, had studied speechmaking, and knew enough about case law to file papers; he could fix anything, and could cut hair; he ran groups, organized events, led workshops, played the guitar, and excelled in almost any sport. But when Karter checked into work in barbering in Massachusetts after his release, he found that he needed to update his skills and get a license, which would cost more than $1,000, money he did not have. And most of his practical skills, such as electrical expertise, also required some sort of certification before he could apply for jobs. He began attending employment fairs and applied online to every posting he could find. And then, like most of the rest of the world, he received automated replies to his résumés and a barrage of e-mails and texts that had nothing to do with job hunting.

Finding a job is critical for parolees. However, per the most recent data available in 2012, only 32 percent of men and women on parole in Massachusetts were working full time.[32] Released prisoners have few resources to help them secure jobs, a situation made worse because of the stigma attached to those with histories of incarceration.[33] In a pivotal 2001 study of five US cities, more than two-thirds of employers said they would not knowingly hire anyone with a criminal background.[34] Additionally, a groundbreaking 2001 project showed that "White applicants without a record were twice as likely to be called back as those with one (34% to 17%) . . . for black applicants that gap rose to almost threefold (14% to 5%)."[35] This study, first conducted in Milwaukee, was repeated in New York City in 2004, with similar results.[36] Formerly incarcerated people, despite the country's rhetoric of "second chances," are often unfairly deemed "untrustworthy," and, depending on where they live, may be restricted from various professions—for example, law, real estate, medicine, nursing, physical therapy, and education.[37] The US Equal Employment Opportunity Commission filed lawsuits in 2012 against several companies such as BMW, charging that "systematic exclusion of people with criminal records was effectively a form of discrimination against black men."[38] In 2015, BMW settled with both monetary relief and employment opportunities.[39]

Such opportunities may be improving in other quarters. Business Insider profiled the CEO of Butterball Farms, Inc., who said hiring formerly incarcerated people makes sense because "they'll be looking out for you since you looked out for them."[40] There are also tax incentives for employers to hire those who've been released from prison within a year before their date of hire.[41] Some states have also enacted so-called "ban the box" legislation, meaning that employers can no longer ask applicants if they have committed a felony. In Massachusetts, restricting employers from asking the criminal-background question on job applications became law in 2010.[42] The objective of this was to put everyone on the same footing at the entry level. But Karter said that employers got around hiring former prisoners by asking to do a background check at the interview stage. A 2008 study in three states showed that, two months after release, more than 70 percent of prisoners who had actively looked for a job said that their criminal histories had affected their job search. Researchers, activists, and policymakers continue arguing to change this, saying that job readiness is not affected by a single arrest or convictions that happened years earlier.[43] By 2015, more than 100 cities and counties from nineteen states had adopted "ban the box" policies.[44]

Karter finally found his first job on Craigslist: moving pumpkins for two months during the Halloween season. It paid $11 an hour, which at the time was higher than the $8 minimum wage in Massachusetts.[45] Since he had been without income for more than a month, Karter leapt at the opportunity and enthusiastically went to work in the pumpkin patch.

On his third day, Karter brought in a form for a work-opportunity tax credit. He had heard that employers could get back 25 percent of his salary for taking part in the program. He told one of his employers that she needed only to fill out this form to be eligible to receive money for hiring one of several targeted groups.[46]

"Which category do you qualify under?" the woman asked.

"Within a year of release from a correctional facility," Karter replied.

"Oh," she said, turning over the form in her hands. "I guess we never asked you about that, huh?"

Karter worked the rest of the day. The next morning, a man he did not know called him before work. "I guess there was not as much work as we thought there was going to be." Karter was let go.

Perhaps Karter had been naive. Perhaps it was just a matter of time. In any case, there would be more jobs through a temp agency, an assembly line of pies at a company where no one spoke English, and some handyman work for a couple of weeks. Karter kept applying for every job he could find. Finally, right before Christmas 2013, he was offered a full-time job at the United Parcel Service. He had to be at work at 3:30 in the morning and he got home after 9 a.m. He would have to head for bed at dinner time. But it was a real job, even if the hours were not the best. Karter just hoped it would last beyond the holidays.

That same month, six years after he wrote his first letter to me, Karter came to Lowell to speak to my prison literature class. He stood in front of my Middlesex Community College students in polished shoes, sporting a vest and tie, looking like the Clark University professor he wanted to become more than the former prisoner he was. He told his story, tearing up when he described Jason's death, his mother's pain, his father's renewal, and his devotion to Chace. Later, my students would write journals filled with shock and admiration at how Karter had studied law behind bars, some with a sense of disbelief—Did he ever really imagine he would be seen without his crime? They saw that Karter was not the stereotype, the one they had formed in their minds that first day in class. Back then, they had said that such men were the caricatures they saw on *Oz* or *Prison Break:* "junkies," "tattooed bodies," "somebody's bitch," "once a con always a con," and "rage addicts."

As Karter stood before them, composed, articulate, an anomaly and yet in many ways representative of all the fallow talent that exists behind bars, he retold the events of that April day in 1993. As he unraveled all the days that followed, the students finally understood what it meant to hold two images in their minds at the same time. Yes, he had murdered a boy; yes, he had become a man capable of a truly meaningful life. It was cognitive dissonance in the form of Karter Reed.

AFTERWORD

When I first met him in 2007, I never would have imagined seeing Karter Reed at a criminal justice forum at Harvard University Law School. But there he was in 2014, in some ways no different from the others who stood in line to ask questions. He was dressed in a white shirt and casual pants, appropriate for a spring day in May. I had helped organize the forum to showcase candidates running for state attorney general. I sat in the front row with my husband as the candidates fielded questions about mandatory minimum sentencing, bail, and police arrests in poor neighborhoods where people of color were the majority.

Karter said nothing about his past as he asked each candidate their position on parole for youth convicted of first-degree murder. He listened to their answers, tempered and predictable. But he wasn't finished. As chairs were being stacked and the video camera packed up, he introduced himself to the candidates. There he stood, shaking hands with Maura Healy, who would be the next attorney general, saying how important it was to get a second chance, that he was one of those lifers who had almost not been released from prison. In fact, the assistant district attorney had attended his parole hearing to testify that Karter should have been sentenced to life without parole. Karter was now in the honors program at the community college, had his own apartment with Lisy, and worked at UPS. He cared about the men sentenced as adolescents, and did not believe they should have been sent to adult prisons. He was able to change his life and said that was true of so many others who'd gone to prison as kids; it was in spite of incarceration, not because of it. Still, not a day went by that he did not think about Jason Robinson, the boy he killed.

There was no reason for anyone to stay—other gatherings and other fundraisers awaited. But Karter spoke, and people listened. They teared up. They saw the change in a man who had suffered and been transformed, who was determined to make meaning of his new, fragile life in the free world. I saw that he was writing his own story.

As Karter wrote in 2011 in a letter to the *Boston Globe*, "What it comes down to in the end . . . is this: Human beings are fallible. We all make mistakes, use poor judgment, and make regrettable decisions. Some of us, unfortunately, go further, and commit unjustifiable or unconscionable acts that bring undeserved heartache and suffering to our victims and their families, something I agree is tragic and unacceptable. But we are not beyond redemption. All of us have the capacity for change, to become productive contributors to our families and society, and to make a difference in the world for the better."

Karter's words are a force for change.

In 2015, Connecticut governor Daniel Malloy took a first-in-the-nation stance on raising the age of adult criminal liability to twenty-one, citing recent brain research and European prisons as influences on his thinking.[1] Malloy's position was backed up with these important stats: as Connecticut raised the age of liability from sixteen to seventeen in 2010, and to eighteen in 2012, crime dropped, and the number of youth in prison decreased.[2] Malloy also put into motion a separate prison for youth, ages eighteen to twenty-five, in order to protect kids from abuse and violence.[3]

Researchers Vincent Schiraldi and Bruce Western of the Program in Criminal Justice Policy and Management at the Harvard Kennedy School, also put forth similar ideas about youth responsibility in 2015. They argued for the US to allow twenty-one-year-olds the "protections and rehabilitative benefits" of juvenile, or what they refer to as "family court."[4] They went beyond the more common practice of calling for change for those who have committed low-level crimes; instead, they decried transferring any juvenile into the "maw of the adult system."[5]

However, these ideas are on paper, and not yet the embodiment of policy change. Today, we still have a system where a boy can learn to shave for the first time in jail.[6] We still create prisons where a girl wonders whether she will ever walk in high heels, own her own computer, or have a baby.[7] And we still have conditions which can be considered Dickensian, are racially biased, and feel so chaotic that values and morals are crushed.[8] "For these are all our children. We will all profit by, or pay for, whatever they become," wrote James Baldwin in a concert program to benefit a boys' school.[9] Today, as much as ever, this rings true.

EPILOGUE BY KARTER REED

What is it like to transition from prison to the free world? Difficult. The irony is that in Massachusetts (and in most states across the country), the state prison system uses the word Correction in its title, though it does little to correct those in its custody and even less to prepare them to be law-abiding citizens. The problem is that in prison, your autonomy and responsibility are stripped from you, and unless you have the foresight to create that responsibility for yourself, you will leave from a world where everything is done for you and enter into a world where nothing, or almost nothing, is done for you. In prison, even with the things you have to do for yourself, there is someone there to tell you to do them, or there is an ever-present consequence for not doing them. But without the constant supervision and rigid structure that dictated their lives on the inside, many—probably most—released prisoners struggle to adapt on the outside. We call this condition "institutionalization."

Webster's dictionary defines institutionalization as being so firmly accustomed to the care and supervised routine of an institution as to make incapable of managing a life outside. While it may not be spoken of much either in or out of prison, most people who have been incarcerated, or have interacted with those who have, would tell you that a certain degree of institutionalization is inevitable.

When I left prison I understood that I was institutionalized, even though I had done everything in my power to prepare myself for life outside. I left far more educated and far more motivated than when I had entered—but I still had little clue how to function as an adult in society. Some of the challenges I faced were trivial, such as trying to acquire an identification and social security card, trying to find work, or to navigate a city I had never been to before. Because I had so much help from my family and friends and transitioned to a residential program, I was spared many of the challenges a lot of returning prisoners face, such as finding stable and affordable housing, and earning enough to purchase food and clothing. Even still, I spent much of my first few weeks feeling uncertain of my every move. I was unsure if I was forgetting something or should have done something differently. I did not ever really know what the next step was.

I left prison only a few years from turning forty, yet had never held a job, never paid taxes, never rented an apartment or been grocery shopping—the list of Nevers was pretty astounding. I had never seen or used the Internet or a cell phone, had never been in an adult relationship, and had never paid any bills—or had any bills to pay for that matter. I was just as prepared as any other released prisoner: I was clueless.

Despite the many uncertainties I faced, there was one thing I was sure about: my education. On May 21, 2015, I achieved the first major goal I had set out to accomplish after my release (from prison): I graduated from college. A week before, I received an award for being the top student in the Liberal Arts department at Quinsigamond Community College. I had made the Dean's List for the fourth consecutive semester and graduated a week later with highest honors and a perfect 4.0 GPA. While it is obvious that I am a non-traditional student in terms of my age, none of my professors had any clue as to the reason for the twenty-year layoff. In fact, many of them often remarked what a pleasure it was to have me in their class on account of my openness, sincerity, and respect.

Following my second semester of straight A's, my school's chapter of the Phi Theta Kappa honor society reached out and invited me to join. There was some paperwork to fill out and it required at least two recommendations from professors, which I took my time soliciting, but nonetheless submitted well before the deadline for that semester. Shortly thereafter, I received notice that the preliminary requirements had been met and I could submit my application. About halfway through the application I came across a clause I had not expected to find. It was an affirmation declaring, under the pains and penalties of perjury, that I had never been convicted of a felony. The asterisk led me to a further clause below that assured me I could overcome that burden as long as I had completed all conditions of my sentence, including any parole or probation, at least two years prior. Considering that I am on lifetime parole, that meant that I would be forever ineligible for admittance into the honor society. I could graduate at the top of my class, receive the congressional medal of honor, be knighted by the queen of England, or win the Nobel Peace Prize, but I cannot be admitted into the Phi Theta Kappa honor society. This is just one of the many "collateral sanctions" that can send returning prisoners into a tailspin, beset by the frustration and indignation that come from working so hard to change, only to be treated as if you had not.

At United Parcel Service (UPS) where I work, only my manager knows about my past—and that is only because he asked me during the promotion process if I had ever been to jail. I had signed a Criminal Offender Record Information (CORI) release granting UPS access to my criminal record when I first applied, so I did not think too much about it when I applied for a promotion. But three days before I was slated to receive the promotion, my manager pulled me aside and told me everything was moving along nicely; they were just waiting for my CORI to come back. "As long as you're not some kind of crazed murderer," he joked, "you should be a supervisor come Monday." If it were not such a serious subject I would have laughed at the irony.

The next morning, the manager called me into his office at the end of the shift and said that they were still waiting on the background check but would proceed without it: "You haven't ever been to jail or anything like that, have you?" he asked.

"Well, actually," I answered, "I have . . . I was just released last August after almost twenty years."

"What?!" he exclaimed, "Are you kidding me? What the hell happened?"

But as I began to answer, he just said, "You know what, it doesn't matter. What's done is done, but Jesus, I wish you had told me."

I explained that I had already submitted two CORI waivers and had even submitted all of my parole information on my initial application. He said that the final decision was not up to him, but we would just have to wait to see what Corporate decides.

I left the interview feeling a bit hopeless and dejected. I thought for sure they would come back and tell me that they could not promote me because of my record. I was going to Nantucket for the weekend, and should have been excited, but the specter of my past was looming in my mind and it was making me miserable. Then on Saturday night my phone began ringing, and I saw it was from my manager. I was afraid to answer it and let it ring until the very last moment before picking it up. When I answered, the manager said, "I am sorry to disturb you over the weekend, but I just wanted to be the first to congratulate you; starting Monday morning you are a supervisor. I'll see you forty-five minutes before the shift."

Although I have not yet had the opportunity or need to confide in anyone regarding my past, I look forward with great anticipation to the moment when I get to see unbelieving and incredulous eyes staring at me in bewilderment; to see the wheels of their minds turning frantically trying to conjure up some explanation; to recall some unmistakable clue they are sure they must have missed. "Surely," they will be thinking, "He cannot possibly be a normal human being. There must be some kind of monster in there he keeps hidden, some kind of crazed animalistic predator who will emerge at some unsuspecting moment." But, of course, they are wrong. I am just a regular guy, someone who could have easily been in far different shoes if I had made one different choice or another.

Almost eighteen months after I was released, my girlfriend and I officially became first-time homeowners. Lisy had moved to Worcester a couple months after we started dating with the plan that I would move in once I had completed my six months at Dismas House in February of 2014. However, her move from an apartment in Southbridge to an apartment in Worcester was not something she intended to be long term. She had already been involved with a realtor and had gone as far as making an offer on a home before we met, but the deal had fallen through. Sometime in the summer, after I had been promoted at UPS, we started talking about looking for a house together, something affordable. Although I was still in school and did not have any significant savings or notable credit history, we nonetheless thought it was in our best interest if we could find something with a mortgage comparable to our current rent, so we began looking.

Since we were looking for something relatively cheap in the Greater Worcester area, there were not too many viable options. One house in particular that we drove by in the adjacent town of Leicester was decent sized, and even more reasonably priced, but was on a rather steep hill and conspicuously overgrown with a myriad of flora, so we did not even stop to inquire further. But after a month or so of slim pickings, Lisy contacted her realtor and asked if we could do a walk through. Despite the jungle-like flora and unkempt exterior, the interior was in surprisingly good condition—it would just take a lot of elbow grease and little bit of know-how to make this deal an absolute steal. Even the realtor agreed without hesitation that we should make an offer. Unfortunately, when she contacted the listing agent, she was told that the seller had received and accepted an offer just the day before—our possible budget dream home had slipped away.

Then something remarkable happened. The deal fell through—it was going to go back on the market, but the listing agent would let us make an offer before it went public. We did another walk through and agreed: this was the one. It took a couple months to get all of our financial ducks in a row, but things have gone remarkably smoothly.

Of course, it would be naïve to think that just because I have put in the effort, everything would go as smoothly as work, school, or buying a house. Nevertheless, it is easy to get caught up in imagining that something magical will happen the day you are released and all of the problems that your family and friends were dealing with will be resolved. But that is not the case. In fact, in some respects, things probably got worse. Particularly with my little brother.

I had a very difficult childhood and adolescence, not so much because of all the things I experienced, but how I reacted to and interpreted those things. A lot of the perceptions that I had of my place in the world were pretty skewed. My brother Chace is like that, only he has a lot more actual reasons to feel like he has repeatedly drawn the short straw.

My brother's relationship with my father is something terribly difficult to describe beyond saying it may be one of the most profoundly dysfunctional relationships to which I have ever borne witness. I have never seen two people who love and need each other so much be at each other's throats more than those two. My dad, probably because he feels so guilty about all of his parental failings, can manage to do almost nothing but berate, ridicule, and insult Chace, first as a misguided attempt to motivate him, and, second, as an indirect lashing out at himself. Nonetheless, my brother bears the brunt of my dad's chastisement with the constant weight of perceived inferiority. In all of our interactions, I sense Chace questioning why I can do no wrong and he can do no right. Like me at his age, his perception is tainted by the distorted notion that the world is somehow against him. When I make mistakes, as I often do, he does not notice them or does not see them as mistakes. He sees the end result of me getting straight A's and graduating with a 4.0 GPA, but he does not see me agonizing over a bad test score, cramming for hours on end, or pulling an all-nighter to finish a paper. He does not yet understand that mistakes can be overcome as long as you are willing to put in the work.

One of the more interesting consequences is that in all of my time outside of prison, including the two years of college (even the ethics and criminology classes), I have yet to encounter the kind of deep, philosophical, and conscientious dialogue that was a regular part of my life inside prison. Although it would be unusual for me to be in a group of people having a conversation where everyone involved had not killed someone or tried to kill someone, it did not seem at all unnatural to hold conversations with these people about everything from the economy to the separation of church and state to childrearing. My friends and I talked extensively about everything imaginable, almost always related to the betterment of society or ourselves—there was a constant dialogue concerning society's ills and an earnest attempt to discover their remedies. The themes were oft repeated and discussed at length. I had countless discussions about political and social reform, the justice system, ethics and morality. This epic journey of self-improvement that we embarked on together has become a solo expedition. I miss my friends, some of them terribly. A few I miss simply because they are my friends and that is human nature, but many I miss because of how they enriched my life, how the interaction I shared with them challenged me to meet and exceed my potential. Despite all of its flaws and shortcomings, there is that one element of the prison system that I cherish—the metaphorical place where those stripped of everything they once cared about are able to find meaning and purpose.

I went into prison a lost, self-absorbed boy, without any sense of who I was or who I wanted to be. I was a rudderless ship at sea, but the moment I found my drive to aspire to something greater, I knew I needed to share that with others. Now, each semester, I go to Middlesex Community College to speak to Professor Trounstine's Voices Behind Bars class, not for myself, but for the students. I see myself in all of them, and for those who have not yet found their way or are unsure of their abilities, I want them to see themselves in me. I also do it because it is critically important for me to have people understand that the mistakes and poor choices people make do not define them. No one should be judged solely on the worst thing they have ever done. I need people to understand that people can change, and I am one of them. More importantly, I represent all of those who have changed, who are struggling to make amends for their past transgressions. When I hold the door for someone at a restaurant or a store, or help someone with their groceries, or do any of the countless small kindnesses I try to do every day, I am doing them because that is who I am, but also because I represent a class of people who deserve to be seen in their best light for a change. When my actions have a positive impact on others, I want them to question whether that inherent goodness is universal. I already know the answer, but I want them to know it the way I do.

Since my release, I have been affiliated with and involved in a community organization called Ex-prisoners and Prisoners Organizing for Community Advancement (EPOCA), actively promoting restorative justice, community reinvestment, CORI reform, job training, and raising the state's minimum wage so that entry-level employees will be able to earn a decent living. I have collected signatures on petitions, attended rallies, delivered speeches / presentations, and facilitated workshops. I have also attended seminars and presentations at Harvard University, Wheelock College, and Lasell College concerning various criminal justice issues, eventually meeting and speaking at length with Maura Healy, now the state's Attorney General. But one of my most meaningful opportunities as an advocate for juveniles came when Professor Trounstine was able to set up a meeting at the state house with Senator William Brownsberger, the chair of the Joint Committee on the Judiciary, and his aides. To receive an audience with such an important person and to hear that my story and advocacy had a favorable impact on him is nothing short of inspirational.

It is my goal to bring awareness to juvenile justice issues and justice issues in general. There are too many misconceptions and too much misinformation out there that prevents healing and restoration. It fosters rejection and prejudice against former prisoners and robs those still in prison of the hope for reconciliation and redemption. The stories of those who have "turned their lives around" are innumerable, but for the most part they go unheard.

I want to shout them from the rooftops until people take notice. I know that I cannot change the past, but the future . . . that's another story.

ACKNOWLEDGMENTS

This book would not have been possible without words, cascading into letter after letter, from Karter Reed. Karter's mother, Sharon Reed, and his father, Derek Reed, allowed me into their lives. For many years, we never knew if Karter would be released.

Heartfelt thanks go to two who helped shape this book, IG Publishing's insightful editor Robert Lasner and press shepherd Elizabeth Clementson. Thanks dearly to those who helped me understand our country's ever-changing laws, Attorneys Jeremy Cohn, Richard Neumeier, and Barbara Dougan. Wordsmith Kaitlyn Johnston stood by my side. Dear friends Sondra Upham and Karen Propp nurtured drafts over the six years I worked on the manuscript. Other supporters who were with me in one stage or another: Judge Joseph Dever, Judith Paige Heitzman, the late Christina Ward, Neeti Madan, Cecilia Cancellaro, Lois Ahrens, Cathryn Delude, Shela Pearl, Rickie Solinger, Caroline Leavitt, and Barbara Helfgott Hyett. Special thanks to publicist Gail Leondar-Wright and Eileen MacDougall who treated this project with reverence.

Many people gave me valuable information for this book including Dr. Robert Kinscherff, Judge Jay Blitzman, and Attorneys Patricia Garin, Armand Fernandes, Joshua Dohan, James Pingeon, and Dana Curhan. Much appreciation goes to the Dartmouth Middle School, Dartmouth Police Station, New Bedford Public Library, and those who taught me the history of New Bedford and Dartmouth: Joseph Thomas, Carl Alves,

Loretta Bourque, Helena Marques, Ken Resendes, and Tom Cadieu, in addition to the many people I spoke to in cafés, shops, and public offices.

My family has always stood behind me, and I am lucky to count among many blessings my husband, Robert Wald, who believed without fail that Karter's story must be told.

NOTES

Introduction

1. Nathanial Romano, SJ, "A Justice That Restores," *Jesuit Post,* May 11, 2013, https://thejesuitpost.org/2013/05/a-justice-that-restores/. The image, an adaptation of a photograph posted on Flickr, originally appeared in Dina Rasor, "War Fraud Whistleblowers under Wraps," November 30, 2009, Truthout, http://truth-out.org/archive/component/k2/item/86962:war-fraud-whistleblowers-under-wraps.
2. The image, adapted by Jared Rodriguez from a photo by Flickr user LizaP, is titled "Lady Sees What She's Paid to See"; see https://secure.flickr.com/photos/truthout/4172417013/in/photostream/.
3. Peter Gelzinis, *Boston Herald*, May 16, 2008.
4. All quotes from Karter Reed are from Karter's correspondence with and interviews by the author from 2007 to 2014.
5. Patrick Griffin, Sean Addie, Benjamin Adams, and Kathy Firestine, "Trying Juveniles as Adults: An Analysis of State Transfer Laws and Reporting," Juvenile Offenders and Victims: National Report Series, Bulletin (Washington, DC: US Department of Justice, Office of Justice Programs, Office of Juvenile Justice and Delinquency Prevention, September 2011), 4, https://www.ncjrs.gov/pdffiles1/ojjdp/232434.pdf.
6. Warren Richey, "Death Penalty Abolished," *Christian Science Monitor*, March 2, 2005.
7. "25th Anniversary of the Convention on the Rights of the Child: Questions and Answers," Human Rights Watch, November 17, 2014,http://www.hrw.org/news/2014/11/17/25th-anniversary-convention-rights-child.
8. Judge Jay D. Blitzman, "Gault's Promise" Barry Law Review, (2007):4; and MacArthur Foundation, Research Network on Adolescent Development & Juvenile Justice, available at http://www.macfound.org/networks/research-network-on-adolescent-development-juvenil/details.

9. Key Facts: Youth in the Justice System, Campaign for Youth Justice, updated April 2012, 4,http://www.campaignforyouthjustice.org/documents/ KeyYouthCrimeFacts.pdf; Liz Ryan and Jason Ziedenberg, The Consequences Aren't Minor: The Impact of Trying Youth as Adults and Strategies for Reform, A Campaign for Youth Justice Report, March 2007 (Washington, DC), 17, http://www.prisonpolicy.org/scans/National_Report_consequences.pdf.
10. Patrick Griffin, Sean Addie, Benjamin Adams, and Kathy Firestine, "Trying Juveniles as Adults: An Analysis of State Transfer Laws and Reporting," Juvenile Offenders and Victims: National Report Series, Bulletin (Washington, DC: US Department of Justice, Office of Justice Programs, Office of Juvenile Justice and Delinquency Prevention, September 2011), 4, https://www.ncjrs.gov/pdffiles1/ojjdp/232434.pdf.
11. Ashley Nellis, *Life Goes On: The Historic Rise of Life Sentences in America* (Washington DC: Sentencing Project, 2013), 1, http://sentencingproject.org/doc/publications/inc_Life%20Goes%20On%202013.pdf.
12. MacArthur Foundation, Research Network.
13. Richard E. Redding, "Juvenile Transfer Laws: An Effective Deterrent to Delinquency?" *Juvenile Justice Bulletin* (2008): 6-8, https://www.ncjrs.gov/pdffiles1/ojjdp/220595.pdf.
14. The Sentencing Project, "The Time is Now to Raise the Age of Criminal Responsibility," sentencingproject.org, Website, http://www.sentencingproject.org/detail/news.cfm?news_id=1939&id=184
15. Ibid.
16. Redding, "Juvenile Transfer Laws,"7.
17. Judge Jay D. Blitzman, "Gault's Promise," 15.
18. Jeremy Travis and Bruce Western, eds., *The Growth of Incarceration in the United States: Exploring Causes and Consequences*, (Washington, D.C.: The National Academies Press, 2014), 2, available at http://www.nap.edu/catalog.php?record_id=18613.
19. Nellis, Life Goes On, 9-10.
20. Ibid.
21. Josh Rovner, "JJDPA Matters: A Look at the Latest Data on Race and Juvenile Justice, The Sentencing Project," JJDPA Matters

(blog), SparkAction.org, April 16, 2014, http://sparkaction.org/content/jjdpa-matters-look-latest-data-race.

22. Tavis Smiley, "Activist-writer Nell Bernstein," *Tavis Talks*, May 27, 2014, http://www.pbs.org/wnet/tavissmiley/interviews/nell-bernstein.
23. Robin L. Dahlberg, "Locking Up our Children: the Secure Detention of Massachusetts Youth Before Arraignment and After Detention," (Boston: American Civil Liberties Union): 20. http://www.aclum.org/sites/all/files/education/locking_up_our_children_web.pdf.
24. "Does Treating Kids like Adults Make a Difference?" *Frontline*, PBS Online, 2001, http://www.pbs.org/wgbh/pages/frontline/shows/juvenile/stats/kidslikeadults.html.
25. Adam Liptak and Ethan Bronner, "Justices Bar Mandatory Life Sentences for Juveniles," *New York Times*, June 25, 2012. In Massachusetts, no sentence of a juvenile to life without parole is permitted. See *Diatchenko v. District Attorney* for Suffolk District Court, 466 Mass. 655 (213).
26. "Death in Prison Sentences for Children," Equal Justice Initiative, Website, accessed November 9, 2013, http://www.eji.org/children-prison/deathinprison.
27. Joshua Rovner, telephone interview by author, April 16, 2014
28. Joshua Rovner, "Slow to Act: State Responses to 2012 Supreme Court Mandate on Life without Parole," *Policy Brief: State Responses to* Miller (Washington DC: Sentencing Project, June 2014), 1, http://sentencingproject.org/doc/publications/jj_State_Responses_to_Miller.pdf.
29. Ibid, 2.
30. Jean Trounstine, "A Moral Imperative: Release Aging and Long-Term Prisoners," Truthout.com (blog), February 10, 2015, http://www.truth-out.org/news/item/29028-a-moral-imperative-release-aging-and-long-term-prisoners.
31. Texas Criminal Justice Coalition, "Support a Meaningful Opportunity for Release for Youth Sentenced to the Texas Department of Criminal Justice," Public Policy Center, Website, accessed September 11, 2015, http://publicpolicycenter.texascjc.org/support-a-meaningful-opportunity-for-release-for-youth-sentenced-to-the-texas-department-of-criminal-justice.

32. Jennifer Gonnerman, "Kalief Browder, 1993-2015," newyorker.com, Website, June 7, 2015, http://www.newyorker.com/news/news-desk/kalief-browder-1993-2015.
33. Ibid.
34. The Sentencing Project, *Raise the Age.*
35. Sam Levin, "California Senate Passes Bill to Limit Youth Solitary Confinement," June 3, 2015, eastbayexpress.com, Website, http://www.eastbayexpress.com/SevenDays/archives/2015/06/03/ california-senate-passes-bill-to-limit-youth-solitary-confinement; and Anne Teigen, "States that Limit or Prohibit Juvenile Shackling and Solitary Confinement," May 6, 2015, http://www.ncsl.org/research/civil-and-criminal-justice/states-that-limit-or-prohibit-juvenile-shackling-and-solitary-confinement635572628.aspx#1.
36. *Roper v. Simmons,* 543 US 551 (2005) (abolishing the death penalty for juveniles); *Graham v. Florida*, 560 US 48 (2010)-(abolishing juvenile life-without-parole sentencing in non-homicide cases); *Miller v. Alabama,* 132 S.Ct. 2455 (2012) (abolishing mandatory juvenile life-without-parole sentencing).
37. Dr. Robert Kinscherff, interview by author, Massachusetts School of Professional Psychology, Natick, Mass., May 10, 2010.
38. Richard A. Mendel, No Place for Kids: The Case for Reducing Juvenile Incarceration (Baltimore: The Annie E. Casey Foundation, 2011), 39, http://www.aecf.org/m/resourcedoc/aecf-NoPlace-ForKidsFullReport-2011.pdf.
39. Jean Trounstine, "Brutal Crimes Don't Justify Bad Laws,"Truthout.com (blog), October 26, 2014, http://truth-out.org/news/item/26951-brutal-crimes-don-t-justify-bad-laws.
40. Blitzman, Gault's Promise, 7.
41. Trounstine, "Brutal Crimes."
42. Massachusetts General Laws 279 § 24
43. Sarah Schweitzer and Michael Levenson, "Mass SJC Bars No-Parole Life Terms for Youth," *Boston Globe*, December 24, 2013.
44. Jean Trounstine, *Shakespeare behind Bars: The Power of Drama in a Women's Prison* (New York: St. Martin's, 2001). Karter's friend Pam eventually was released on parole.
45. Adrian Nicole LeBlanc,"A Woman behind Bars Is Not a Dangerous Man," *New York Times Magazine,* June 2, 1996.

46. Michelle Alexander, in *The New Jim Crow: Mass Incarceration in the Age of Colorblindness,* rev. ed. (New York: New Press, 2012) sheds light on such prisoner stereotypes.
47. See, e.g. Howie Carr, *Boston Herald*, May 18, 2008; Jordana Hart and John Ellement, "Classroom Killing Aftermath: Three Defendants Are Arraigned," *Boston Globe*, April 14, 1993.
48. The articles about Karter Reed's crime are mentioned throughout this book, notably in Chapters Three through Five; quotes from prosecutors came from the arraignment, hearings, and trial, gleaned from transcripts and news articles, as well as from interviews with defense attorneys as noted; material from school officials came from news articles and interviews, as noted.

Chapter 1

1. Diego Ribideneiro, "1 in 3 Mass. High school boys armed, survey finds," *Boston Globe*, Jan. 9, 1993.
2. Raymond Hernandez, "For Many Youths, Carrying Knives Keeps Fear Away, *New York Times*, May 23, 1993; "Fear Led Students to Put Knife in ORR Locker, Family Says," *Standard-Times*, March 6, 1993.
3. "Fear Led Students," *Standard Times*.
4. Janita Poe and Cameron McWhirter, "Gun Entered Students Feud, Police Say," *Chicago Tribune*, September 19, 1993.
5. Karter Reed, "Why Not Carry Weapons," was written at MCI-Shirley for the Toastmasters public speaking program.
6. "MCI-Shirley," Executive Office of Public Safety and Security, 2014, http://www.mass.gov/eopss/law-enforce-and-cj/prisons/doc-facilities/mci-shirley.html.
7. Ibid.
8. Keri Blankinger, "Graduation Behind Bars," IV League: The Blog Behind the Memoir (blog); accessed December 23, 2014, http://keriblakinger.com/2014/12/22/graduation-behind-bars/
9. James A. Fox, "Life without Parole: Right for Some; Wrong for Others," Crime and Punishment (blog), Boston.com, November 8, 2012, http://www.boston.com/community/blogs/crime_punishment/2012/11/rethinking_life_without_parole.html. Fox's blog post is adapted

from Ashley Nellis, "Throwing Away the Key: The Expansion of Life without Parole Sentences in the United States," *Federal Sentencing Reporter* 23, no. 1 (October 2010): 27–32.

10. "Frequently Asked Questions About the DOC," 2015, Official Website of the Executive Office of Public Safety and Security, http://www.mass.gov/eopss/agencies/doc/faqs-about-the-doc.html
11. "Minor Transgressions, Major Consequences: A Picture of 17-year-olds in the Massachusetts Criminal Justice System, Citizens for Juvenile Justice, December 2011, http://www.cfjj.org/minortransgressions.php.
12. Maurice Chammah, "The 17-Year-Old Adults: States are raising the age of who counts as an adult, but it's no simple task," The Marshall Project, June 3, 2015, https://www.themarshallproject.org/2015/03/03/the-17-year-old-adults.
13. Ibid.
14. Jean Trounstine, "Keep Kids Out of Handcuffs," Truthout.com (blog), May 15, 2015, http://www.truth-out.org/news/item/30713-keep-kids-out-of-handcuffs.
15. American Bar Association, "Part 1: The History of Juvenile Justice," Dialogue on Youth and Justice, 2007, 4-5, http://www.americanbar.org/content/dam/aba/migrated/publiced/features/ DYJfull.authcheckdam.pdf ADD
16. Ibid., 4.
17. Ibid., 5.
18. Chai Woodham, "Eastern State Penitentiary: A prison with a Past," Smithsonianmag.com, Website, September 30, 2008, http://www.smithsonianmag.com/history/eastern-state-penitentiary-a-prison-with-a-past-14274660/?no-ist.
19. Sanford J. Fox, "The Early History of the Court," Stanford Law Review, vol. 6, no. 3 (Winter 1996): 30.
20. Ibid.
21. Charles Richmond Henderson, "Papers," (Box 2, Folder 10), Special Collections Research Center, University of Chicago Library, available online at http://www.socialwelfarehistory.com/corrections/pennsylvania-prison-society/.
22. Fox, "The Early History," 30; Sanford J. Fox, "Juvenile Justice Reform: An Historical Perspective," Stanford Law Review, vol. 22 (June 1970): 1188-1189.

23. Fox, "Juvenile Justice Reform," 1193.
24. bid., 1190-1191.
25. Nell Bernstein, *Burning Down the House* (New York: The New Press, 2014), 39.
26. Alexander W. Pisciotta, "Race, Sex and Rehabilitation: A Study of Differential Treatment in the Juvenile Reformatory, 1825-1900," *Crime and Delinquency*, (April 1983): 254.
27. Ibid., 257.
28. Oliver Warner, Public Documents of Massachusetts: Being the Annual Reports of Various Public Offices and Institutions, for the year 1865, vol. IV, no. 19-38 (Boston: Wright and Potter, 1866): 103-4.
29. Pisciotta, "Race, Sex and Rehabilitation," 258.
30. Ibid., 260, 264.
31. Judge Jay D. Blitzman, "Gault's Promise," 9 *Barry Law Review*, (2007): 71.
32. Fox, "Juvenile Justice Reform," 1192.
33. The Massachusetts Juvenile Justice System of the 1990's: Rethinking a National Model, Report of the Boston Bar Association's Juvenile Task Force on the Juvenile Justice System, 5, http://www.bostonbar.org/prs/reports/majuvenile94.pdf.
34. Ibid., 5-6.
35. Jeffrey A. Butts and Ojmarrh Mitchell, "Brick by Brick: Dismantling the Border Between Juvenile and Adult Justice," Criminal Justice 2000, vol. 2, 168-174, available at http://www.urban.org/sites/default/files/alfresco/publication-pdfs/1000234-Brick-by-Brick-Dismantling-the-Border-Between-Juvenile-and-Adult-Justice.PDF.
36. Juvenile Justice Legal Issues: History," Executive Office of Health and Human Services, 2015, http://www.mass.gov/eohhs/gov/laws-regs/dys/juvenile-justice-legal-issues.html.
37. Butts and Mitchell, "Brick by Brick," 174-175.
38. Blitzman, "Gault's Promise," 71.
39. Ibid.
40. Reggie Sheffield, "Ferrer Gets at Least 15 Years for Shooting at Fourteen," *New Bedford Standard-Times*, May 11, 1995.
41. New Bedford Police Department, abstract to "Juvenile Violence Project (1997)", Center for Problem-Oriented Policing, p. 2, http://www.popcenter.org/library/awards/goldstein/1997/97-48.pdf.

42. Urban Dictionary, s.v. "New Bedford," posted by O Corajoso, April 9, 2009, http://www.urbandictionary.com/author.php?author=O_Corajoso; Curt Brown, "New Bedford Saw 15 Overdoses in a 24-hour Period, Southcoast Today, March 8, 2014, http://www.southcoasttoday.com/article/20140308/News/403080331.
43. Herman Melville, *Moby-Dick* (New York: Bantam Classics, 1981), 32.
44. Ibid., 14.
45. Ibid.
46. "The City's Evolution—from Old Dartmouth to New Bedford, Whaling Metropolis of the World, New Bedford Whaling Museum, Website, http://www.whalingmuseum.org/learn/research-topics/citys-evolution.
47. Ibid., "Cultural Communities and Identity," http://www.whalingmuseum.org/learn/research-topics/cultural-communities.
48. Lynn Ruggieri, "Michael Bianco Inc.—Immigrant Workers to Save Costs," Journal of Business Case Studies, vol. 7, no. 4 (July, August 2011): 91.
49. New Bedford Labor Commission, "History of New Bedford," Ports of New Bedford, Website, http://www.portofnewbedford.org/cruise/about-the-harbor/history.php.
50. The 1928 New Bedford Textile Strike Collection (MC 9), University of Massachusetts at Dartmouth, Claire T. Carney Library Archives and Special Collections, available at http://www.lib.umassd.edu/archives/findaids/MC9.pdf; Joe Silva, "New Bedford's Forgotten History: 1928 Textile Strike, NewBedfordGuide.com (blog), April 4, 2013, http://www.newbedfordguide.com/new-bedford-1928-textile-strike/2013/04/04.
51. Ibid.
52. Hans Schatte, "An Economy in Crisis, Re-tooling for the Next Generation," *Standard-Times*, April 25, 1993.
53. Ibid.
54. Beth Siegel, Barbara Baran, and Suzanne Teegarden, "Small Cities, Big Challenges," *Commonwealth Magazine*, Spring 2001, http://www.commonwealthmagazine.org/Voices/Considered-Opinion/2001/Spring/Small-cities-face-big-economic-challenges.aspx.

55. "Weld's Governor's Hispanic Advisory Commission," Standard-Times, June 6, 1993.
56. Mass. Juv. Justice System 1990's, 3.
57. Ibid.
58. Ibid.
59. Fox, "Juvenile Justice Reform," 1229-1233.
60. Ibid., 1235.
61. Mass. Juv. Justice System 1990's, 8-9.
62. Ibid., 9.
63. Fox, "Juvenile Justice Reform," 1233.
64. Ibid., 1235.
65. Ibid.
66. Butts and Mitchell, "Brick by Brick," 176.
67. Blitzman, "Gault's Promise," 72.
68. Ibid.
69. Mass. Juv. Justice System 1990's, 7. For more on *Kent v. United States,* see ABA, "Part 1: History of Juvenile Justice," 6.
70. Mass. Juv. Justice System 1990's, 8. For more on In re Gault, see ABA, "Part 1: History of Juvenile Justice," 6-7.
71. ABA, "Part 1: History of Juvenile Justice," 7.
72. Ibid., 8; Philip W. Harris, Wayne N. Welsh, and Frank Butler, "A Century of Juvenile Justice," *The Nature of Crime: Continuity and Change*, vol. 1 (2000): 364, https://www.ncjrs.gov/criminal_justice2000/vol_1/02h.pdf.
73. Ibid.
74. William J. Bennett, John J. Dilulio, and John P. Walters, *Body Count: Moral Poverty . . . and How to Win America's War Against Crime and Drugs* (New York: Simon and Schuster, 1996), 27.
75. Harris, et al., "Century of Juvenile Justice," 178.
76. Key Facts: Youth in the Justice System, Campaign for Youth Justice, updated April 2012, 3, http://www.campaignforyouthjustice.org/documents/Transfertalkingpoints.pdf.
77. Blitzman, "Gault's Promise," 73-4; Richard E. Redding, "Juvenile Transfer Laws: An Effective Deterrent to Delinquency?" Juvenile Justice Bulletin (2008): 7-8, https://www.ncjrs.gov/pdffiles1/ojjdp/220595.pdf; Patrick Griffin, Sean Addie, Benjamin Adams, and Kathy Firestine, "Trying Juveniles as Adults: An Analysis

of State Transfer Laws and Reporting," Juvenile Offenders and Victims: National Report Series, Bulletin (Washington, DC: US Department of Justice, Office of Justice Programs, Office of Juvenile Justice and Delinquency Prevention, September 2011), 1, https://www.ncjrs.gov/pdffiles1/ojjdp/232434.pdf.

78. Robert Kinscherff, "The Issue," Juvenile Justice & the Adolescent Brain: Is Healthy Neurodevelopment a Civil Right? An event sponsored by the MGH Center for Law, Brain & Behavior, March 15, 2015, https://vimeo.com/122451609.
79. Social Explorer, US Census Bureau, Social Explorer Dataset, Census 1990, New Bedford, SE:T-13; SE:T-14. Document sent to the author from Middlesex Community College Library, Lowell, MA.
80. Ibid., SE:T-13.
81. Ibid., SE:T-12.
82. Loretta Bourque, interview by author, New Bedford, Mass., August 8, 2011.
83. Helena Marques, interview by author, New Bedford, Mass., July 12, 2011.
84. Ibid.
85. Ken Resendes, interview by author, New Bedford, Mass., July 17, 2011.
86. Stephen Kurkjian, "Drug Dealers Favor Mass. Real Estate," *Boston Globe*, August 4, 1989.
87. Schatte, "Economy in Crisis."
88. Ibid.
89. Siegel, "Small Cities."
90. Schatte, "Economy in Crisis."
91. Ibid.
92. Elizabeth Neuffer, "Crime, Despair on Rise as Recession Deepens," *Boston Globe*, May 18, 1991.
93. Sharon Reed, interview by author, New Bedford, Mass., July 12 and 19, 2011. Derek Reed, interview by author, Burlington, Mass., August 9, 2011.

Chapter 2

1. Ibid., 8.
2. Catherine L. Bagwell and Michelle E. Schmidt, *Friendships in Childhood & Adolescence*, (New York: The Guilford Press, 2011): 186.

3. Ron H. J. Schote et al., "Stability in Bullying and Victimization and Its Association with Social Adjustment in Childhood and Adolescence," Journal of Abnormal Child Psychology 35, no. 2 (April 2007): 217–28, http://www.ncbi.nlm.nih.gov/pmc/articles/PMC1915632.
4. "In re: Karter Reed," Probable Cause-Part B-Day 6, Bristol County Juvenile Court, DL 9303350, DL 9300352–4, DL9300357, DL 9300360, DL 9300366, transcript, 17.
5. Solangel Maldonado, "Recidivism and Paternal Engagement," *Family Law Quarterly* 40, no. 2 (Summer 2006):196.
6. Tom Cadieux, telephone interview by author, Dartmouth, MA., July 21, 2011.
7. Lola Ogunnaike, "A Skateboard Hero Who Fell to Earth," *New York Times*, August 21, 2003.
8. Tom Coakley and John Ellement, "Details Emerge on Youths' Lives," *Boston Globe*, April 14, 1993.
9. Cadieux, interview.
10. Jordana Hart and John Ellement, "Classroom Killing Aftermath: Three Defendants Are Arraigned," *Boston Globe*, April 14, 1993.
11. "Friends of Defendants in Dartmouth Slaying Fear Revenge Attacks," *Boston Globe*, April 15, 1993.
12. Coakley and Ellement, "Details Emerge."
13. Hart and Ellement, "Classroom Killing Aftermath."
14. Sara Reimer, "No Gang Tied to Killing, Just Three Rare Friends," *New York Times*, April 23, 1993.
15. Aljean Harmetz, "Making 'The Outsiders,' A Librarian's Dream, *New York Times*, March 23, 1983.
16. Derek Reed, interview by author, Burlington, Mass., August 9, 2011.
17. Bruce Western and Becky Potts, Collateral Costs: Incarceration's Effect on Economic Mobility, (Washington D.C.: Pew Charitable Trusts 2010), 18. http://www.sentencingproject.org/doc/publications/cc_Parents%20in%20State%20Prisons%20Fact%20Sheet.pdf.
18. Ibid.
19. Patricia Allard and Judith Greene, Children on the Outside: Voicing the Pain and Human Costs of Parental Strategies, (Brooklyn, New York: Justice Strategies 2011), i, http://www.justicestrategies.org/sites/default/files/publications/JS-COIP-1-13-11.pdf.

20. Ibid., i–iv.
21. Michael Leo Owens, "Mass incarceration Does Injustice to Millions of American Children," *The Guardian*, August 19, 2013.
22. Jackson Katz, Tough Guise: Violence, Media, and he Crisis in Masculinity, 57 minute documentary film, dir. Sut Jhaly, 1999, http://thoughtmaybe.com/tough-guise/.
23. Ibid.
24. Community Overcoming Relationship Abuse, "Effects on Children and Teens," corasupport.org, Website, 2015, http://www.corasupport.org/about-domestic-violence/effects-on-children-teens/
25. Allard and Greene, "Specialists Seek," 24-26.
26. Ibid., 28.
27. Patricia Allard and Judith Greene, Children on the Outside, 34.
28. Ibid,5.
29. Ibid., 9.
30. Ibid, "All the Wrong Lessons," 37.
31. Cadieux, interview.
32. *Commonwealth v. Reed,* No. 34575-77, Bristol County Superior Court (February 6, 1995), transcript, 1:210.
33. Information obtained from Beth Streck's Facebook page, accessed June 12, 2009, from https://www.facebook.com/beth.streck.
34. *Commonwealth v. Reed,* transcript, 1:210.
35. Ibid., 1:59.
36. Ibid., 1:210–17.
37. Ibid., 1:191, 6:82.

Chapter 3

1. Nick Wing, "When The Media Treats White Suspects And Killers Better Than Black Victims," Huffington Post, Website, August 8, 2014, http://www.huffingtonpost.com/2014/08/14/media-black-victims_n_5673291.html.
2. Ibid.
3. Richard Prince, "How Media Have Shaped our Perception of Race and Crime," The Root, Blog, September 4, 2014, http://www.theroot.com/blogs/journalisms/2014/09/how_media_have_shaped_our_perception_of_race_and_crime.html.

4. Moira Peelo et al., "Newspaper Reporting and the Public Construction of Homicide," *British Journal of Criminology* 44 (2004): 274.
5. Sara Rimer, "Model School tries to Cope with Killing in a Classroom." *New York Times*, April 21, 1993, online version available at http://www.nytimes.com/1993/04/14/us/model-school-tries-to-cope-with-killing-in-a-classroom.html.
6. Office of Housing and Community Development, Analysis of Impediments Report, 2006 (2006), 9–17, http://www.newbedford-ma.gov/community-development/wp-content/uploads/sites/34/Analysis_Impediments_Full_Document.pdf.
7. Tom Cadieux, telephone interview by author, Dartmouth, MA, July 21, 2011.
8. Social Explorer, US Census Bureau, Social Explorer Dataset, Census 1990, Dartmouth, SE:T-1; SE:T-12; SE:T-45, Document sent to the author from Middlesex Community College Library, Lowell, Massachusetts.
9. Social Explorer, US Census Bureau, Social Explorer Dataset, Census 1990, Dartmouth, SE: T93; Census 2000, Dartmouth, SE: TDocuments sent to the author from Middlesex Community College Library, Lowell, Massachusetts.
10. Jordana Hart and John Ellement, "Classroom Killing Aftermath: Three Defendants Are Arraigned," *Boston Globe*, April 14, 1993.
11. Cadieux, interview.
12. "Top Scoring Schools on the 10th-Grade MCAS," 2013 MCAS Results, Boston.com, http://www.boston.com/news/special/education/mcas/scores13/10th_top_schools.html.
13. Editorial Staff, "Education Deficit," *New Bedford Standard-Times*, April 29, 1993.
14. Sara Reimer, "No Gang Tied to Killing, Just Three Rare Friends," *New York Times*, April 23, 1993.
15. Cadieux, interview.
16. Pete Clare, "Dartmouth High Enrollment," Schooldigger.com, Website, http://www.schooldigger.com/go/MA/schools/0402000540/school.aspx.
17. Cadieux, interview.
18. Sean P. Murphy, "Increasing Violence among Teenagers Causes Alarm," *Boston Globe*, April 20, 1993.

19. B. Adams and C. Puzzanchera, Juvenile Justice System: A National Snapshot (Pittsburgh: National Center for Juvenile Justice, 2007), 1, http://www.modelsforchange.net/publications/132/National_Statistics_System_Snapshot.pdf.
20. Howard Snyder, Melissa Sickmund, and Eileen Poe-Yamagata, "Statistics Summary," Juvenile Offenders and Victims: 1996 Update on Violence, (Washington, D.C.: Office of Juvenile Justice and Delinquency Prevention, February 1996), 27-28, https://www.ncjrs.gov/pdffiles/90995.pdf.
21. Ibid, 28.
22. Jennifer Tanner, "Bennett, William J., John J. DiIulio, Jr., and John P. Walters: Moral Poverty Theory," Encyclopedia of Criminological Theory, eds. Francis T. Cullen & Pamela Wilcox (Thousand Oaks: Sage Publications, Inc. 2010) 83-86.
23. Retro Report, "The 'Superpredator' Scare," *New York Times* video, 10:35, April 6, 2014, http://www.retroreport.org/video/the-superpredator-scare.
24. Office of Juvenile Justice and Delinquency Prevention Statistical Briefing Book, Online, July 01, 1999. http://www.ojjdp.gov/ojstatbb/structure_process/qa04107.asp?qaDate=19990701.
25. Retro Report, "Superpredator."
26. Hart and Ellement, "Classroom Killing"
27. David Cantor and Mareena McKinley Wright, School Crime Patterns: A National Profile of US Public High Schools Using Rates of Crime Reported to the Police, US Department of Education report #EA96055001 (August 2002), 7.
28. Manley, "Dartmouth Parents."
29. Officers at Dartmouth (Mass.) Police Station, interview by author, September 20, 2011.
30. Ibid.
31. *Commonwealth v. Thomas,* Collet, and Reed, Probable Cause-Part A, DL 9300331, DL 9303355, DL 9300360, DL 9300356, DL 9300358, DL 9300359, DL 9300361, DL 9300362, DL 9300363, DL 9300364, DL 9300365, DL 9300352, DL 9300350, DL 9300366, DL 9300354, DL 9300357, Bristol Juvenile Court (June 24, 1993), transcript, 4.
32. Hart and Ellement, "Classroom Killing."

33. *Commonwealth v. Thomas,* Collet, and Reed, Probable Cause-Part A, DL 9300331, DL 9303350, DL 9300352, DL 9300353, DL 9300359, DL 9300360, DL 9300366, Bristol Juvenile Court (June 21, 1993), transcript, 159.
34. Ibid., 163.
35. Ibid., 161.
36. *Commonwealth v. Thomas,* Collet, and Reed, Probable Cause-Part A, DL 9300331, DL 9303350, DL 9300352, DL 9300353, DL 9300359, DL 9300360, DL 9300366, Bristol Juvenile Court (July 12, 1993), transcript, 22–23.
37. Ibid.
38. *Commonwealth v. Thomas,* Collet, and Reed, Probable Cause-Part A, DL 9300331, DL 9303350, DL 9300352, DL 9300353, DL 9300359, DL 9300360, DL 9300366, Bristol Juvenile Court (June 22, 1993), transcript, 9.
39. *Commonwealth v. Reed,* No. 34575-77, Bristol Superior Court (February 13, 1995), transcript, 6:94.
40. *Commonwealth v. Thomas,* Collet, and Reed, Probable Cause-Part A, DL 9300331, DL 9303355, DL 9300360, DL 9300356, DL 9300358, DL 9300359, DL 9300361, DL 9300362, DL 9300363, DL 9300364, DL 9300365, DL 9300352, DL 9300350, DL 9300366, DL 9300354, DL 9300357, Bristol Juvenile Court (June 23, 1993), transcript, 170–71.
41. Ibid., 170; Cadieux, interview.
42. Cadieux, interview.
43. *Commonwealth v. Reed,* No. 34575-77, Bristol Superior Court (May 19, 1995), transcript, 1:199–200.
44. Ibid., 200–202.
45. *Commonwealth of Massachusetts v. Nigel Thomas,* Gator Collet, and Karter Reed, Probable Cause-Part A (June 24, 1993), transcript, 4–5.
46. *Commonwealth v. Thomas,* Collet, and Reed, Probable Cause-Part A (June 22, 1993), transcript, 133–44.
47. Ibid.
48. "Collet Warns Students about Bad Decisions," The Item, December 3, 2005, http://www.telegram.com/apps/pbcs.dll/article?AID=/20051223/001-FRONTPAGE/512230762&LID=001.

49. *Commonwealth v. Thomas,* Collet, and Reed, Probable Cause-Part A (June 23, 1993), transcript, 172.
50. *Commonwealth v. Reed,* No. 34575-77, Bristol Superior Court (February 13, 1995), transcript, 6:105.
51. Obituary of Jason P. Robinson, *New Bedford Standard-Times,* April 13, 1993.
52. Ibid.
53. *Commonwealth v. Reed,* Bristol Superior Grand Jury Testimony, Fall River Superior Courthouse (June 8, 1994), transcript, 14.
54. Ibid., 20.
55. Jordana Hart, "Police Seek to Halt School Violence: Friends of Defendants in Dartmouth Slayings Fear Attack," *Boston Globe,* April 15, 1993. Juvenile court hearing transcripts also contain various testimonies from students.

Chapter 4

1. *Commonwealth v. Reed,* Bristol County Superior Grand Jury Testimony, Fall River Superior Courthouse (June 8, 1994), transcript, 26.
2. Sharon Reed, interview by author, New Bedford, Mass., July 12 and 19, 2011.
3. Ibid.
4. Derek Reed, interview by author, Burlington, Mass., August 9, 2011.
5. *Commonwealth of Massachusetts v. Thomas,* Collet, and Reed, DL 9300331, DL 9303350, DL 9300352, DL 9300353–59, DL 9300360–66, Bristol County Juvenile Court (June 21, 1993), transcript, 4–5.
6. Editorial, "Juvenile Miranda Waiver and Parental Rights," *Harvard Law Review* 126, no. 8 (June 2013): 2359–61.
7. ACLU, Children's Law Center and Office of Ohio State Public Defender, "Ensuring Access to Counsel in Ohio: Why Youth Waive Their Right to Counsel," *Fact Sheet,* March 2006, 1–2, https://www.aclu.org/sites/default/files/pdfs/ohiowhykidswaive20060309.pdf.
8. Tamar Birckhead, "The Role of Parent during Juvenile Interrogation," Juvenile Justice Blog, August 7, 2012, http://juvenilejusticeblog.web.unc.edu/2012/08/07/the-role-of-the-parent-during-juvenile-interrogation/.

9. Allison D. Redlich, Melissa Silverman, Julie Chen, and Hans Steiner, "Chapter Five," The Police Interrogation of Children and Adolescents, January 21, 2004, 110, http://www.albany.eu/scj/documents/Chapter05Lassiter.pdf.
10. Editorial, "Juvenile Miranda Waiver," 2360-61.
11. Judith B. Jones, "Access to Counsel," Juvenile Justice Bulletin (June 2004): 15-16, https://www.ncjrs.gov/pdffiles1/ojjdp/204063.pdf
12. Laurence Steinberg, "Network on Adolescent Development and Juvenile Justice," macfound.org, Website, 2015, https://www.macfound.org/media/article_pdfs/HCD_NET_DEVELOPMENT_JUVENILE_JUSTICE.PDF.
13. Ibid.
14. Birckhead, "Role of Parent;" Editorial, "Juvenile Miranda Waiver," 2372.
15. Youth Advocacy Division of the Committee for Public Counsel Services, "Juveniles Over age 14," An Overview of Massachusetts Law: Miranda and Juveniles, 12, https://www.publiccounsel.net/ya/wp-content/uploads/sites/6/2014/08/Miranda-Outline-January.2015.pdf.
16. Ibid.
17. The Youth Law T.E.A.M. of Indiana, "Your Child and the Juvenile Court," A Guide for Parents to the Juvenile Justice System in Indiana (Indianapolis: 2006), 6, http://www.youthlawteam.org/files/2006parentEnglish.pdf.
18. Birckhead, "Role of Parent."
19. Hillary B. Farber, "The Role of the Parent/Guardian in Juvenile Custodial Interrogations: Friend or Foe?" American Criminal Law Review 41, no. 3 (2004): 1291; Birrckhead, "Role of Parent."
20. Farber, "The Role of the Parent/Guardian:" 1311.
21. ACLU, "Ensuring Access to Counsel."
22. Barry C. Feld, "Police Interrogation of Juveniles An Empirical Study of Policy and Practice," *Journal of Criminal Law and Criminology* 97, no. 1, (Fall 2006): 227, http://scholarlycommons.law.northwestern.edu/cgi/viewcontent.cgi?article=7256&context=jclc.
23. Hillary B. Farber, "Do You Swear to Tell the Truth, the Whole Truth, and Nothing but the Truth Against your Child?" 43 *Loy.L.A.L.Rev.* 551 (2010), 569-71, http://scholarship.law.umassd.edu/cgi/viewcontent.cgi?article=1058&context=fac_pubs.

24. Rick Hampsen, "You Have the Right to Counsel, or Do You?" *USA Today,* March 12, 2013.
25. Gabrielle Gurley, "Public Defender Blues," *Commonwealth Magazine,* Winter 2014, http://commonwealthmagazine.org/uncategorized/004-public-defender-blues/.
26. Massachusetts Laws, c. 211D, sec. 2, 2A.
27. *Gideon v. Wainright,* 372 US 335 (1963), https://www.law.cornell.edu/supremecourt/text/372/335.
28. Hampsen, "Right to Counsel;" Andrew Cohen, "How Americans Lost the Right to Counsel 50 Years After 'Gideon, theatlantic.com, Website, March 13, 2013, http://www.theatlantic.com/national/archive/2013/03/how-americans-lost-the-right-to-counsel-50-years-after-gideon/273433/.
29. Kathleen Michon, J.D., "Juvenile Delinquency: What Happens in a Juvenile Case?" nolo.com, Website, http://www.nolo.com/legal-encyclopedia/juvenile-delinquency-what-happens-typical-case-32223.html
30. Citizens for Juvenile Justice, Data Points, December 2011, 4, http://www.cfjj.org/pdf/Data%20Points%202011.pdf.
31. The Massachusetts Juvenile Justice System of the 1990's: Rethinking a National Model, Report of the Boston Bar Association's Juvenile Task Force on the Juvenile Justice System, App. II, vi–viii, http://www.bostonbar.org/prs/reports/majuvenile94.pdf; Massachusetts Department of Youth Services, "Description of Training Organization," Site Visit Report, n.d.. http://www.excelsior.edu/c/document_library/get_file?uuid=1be3688e-6bfb-4f98-afaa-fe0de42b0a93
32. Inimai M. Chettiar, "The Many Causes of America's Decline in Crime," theatlantic.com, Website, February 11, 2015, http://www.theatlantic.com/politics/archive/2015/02/the-many-causes-of-americas-decline-in-crime/385364/.
33. Dana Goldstein, "10 (Not Entirely Crazy) Theories Explaining the Great Crime Decline," The Marshall Project, Website, November 24, 2014, https://www.themarshallproject.org/2014/11/24/10-not-entirely-crazy-theories-explaining-the-great-crime-decline; Citizens for Juvenile Justice, Unlocking Potential: Addressing the Overuse of Detention in Massachusetts, March 2014, 10, http://www.cfjj.org/pdf/Unlocking%20Potential%20-March%20

2014-DIGITAL.pdf.; Justin Wolvers, "Perceptions Haven't Caught Up to Decline in Crime," *New York Times*, September 16, 2014.
34. Citizens for Juvenile Justice, Unlocking Potential, 10.
35. Ibid., 12.
36. "Juvenile Justice Legal Issues: Juvenile Deliquincy," Executive Office of Health and Human Services, 2014, http://www.mass.gov/eohhs/gov/laws-regs/dys/juvenile-justice-legal-issues.html.
37. "Justice for Kids," Citizens for Juvenile Justice, accessed June 15, 2013, http://www.cfjj.org/justiceforkids.php.
38. Michael deCourcy Hinds, "Number of Killings Soars In Big Cities Across US," *New York Times*, July 18, 1990.
39. Ibid.
40. Ibid.
41. Clyde Haberman, "When Youth Violence Spurred the Superpredator Fear," *New York Times*, April 6, 2014.
42. "The Superpredator Myth, 20 Years Later," Equal Justice Initiative, Website, April 7, 2014, http://www.eji.org/node/893.
43. Hinds, "Killings."
44. Ibid.
45. Retro Report, "The Superpredator Scare," *New York Times* Video, April 6, 2014, http://www.nytimes.com/2014/04/07/us/politics/killing-on-bus-recalls-superpredator-threat-of-90s.html?_r=0.
46. Ibid.
47. Jonathan D. Salant, "Youths Shouldn't Be Tried as Adults, Study Says," Associated Press, March 3, 2003, http://www.commondreams.org/headlines03/0303-04.htm.
48. "Fact Sheet: Trends in US Corrections," (Washington, DC: The Sentencing Project, 2012), 1, http://sentencingproject.org/doc/publications/inc_Trends_in_Corrections_Fact_sheet.pdf.
49. Until They Die a Natural Death: Youth Sentenced to Life without Parole in Massachusetts (Lynn, MA: Children's Law Center of Massachusetts, September 2009), 8, http://www.clcm.org/UntilTheyDieaNaturalDeath9_09.pdf.
50. Richard A. Mendel, No Place for Kids: The Case for Reducing Juvenile Incarceration (Baltimore: The Annie E. Casey Foundation, 2011), 3, http://www.aecf.org/m/resourcedoc/aecf-NoPlaceForKidsFullReport-2011.pdf.
51. Ibid.

52. "Federal Government Increases Pressure on States to Stop Prison Rape," Equal Justice Initiative, Website, February 17, 2014, http://www.eji.org/node/876.
53. American Civil Liberties Union, "Youth Solitary Confinement: The Prison Rape Elimination Act (PREA)," aclu.org, Website, accessed by author October 25, 2015, https://www.aclu.org/files/assets/4%204%20PREA%20Two%20Pager.pdf ; Citizens for Juvenile Justice,
54. Jason Ziedenberg, You're an Adult Now: Youth in Adult Criminal Justice System, (Washington, D. C., National Institute of Corrections 2011): 10, http://static.nicic.gov/Library/025555.pdf.
55. Ibid.: 14.
56. Jackie Davis, "'Raise the Age' effort fails; youth can still be prosecuted and tried as adults," *The Legislative Gazette,* Website, June 29, 2015, http://www.legislativegazette.com/Articles-Top-Stories-c-2015-06-29-92275.113122-Raise-the-Age-effort-fails-youth-can-still-be-prosecuted-and-tried-as-adults.html
57. Maurice Chammah, "The 17-Year-Old Adults," *The Marshall Project,* Website, June 3, 2015, https://www.themarshallproject.org/2015/03/03/the-17-year-old-adults
58. "Death in Prison Sentences for Children," *Equal Justice Initiative,* Website, accessed by author November 9, 2013, http://www.eji.org/childrenprison/deathinprison; *Miller v. Alabama,* 132 S. Ct. 2455 (2012).
59. "Death in Prison."
60. Sarah Schweitzer and Michael Levenson, "Mass SJC Bars No-Parole Life Terms for Youth," *Boston Globe*, December 24, 2013.
61. "Children in Prison," Equal Justice Initiative, Website, accessed October 25, 2015, http://www.eji.org/childrenprison.
62. Ward and Ryan, Snapshot.
63. As seen in a photo by Mike Valeri on the front page, *New Bedford Standard-Times,* April 13, 1993.
64. "Hon. Armand Fernandes, Jr. Elected Chair of the New Bedford Whaling Museum," New Bedford Whaling Museum, http://www.whalingmuseum.org/press-room/releases/hon-armand-fernandes-jr-elected-chair-new-bedford-whaling-museum-06-07-2013.
65. Hon. Joseph Dever, interview by author, Boston, Mass., October 29, 2013.

66. Attorney Barbara Dougan, interview by author, Arlington, Mass., December 30, 2013.
67. Hon. Jay Blitzman, First Justice, Juvenile Court, interview by author, Lowell, Mass., September 17, 2013; As of the 1991 amendment, murder one for juveniles was punishable by a maximum of 20 years, at least 15 years of which had to be served. Murder two for juveniles was punishable by a maximum of 15 years, at least 10 of which had to be served.
68. *Commonwealth v. Reed,* No. 34575-77 (Bristol County Superior Court, February 14, 1995), transcript, vol. 7:79–80.
69. Jordana Hart and John Ellement, "Classroom Killing Aftermath: Three Defendants Are Arraigned," *Boston Globe*, April 14, 1993.
70. Massachusetts Historical Society, "Long Road to Justice: The African-American Experience in the Massachusetts Courts," Website, accessed January 6, 2014, http://www.masshist.org/longroad/03participation/judges.htm.
71. MacArthur Foundation, Research Network on Adolescent Development & Juvenile Justice, available at http://www.macfound.org/networks/research-network-on-adolescent-development-juvenil/details.
72. Ibid.
73. The Massachusetts Juvenile Justice System of the 1990's: Rethinking a National Model, Report of the Boston Bar Association's Juvenile Task Force on the Juvenile Justice System, 20-25, https://www.bostonbar.org/prs/reports/majuvenile94.pdf; Kinscherff, interview.
74. "Dartmouth Trio," New Bedford Standard-Times.
75. Jeffrey Burt, "He's Got No Remorse," *New Bedford Standard-Times*, April 14, 1993.
76. "Moral Compass Goes Off Course," *New Bedford Standard-Times*, April 18, 1993.
77. Patricia Nealon, "Dartmouth High Student Stabbed to Death in Class," *Boston Globe*, April 13, 1993.
78. Paul Langner, "Witness Says Boys Joyful after Murder," *Boston Globe*, February 9, 1995.
79. *Commonwealth v. Reed,* No. 34575-77, Bristol County Superior Court (February 13, 1995), transcript, 6:116–22.
80. Lynda Gorov, "Help Often Crowded Out for DYS' Charges," *Boston Globe*, May 24, 1993.

81. The Massachusetts Juvenile Justice System of the 1990's, Appendix II, vii.
82. Lisa E. Brooks, Amy L. Solomon, Sinead Keegan, Rhiana Kohl, and Lori Lahue, Prisoner Reentry in Massachusetts (Washington, DC: Urban Institute Justice Policy Center, 2005), 30, http://www.urban.org/uploadedPDF/411167_Prisoner_Reentry_MA.pdf.
83. Robin L. Dahlberg, "Appendix C," Locking Up Our Children: The Secure Detention of Youth After Arraignment and Before Adjudication, (Boston: American Civil Liberties Union, May 2008): 45, https://aclum.org/app/uploads/2015/06/reports-locking-up-our-children.pdf.
84. Gorov, "Help Often Crowded Out."
85. Lynda Gorov, "Risky business at DYS Workers face daily dangers amid soaring number of detained youths," *Boston Globe*, June 29, 1993.
86. Richard A. Mendel, No Place for Kids: The Case for Reducing Juvenile Incarceration (Baltimore: The Annie E. Casey Foundation, 2011), 2, http://www.aecf.org/m/resourcedoc/aecf-NoPlaceForKidsFullReport-2011.pdf.
87. Bobby Allyn, "Tenn. Detention Facility Explores How To Control Rough Teens," Nashville Public Radio, NPR Website, September 30, 2014, http://www.npr.org/2014/09/30/352661336/tenn-detention-facility-explores-how-to-control-rough-teens.
88. Barry Holman and Jason Ziedenberg, The Dangers of Detention: The Impact of Incarcerating Youth in Detention and Other Secure Facilities (Justice Policy Institute, Washington D.C., June 2011): 2, 5, 7-8, http://www.justicepolicy.org/images/upload/06-11_rep_dangersofdetention_jj.pdf.
89. Citizens for Juvenile Justice, Unlocking Potential, 2.
90. Ibid., 5.
91. Allyn, "Tenn. Detention."
92. Richard A. Mendel, The Missouri Model: Reinventing the Practice of Rehabilitating Youthful Offenders, (Baltimore: The Annie E. Casey Foundation, 2010): 25, http://static1.1.sqspcdn.com/static/f/658313/9749173/1291845016987/aecf_mo_fullreport_webfinal.pdf?token=2I4Oc1jyutMBcjOlbah4OFC4ku0%3D.
93. The Massachusetts Juvenile Justice System of the 1990's, 12.

94. NPR Staff, "'Burning Down The House' Makes The Case Against Juvenile Incarceration," Fresh Air, NPR Website, June 4, 2014, http://www.npr.org/2014/06/04/318801651/burning-down-the-house-makes-the-case-against-juvenile-incarceration.
95. Jenny Gold, "In Juvenile Detention, Girls Find Health System Geared To Boys," Kaiser Health News, NPR Website, November 26, 2012, "http://www.npr.org/sections/health-shots/2012/11/26/165913879/in-juvenile-detention-girls-find-health-system-geared-to-boys.
96. Mariame Kaba, "Supporting Girls in Conflict with the Law," Prison Culture: How the PIC Structures Our World (blog), December 13, 2010, http://www.usprisonculture.com/blog/2010/12/13/supporting-girls-in-conflict-with-the-law/.
97. *Commonwealth v. Reed,* transcript, 6:130.
98. Jordana Hart, "Dartmouth Youth Remembered," *Boston Globe*, April 16, 1993.
99. Effrain Hernandez Jr., "Southeastern Mass. Residents Seek Emotional Recovery from Violence," *Boston Globe*, April 29, 1993.

Chapter 5

1. Chesa Boudin, Trevor Stutz and Aaron Littman, "Prison Visitation: A Fifty State Survey," Prison Legal News, Website, May 15, 2013, https://www.prisonlegalnews.org/news/2013/may/15/prison-visitation-a-fifty-state-survey/.
2. Ibid.
3. Ibid.
4. Leslie A. Gordon, "Is video visitation helpful or harmful for prisoners and their families?" ABA Journal, Website, October 1, 2015, http://www.abajournal.com/magazine/article/is_video_visitation_helpful_or_harmful_for_prisoners_and_their_families.
5. Ibid.
6. In re: Karter Reed,"Transfer-Part B-Day III, Bristol County Juvenile Court, DL 9303350, DL 9300352–4, DL9300357, DL 9300360, DL 9300366, transcript, 8-28.
7. Nell Bernstein, Burning Down the House (New York: The New Press, 2014), 40-1.

8. In re: Karter Reed,"Transfer-Part B-Day III, 13-20.
9. *Commonwealth v. Reed,* No. 34575-77, Bristol County Superior Court (February 14, 1995), transcript, 7: 47.
10. Hon. Jay Blitzman, First Justice, Juvenile Court, interview by author, Lowell, Mass., September 17, 2013.
11. Randy Borum and Randy Otto, "Evaluation of Youth in the Juvenile Justice System," Mental Health Law and Faculty Policy Publications, Paper 394, (2004): 873-4, http://scholarcommons.usf.edu/cgi/viewcontent.cgi?article=1393&context=mhlp_facpub.
12. Dr. Laurence Steinberg, "Should the Science of Adolescent Brain Development Inform Legal Policy?" (Lecture, Harvard University, Cambridge MA., November 13, 2015).
13. Juvenile Justice: MacArthur Foundation, "Bryan Stevenson on Juveniles Sentenced to Life Without Parole,"YouTube video, available at http://modelsforchange.net/newsroom/343.
14. The Massachusetts Juvenile Justice System of the 1990's: Rethinking a National Model, Report of the Boston Bar Association's Juvenile Task Force on the Juvenile Justice System, 21-22, http://www.bostonbar.org/prs/reports/majuvenile94.pdf.
15. Susan Buratto and Stephen Dinwiddie, "Juvenile Forensic Psychiatric Evaluations," AMA Journal of Ethics (formerly Virtual Mentor) 15, no. 10 (October 2013): 860-865, http://journalofethics.ama-assn.org/2013/10/hlaw1-1310.html.
16. Ibid.
17. Ibid.
18. Ibid.
19. "In re: Karter Reed," Transfer-Part B-Day IV, Bristol County Juvenile Court, DL 9303350, DL 9300352–4, DL9300357, DL 9300360, DL 9300366, transcript, 77.
20. Depending on the sentence he received, and an evaluation by the juvenile facility, he could be released, or go to the Department of Corrections. Craig Barger testified that such bifurcated sentences had occurred: "In re: Karter Reed,"Transfer-Part B-Day II, Bristol County Juvenile Court, DL 9303350, DL 9300352–4, DL9300357, DL 9300360, DL 9300366, transcript, 14-16.
21. "In re: Karter Reed,"Transfer-Part B-Day IV, 71–72.
22. Marc Miller and Norval Morris, "Predictions of Dangerousness:

Ethical Concerns and Proposed Limits," Notre Dame Journal of Law, Ethics & Public Policy 2, no. 2 (1987): 393-403.

23. Ibid.
24. "In re: Karter Reed,"Transfer-Part B-Day IV, 62.
25. "In re: Karter Reed," Transfer-Part B-Day V, Bristol County Juvenile Court, DL 9303350, DL 9300352–4, DL9300357, DL 9300360, DL 9300366, transcript, 168–69.
26. Ibid., 173.
27. Ibid., 185–86.
28. Ibid., 208.
29. Stephen Porter et al.,"Memory for murder: A psychological perspective on dissociative amnesia in legal contexts," International Journal of Law and Psychiatry 24 (2001): 29-31.
30. "In re: Karter Reed," Transfer-Part B-Day V, Bristol County Juvenile Court, DL 9303350, DL 9300352–4, DL9300357, DL 9300360, DL 9300366, transcript, 220.
31. Stephen Porter, "Memory for Murder," 24-5.
32. "In re: Karter Reed,"Transfer-Part B-Day V, 215-16.
33. Ibid., 229-233.
34. Ibid., 251-3.
35. Ibid, 200-256.
36. "In re: Karter Reed," Probable Cause-Part B-Day 6, Bristol County Juvenile Court, DL 9303350, DL 9300352–4, DL9300357, DL 9300360, DL 9300366, transcript, 17.
37. Ibid., 17–18, 56.
38. Ibid., 96.
39. *Commonwealth v. Karter Reed,* No. 34575-77, Bristol County Superior Court (January 25, 1995), transcript of pre-trial motions, 1:6.
40. Children's Law Center of Massachusetts, Until They Die a Natural Death: Youth Sentenced to Life without Parole in Massachusetts (Lynn, Mass.: By the author, September 2009), 6, http://www.clcm.org/UntilTheyDieaNaturalDeath9_09.pdf.
41. Charles Crowley, "History," Bristol County Sheriff's Office, accessed January 2, 2013, http://www.bcso-ma.us/history.htm.
42. Human Rights Watch and the American Civil Liberties Union, Growing Up Locked Down: Youth in Solitary Confinement in Jails

and Prisons Across the United States, October 2012, 1-3, http://www.hrw.org/sites/default/files/reports/us1012ForUpload.pdf.
43. Ibid.
44. American Civil Liberties Union, "Solitary Confinement Harms Children," Stop Solitary: Ending the Solitary Confinement of Youth in Juvenile Detention Centers and Correctional Facilities, n.d., accessed by author November 14, 2015, https://juvjustice.org/sites/default/files/ckfinder/files/Ending%20the%20Solitary%20Confiement%20of%20Youth%20in%20Juvenile%20Detention%20and%20Correctional%20Facilities.pdf.
45. Ibid.
46. "Solitary Should be Banned in Most Cases, UN Expert Says," UN News Centre, Website, October 18, 2011, http://www.un.org/apps/news/story.asp?NewsID=40097#.VklCWL8f2FZ.
47. Dana Liebelson, "This Is What Happens When We Lock Children in Solitary Confinement," Mother Jones, January/February 2105, http://www.motherjones.com/politics/2014/01/juveniles-kids-solitary-confinement-ohio-new-york.
48. Ibid.
49. Eli Hager and Gerald Rich, "Shifting Away from Solitary," The Marshall Project, Website, December 23, 2014, https://www.themarshallproject.org/2014/12/23/shifting-away-from-solitary.
50. Dana Liebelson, "In 10 States, Children Can Be Punished With Indefinite Solitary Confinement," Huffingon Post, Website, November 2, 2015, http://www.huffingtonpost.com/entry/children-solitary-confinement_5637991fe4b00aa54a4ee011.
51. Victoria Law, "For Advocates, Push to End Solitary Confinement in Prison Only Begins With Youth Isolation," Truthout.com (blog), June 6, 2015, http://www.truth-out.org/news/item/31166-for-advocates-push-to-end-solitary-confinement-in-prison-only-begins-with-youth-isolation.
52. Liebelson, "This is What," Mother Jones.
53. "Collet Warns Students about Bad Decisions," The Item: Serving Clinton, Berlin, Bolton, Boylston, Lancaster and Sterling, December 23, 2005, available at, http://www.telegram.com/apps/pbcs.dll/article?AID=/20051223/001-FRONTPAGE/512230762&LID=001.

54. By the time Karter's case was sent to superior court, Nigel was a year into his sentence, having pleaded delinquent to a reduced charge of manslaughter. He had moved to his father's home in Denmark to serve a probation term and receive counseling. Although he was not allowed to return to the United States until he turned eighteen years old, Nigel would never see the inside of a prison. His admission and conviction of manslaughter would not be allowed as evidence at Karter's trial, although Fernandes worked hard to obtain the documents.
55. Maureen Boyle, "Judge Hely noted for Ability, Diligence," SouthCoast Today, Website, http://www.southcoasttoday.com/article/19980412/News/304129991.
56. Hon. Armand Fernandes, interview by author, New Bedford, Mass., October 12, 2012.
57. Deborah LaBelle and Anlyn Addis, Basic Decency: Protecting the Human Rights of Children, (Michigan: American Civil Liberties Union, 2012) 12-14, http://www.aclumich.org/sites/default/files/file/BasicDecencyReport2012.pdf.
58. Ibid., 13.
59. Ibid.
60. Ibid., 12-14.
61. Jean Trounstine, "Keep Kids out of Handcuffs," Truthout.com (blog), May 15, 2015, http://www.truth-out.org/news/item/30713-keep-kids-out-of-handcuffs.
62. Laura Tonch, "States Start Trend of Recognizing Parent-Child Privilege," Campbell Law Observer, Website, November 12, 2014, http://campbelllawobserver.com/states-start-trend-of-recognizing-parent-child-privilege/; Laura Tonch, "Should 'Every Man's Evidence' include Mom and Dad's?" Campbell Law Observer, Website, October 29, 2014, http://campbelllawobserver.com/should-every-mans-evidence-include-mom-and-dads/.
63. Deborah LaBelle, Basic Decency, 13.
64. *Commonwealth v. Reed,* No. 34575-76, Bristol County Superior Court (February 6, 1995), transcript, 1:125–27.
66. Ibid., 126.
67. Ibid., 151.
68. Ibid., 153.

69. *Commonwealth v. Reed,* No. 34575-77, Bristol County Superior Court (February 14, 1995), transcript, 7: 29-31.
70. *Commonwealth v. Reed,* No. 34575-76, Bristol County Superior Court (February 6, 1995), transcript, 1: 202–3.
71. Dr. Lida C. Landricho et al., "Egocentrism and Risk-Taking Among Adolescents," *Asia Pacific Journal of Multidisciplinary Research 2,* no. 3 (2014): 132.
72. *Commonwealth v. Reed,* No. 34575-77, Bristol County Superior Court (February 14, 1995), transcript, 7: 43.
73. Ibid., 44.
74. Ibid., 79–80.
75. Ibid., 97–107.
76. *Commonwealth v. Reed,* 34575-77, 120-21.
77. Ibid., 124.
78. Ibid., 127-28.
79. Sharon Reed, interview by author, New Bedford, Mass., July 12, 2011.
80. *Commonwealth v. Reed,* No. 34575-77, Bristol County Superior Court (February 15, 1995), transcript, 8:14.
81. Patrick O'Shea, "A Tour Through the Circles of Hell," *Odyssey,* (Spring 1993): 34, available at http://www.realcostofprisons.org/writing/oshea_circles_of_hell.pdf.

Chapter 6

1. Children's Law Center of Massachusetts, Until they Die, 22.
2. Ryan Grim, "American Horror Story: Children Are Being Housed In Adult Prisons Across The Country. It Has To Stop," Huffington Post, Website, July 1, 2015, http://www.huffingtonpost.com/2015/07/01/children-in-adult-prison_n_7702012.html
3. R. Daniel Okonkwo, "Prison Is a Poor Deterrent, and a Dangerous Punishment," *New York Times*, September 18, 2013.
4. Ibid., 23.
5. Ibid.
6. Ibid., 22.
7. Commission and Contributors, "Treating Trauma," National Prison Rape Elimination Commission Report, (Washington D.C.: National

Criminal Justice Reference Service, June 2009), 129, https://www.ncjrs.gov/pdffiles1/226680.pdf.

8. Commission and Contributors, "Executive Summary," National Prison Rape Elimination Commission Report, (Washington D.C.: National Criminal Justice Reference Service, June 2009), 14, https://www.ncjrs.gov/pdffiles1/226680.pdf; Personal conversations of prisoners with author while teaching at Framingham Women's Prison, 1987-1994.
9. Malika Saada Saar et al., "Introduction" The Sexual Abuse to Prison Pipeline, the Girls' Story, (Washington D.C.: Center on Poverty and Inequality, 2015), 5, http://rights4girls.org/wp-content/uploads/r4g/2015/02/2015_COP_sexual-abuse_layout_web-1.pdf.
10. Kelly Virella, "Male Guards, Female Inmates And Sexual Abuse In NYS Prisons," citylimits.org, Website, May 3, 2011, http://citylimits.org/2011/05/03/male-guards-female-inmates-and-sexual-abuse-in-nys-prisons/.
11. "Unequal Risk: Vulnerability and Victimization," National Prison Rape Report, 73.
12. Ibid., 74.
13. Joseph Mayton, "Transgender inmates to be housed by gender preference in San Francisco jail," The Guardian, Website, September 11, 2015, http://www.theguardian.com/us-news/2015/sep/11/san-francisco-jail-transgender-inmates-gender-preference.
14. James Swift, "As Prisons Prepare for PREA, Impact on Youthful Inmates May Be Major," Juvenile Justice Information Exchange, Website, August 19, 2013, http://jjie.org/as-prisons-prepare-for-prea-impact-on-youthful-inmates-may-be-major/; Dierdre Bannon,"PREA at a Crossroads,"The Crime Report, Website, April 26, 2015, http://www.thecrimereport.org/news/inside-criminal-justice/2015-08-prea-at-a-crossroads.
15. Ted Roeffels, "Similar Accounts in Teen Prison Rape Lawsuit Challenge State's Defense, Bridge Magazine, April 14, 2015, available at http://www.mlive.com/news/index.ssf/2015/04/similar_accounts_in_teen_priso.html; The Department of Correction would deny all claims, the lawsuit would be thrown out, and as of 2015, the prisoners had no justice, see Khalil Aljahal, "Teen Prison Rape Lawsuit Thrown Out Because Prisoners Excluded

from Michigan Civil Rights Law, mlive.com, Website, August 26, 2015, http://www.mlive.com/news/detroit/index.ssf/2015/08/teen_prison_rape_lawsuit_throw.html.

16. By Josie Duffy, "Michigan Court Says Juveniles can be Raped and Abused in Prison, Daily Kos, Website, August 28, 2015, http://www.dailykos.com/story/2015/8/28/1416084/-Michigan-court-says-juveniles-can-be-raped-and-abused-in-prison.
17. "When Children are Involved," National Prison Rape Report, 156.
18. T.J. Parsell, "In Prison, Teenagers Become Prey," *New York Times*, June 5, 2012.
19. Children's Law Center of Massachusetts, Until they Die, 22.
20. Ibid,, 23.
21. "Unequal Risk: Vulnerability and Victimization," National Prison Rape Report, 69.
22. Vincent Schiraldi and Jason Zeidenberg, The Risks Juveniles Face When They Are Incarcerated With Adults (Justice Policy Institute, 1997): 3, http://www.justicepolicy.org/images/upload/97-02_REP_RiskJuvenilesFace_JJ.pdf.
23. *Roper v. Simmons,* 543 US 551, 570 (2005).
24. Names of prisoners have been changed to protect their identity.
25. Okonkwo, "Prison Is a Poor Deterrent."
26. Tracy Barnhart, "Why do youth join prison gangs?" policeone.com, Website, http://www.policeone.com/corrections/articles/1681985-Why-do-youth-join-prison-gangs/.
27. Ibid.
28. David Skarbuck, The Social Order of the Underworld: How Prison Gangs Govern the American Penal System, (Oxford: Oxford University Press, 2014): 27.
29. Gary Fields and Erica E. Phillips, "The New Asylums: Jails Swell with the Mentally Ill," Wall Street Journal, September 25, 2013; Susan Starr Sered and Maureen Norton-Hawk, Can't Catch a Break: Gender, Jail, Drugs, and the Limits of Personal Responsibility, (Oakland: University of California Press, 2014).
30. Malika Saada Saar et al., "Girls Paths of Abuse into the Criminal Justice System,"The Sexual Abuse to Prison Pipeline, the Girls' Story, (Washington D.C.: Center on Poverty and Inequality, 2015), 12, http://rights4girls.org/wp-content/uploads/r4g/2015/02/2015_COP_sexual-abuse_layout_web-1.pdf.

31. Ibid.
32. Susan Sered, "Incarceration by any Other Name: a Return to the Cuckoo's Nest?" susan.sered.name (blog) May 21, 2014, http://susan.sered.name/blog/incarceration-by-any-other-name-a-return-to-the-cuckoos-nest/
33. Fields, "The New Asylums;" Sered, "Incarceration;" Susan Sered, "Our Prisons are Drugging Women," Salon, Website, August 8, 2013, http://www.salon.com/2013/08/08/are_americas_prisons_drugging_women/.
34. Campaign for Youth Justice, *Jailing Juveniles: The Dangers of Incarcerating Youth in Adult Jails in America,* (Washington D.C.: Campaign for Youth Justice, November 2007):15 http://www.campaignforyouthjustice.org/Downloads/NationalReportsArticles/CFYJ-Jailing_Juveniles_Report_2007-11-15.pdf.
35. During a trip to a local jail in Massachusetts, an officer made this comment to me.
36. Virella, "Male Guards, Female Inmates And Sexual Abuse."
37. Matt DeLisi and Peter J. Connis, *Violent Offenders: Theory, Research Policy, and Practice,* (Burlington, MA: Jones & Bartlett Learning; 2 edition, July 2011): 443
38. Elizabeth P. Shulman and Elizabeth Cauffman, "Coping while Incarcerated: A Study of Male Juvenile Offenders," *Journal of Research on Adolescence* 21, no. 4 (December 2011): 818-826.
39. Cougar Newquist, "Life Behind Bars as a Convicted Sex Offender," prisonwriters.com, Website, accessed by author November 23, 2015, http://www.prisonwriters.com/life-behind-bars-as-a-convicted-sex-offender/.
40. Julia T. Rickert, "Denying Defendants the Benefit of a Reasonable Doubt: Federal Rule of Evidence 609 and Past Sex Crime Convictions," *Journal of Criminal Law and Criminology 100*, no. 1 (Winter 2010): 213.
41. Michael S. James, "Prison Is Living Hell for Pedophiles," ABC News Online, August 26, 2003, http://abcnews.go.com/US/story?id=90004.
42. Ken McGregor, "'Culture' of older inmates getting young prisoners to bash alleged paedophiles, court told," adelaidenow.com.au, Website, October 8, 2015, http://www.adelaidenow.com.au/news/south-australia/culture-of-older-inmates-getting-

young-prisoners-to-bash-alleged-paedophiles-court-told/story-fni6uo1m-1227562242861?sv=6b91845abbd8b7ba4f1ea89d4e924 64b.

43. Angela Davis, "Globalization and the Prison Industrial Complex" (lecture, Babson College, Wellesley, Mass., February 27, 2014).
44. Dana Liebelson, "Cruel and all-too-unusual punishment: A Terrifying Look at Life in Prison—as a Kid," Huffington Post, Website, July 1, 2015, http://highline.huffingtonpost.com/articles/en/cruel-and-all-too-usual/.
45. Nigel Williams and Lara Natale, "Youth Crime in England and Wales," Civitas Crime Factsheets, (2010-12): 7, http://www.civitas.org.uk/crime/comments.php.
46. Amelia Gentleman, "Life in a Young Offenders' Institution," The Guardian, November 21, 2011.
47. Ibid; Williams and Natale, "Youth Crime."
48. Children's Law Center of Massachusetts, "Until they Die," 29.
49. Richard A. Mendel, No Place for Kids: The Case for Reducing Juvenile Incarceration (Baltimore: The Annie E. Casey Foundation, 2011), 32-34, http://www.aecf.org/m/resourcedoc/aecf-NoPlaceForKidsFullReport-2011.pdf.
50. Richard A. Mendel, The Missouri Model: Reinventing the Practice of Rehabilitating Youthful Offenders, (Baltimore: The Annie E. Casey Foundation, 2010): 11, 19, http://static1.1.sqspcdn.com/static/f/658313/9749173/1291845016987/aecf_mo_fullreport_webfinal.pdf?token=2I4Oc1jyutMBcjOlbah4OFC4ku0%3D.
51. Ibid., 23-40.
52. Ibid., 18.
53. Ibid., 14.
54. The Annie E. Casey Foundation, "Reducing Youth Incarceration in the United States, Data Snapshot, (February 2103): 1, http://www.aecf.org/m/resourcedoc/AECF-DataSnapshotYouthIncarceration-2013.pdf.
55. Ibid., 42.
56. "MCI Norfolk," Official Website of the Executive Office of Public Safety and Security, 2014, http://www.mass.gov/eopss/law-enforce-and-cj/prisons/doc-facilities/mci-norfolk.html.
57. "Timeline," Malcolm-x.org, http://www.malcolm-x.org/bio/timeline.htm.

58. Project Youth brochure from 1997 given to Karter in prison, sent to me by Karter Reed.
59. Gail Jennes, "Saved from the Electric Chair, Hank Arsenault Warns Kids That Crime Pays Only in Heartbreak," People Magazine, October 23, 1978, http://www.people.com/people/archive/article/0,,20072012,00.html.
60. Ibid; John Winters, "Students Get Straight Story from Prisoners;" The Sun Chronicle, Website, November 2, 2001, http://www.thesunchronicle.com/students-get-straight-story-from-prisoners/article_b1d1efbf-060d-5729-8b68-3c6a0a8268e8.html
61. Jennes, "Saved from the Electric Chair;" Project Youth brochure from 1999 given to Karter in prison, sent to me by Karter Reed.
62. Winters, "Students Get Straight Story."
63. Project Youth brochure from 1999.
64. James Austin, Kelly Dedel Johnson, and Maria Gregoriou, Juveniles in Adult Prisons and Jails: A National Assessment (Washington, DC: US Department of Justice, October 2000), x, https://www.ncjrs.gov/pdffiles1/bja/182503.pdf.

Chapter 7

1. "Juveniles with Life Sentences," Official Website of the Executive Office of Public Safety and Security, 2016, www.mass.gov/eopss/agencies/parole-board/juveniles-with-life-sentences.html; Will Brownsberger, "Sentencing Juvenile for Murder," willbrownsberger.com, Website, July 7, 2014, http://willbrownsberger.com/juvenile-first-degree-murder-senate-2246/.
2. Massachusetts Laws, chapter 279, section 24.
3. Joshua Rovner, "Slow to Act: State Responses to 2012 Supreme Court Mandate on Life without Parole," Policy Brief: State Responses to Miller (Washington DC: Sentencing Project, June 2014), 2, http://sentencingproject.org/doc/publications/jj_State_Responses_to_Miller.pdf.
4. Ibid.
5. Ibid.
6. Ibid., 1; Maggie Clark, "After Supreme Court Ruling, States Act on Juvenile Sentences,"Pew Charitable Trusts, Website, August 26, 2013, http://www.pewtrusts.org/en/research-and-analysis/blogs/

stateline/2013/08/26/after-supreme-court-ruling-states-act-on-juvenile-sentences.

7. Natasja Sheriff, "UN Expert Slams US as Only Nation to Imprison Kids for Life Without Parole," Aljazeera America, Website, March 9, 2015, http://america.aljazeera.com/articles/2015/3/9/un-expert-slams-us-as-only-nation-to-sentence-kids-to-life-without-parole.html
8. Erin Heffernan, "New Law Puts Killer who Got Life Sentence as a Teen on Path to Parole," *Seattle Times*, June 21, 2014.
9. Ibid.
10. Liz Ryan and Jason Zeidenberg, *The Consequences Aren't Minor: The Impact of Trying Youth as Adults and Strategies for Reform* (Washington D.C.: Campaign for Youth Justice, March 2007), 29, http://www.campaignforyouthjustice.org/documents/CFYJNR_ConsequencesMinor.pdf.
11. *Programs in Correctional Settings: Innovative State and Local Programs*, Bureau of Justice Assistance Monograph NCJ17008 (Washington, DC: US Department of Justice, Office of Justice Programs, June 1998), 121–26, https://www.ncjrs.gov/pdffiles/170088.pdf; Karla Navarrete, "Arizona Inmates Training Wild Horses," azfamily.com, Website, April 27, 2015, http://www.azfamily.com/story/28910075/arizona-inmates-taming-wild-horses.
12. Programs in Corr. Settings, 64-68; With George Mumford, mindfulness coach, there were also informal conversations during mindfulness work with author and students in Changing Lives Through Literature Program in 1996.
13. Annual Report 2011 (Milford: Massachusetts Department of Correction, August 2012), 47, http://www.mass.gov/eopss/docs/doc/annual-report-2011-final-08-01-12.pdf.
14. Nellis, *The Lives of Juvenile Lifers,* 23-4.
15. Obituary of Larry Apsey, Transformer: Newsletter of Alternatives to Violence Project Newsletter, Winter 1997, 3, http://thetransformer.us/97-4.pdf#zoom=100.
16. "How We Help," Alternatives to Violence Project Massachusetts, http://www.avpma.org/about.
17. "A Short History," Alternatives to Violence Project Massachusetts, Website, access by author, December 7, 2015, http://www.avpma.

org/about; "AVP on the Inside," Alternatives to Violence Project USA, Website, access by author December 7, 2015, http://avpusa.org/what-we-do/avp-in-prisons/.

18. Ryan and Zeidenberg, Consequences Aren't Minor, 14.
19. Ibid., 52.
20. Key Facts: Youth in the Justice System, Campaign for Youth Justice, updated April 2012, 3, http://www.campaignforyouthjustice.org/documents/KeyYouthCrimeFacts.pdf.
21. *Until They Die a Natural Death: Youth Sentenced to Life without Parole in Massachusetts* (Lynn, MA: Children's Law Center of Massachusetts, September 2009), 22-24, http://www.clcm.org/UntilTheyDieaNaturalDeath9_09.pdf.
22. Joan Petersilia, "Parole and Prisoner Reentry in the United States," pt. 1, Perspectives, Summer 2000, 36, http://www.appa-net.org/eweb/resources/ppcsw_10/docs/su00appa32.pdf.
23. Annual Statistical Report 2007 (Natick: Massachusetts Parole Board, n.d.), 4, http://www.mass.gov/eopss/docs/pb/2007annualreport.pdf.
24. Ibid.
25. Petersilia, "Parole and Prisoner Reentry," 36.
26. Ibid., 37.
27. "Historical Context," in *The Future of Parole as a Key Partner in Assuring Public Safety,* Parole Essentials: Practical Guides for Parole Leaders No. 5 (Washington, DC: US Department of Justice, National Institute of Corrections, July 2011), 1–2, http://static.nicic.gov/Library/024201.pdf.
28. Ibid., 2.
29. "Criminal Justice Fact Sheet," NAACP, http://www.naacp.org/pages/criminal-justice-fact-sheet; The Pew Center on the States, "A Snapshot of Prison Growth," in One in 100: Behind Bars in America 2008 (Washington, DC: The Pew Charitable Trust, 2008), 5, http://www.colorado.gov/ccjjdir/Resources/Resources/Ref/PEW_OneIn100.pdf.
30. Parole Practices in Massachusetts and Their Effect on Reintegration (Boston: Boston Bar Association Task Force on Parole and Community Reintegration, August 2002), 2, http://www.bostonbar.org/prs/reports/finalreport081402.pdf.

31. Katherine Bradley and R. B. Oliver, The Role of Parole, Policy Brief (Boston, MA: Community Resources for Justice, July 2001), 2, http://www.crj.org/page/-/cjifiles/THE%20ROLE%20OF%20PAROLE.pdf.
32. Administration of the Government, Massachusetts General Laws, sec. 127.130, https://malegislature.gov/Laws/GeneralLaws/PartI/TitleXVIII/Chapter127/Section130.
33. Ashley Nellis, Life Goes On: The Historic Rise in Life Sentences in America, (Washington, D.C.: Sentencing Project, 2013), 1–5.
34. Rovner, "Slow to Act:" 3.
35. *Henry Montgomery v. State of Louisiana,* 136, S.Ct. 718 (2016)
36. Denying Parole at First Eligibility: How Much Public Safety Does It Actually Buy? A Study of Prisoner Release and Recidivism in Michigan (Lansing, MI: Citizens Alliance on Prisons and Public Spending, August 2009), 1–2, http://www.capps-mi.org/wp-content/uploads/2009/08/Denying-parole-at-first-eligibility-2009.pdf.
37. Ibid., 4.
38. Robert Weisbergh, Debbie A. Mukamal, and Jordan D. Segall, Life in Limbo: An Examination of Parole Releases for Prisoners Serving Life Sentences with the Possibility of Parole in California, (Stanford Law School, CA: Stanford Criminal Justice Center, September 2011), 21, http://www.law.stanford.edu/sites/default/files/child-page/164096/doc/slspublic/SCJC_report_Parole_Release_for_Lifers.pdf.
39. Ibid., 17.
40. Ibid.
41. Ibid.
42. Gordon Haas and Lloyd Fillion, *Life Without Parole: A Reconsideration* (Norfolk, MA.:Norfolk Lifers Group, November 2010), 21-2, http://realcostofprisons.org/materials/Haas_LWOP.pdf.
43. "Frequently Asked Questions About the DOC," Executive Office of Public Safety and Security, 2015, http://www.mass.gov/eopss/agencies/doc/faqs-about-the-doc.html; "Frequently Asked Questions," Executive Office of Public Safety and Security, 2015, http://www.mass.gov/eopss/agencies/parole-board/frequently-asked-questions.html.

Chapter 8

1. Attorneys at Prisoners' Legal Services (PLS) and Attorney Patricia Garin, "E. The Process of Gaining Release After a Grant of Parole," White Paper: The Current State of Parole in Massachusetts, February 2013, http://www.plsma.org/critical-current-legislation/parole-white-paper.
2. Research and Planning Division, January 1, 2008 Inmate Statistics, Publication No. 08-122-02.DOC (Boston: MA Department of Correction),v,http://www.mass.gov/eopss/docs/doc/research-reports/jan-1-population/112008.pdf.
3. Executive Office of Public Safety, 103-420 CMR: Department of Correction, available at http://www.mass.gov/courts/docs/lawlib/101-103cmr/103cmr420.pdf.
4. Prisoners' Legal Services of Massachusetts, "Classification," Website, 2015, http://www.plsma.org/prisoner-self-help/prison-procedures/classification/.
5. PLS and Attorney Patricia Garin, "D. The Effect of Lower Parole Rates," White Paper.
6. Ibid.
7. Pew Charitable Trusts, *Max Out: The Rise in Prison Inmates Released Without Supervision* (Washington D.C., Pew Charitable Trusts, June 2014), 4, http://www.pewtrusts.org/~/media/assets/2014/06/04/maxout_report.pdf.
8. Stephen Kurkjian, "State's Toughened Crime Policy Has Downside," *Boston Globe*, January 25, 2004.
9. Governor's Commission on Correction Reform, Strengthening Public Safety, Increasing Accountability, and Instituting Fiscal Responsibility in the Department of Correction (Boston, Mass., June 30, 2004), 36-37, http://www.mass.gov/eopss/docs/eops/govcommission-corrections-reform.pdf
10. Massachusetts Parole Board, "Karter Reed Record of Decision W-58026," April 18, 2008. This was sent to me by Karter Reed.
11. Jessica Fargen, "Early Release Stuns Teen Victim's Family," *Boston Herald*, May 16, 2008.
12. Curt Brown, "Karter Reed, Convicted of 1993 DHS Stabbing, is Granted Parole," SouthCoastToday.com, May 15, 2008.

13. Ibid.
14. "Man Convicted in Classroom Stabbing Granted Parole," WBZTV.com, May 15, 2008, http://wbztv.com/local/Dartmouth.high.school (page no longer available).
15. "Parole Sought by Man Convicted in High School Stabbing Death," CW56.com, March 12, 2008, http://www.cw56.com/news/articles/local/MI3191 (page no longer available).
16. For example, see Howie Carr, "Hard to Miss Duke When his Cons Won't Go Away, *Boston Herald*, March 25, 2005; Howie Carr, "Bench Helped the Celtics but Hurts You;" *Boston Herald*, June 22, 2008.
17. Howie Carr, "The Parole Board Is Open under New Management—Liberal Bleeding-Heart Management," *Boston Herald*, May 18, 2008.
18. Ibid.
19. A Study of Parole Board Decisions for Lifers, 2008 (Norfolk, MA: Lifers' Group Inc., MCI-Norfolk, April 2009), 3, http://realcostofprisons.org/materials/2008StudyofParoleBoardDecisionsforLifers.pdf.
20. Keith Wallington, "Fact Sheet: Maryland's Policies Around Parole-Eligible Life Sentences," Justice Policy Institute, January 13, 2015, http://www.justicepolicy.org/uploads/justicepolicy/documents/documentary_factsheet.pdf.
21. Beth Schwartzapfel, "How to Investigate Parole Release Rates in Your State," The Marshall Project, Website, July 10, 2015, https://www.themarshallproject.org/2015/07/10/how-to-investigate-parole-release-rates-in-your-state#.IHiXstxPN.
22. PLS and Attorney Patricia Garin, "Institute a Mechanism for Presumptive Parole,"White Paper; Gordon Haas, The Massachusetts Parole Board 2012, a Report, 2-3, accessed by author January 8, 2016, http://www.cjpc.org/2012/MA-Parole-Board-2012.pdf.
23. "Boston Pre-Release Center," Executive Office of Public Safety and Security, 2014, http://www.mass.gov/eopss/law-enforce-and-cj/prisons/doc-facilities/boston-pre-release-center.html.
24. Ibid.
25. Gina Papagiorgakis, Three Year Recidivism Rates: 2011 Release Cohort, No. 15-161-DOC (Boston, MA, Massachusetts

Department of Correction, August 2015), 5, http://www.mass.gov/eopss/docs/doc/research-reports/recidivism/recidivism-rates-2011-releases-3year.pdf.

26. "Boston Pre-Release Center," Official Website of the Executive Office of Public Safety and Security, http://www.mass.gov/eopss/law-enforce-and-cj/prisons/doc-facilities/boston-pre-release-center.html.
27. MIT Center for Civic Media, Between the Bars: Human Stories from Prison, Website, accessed by author December 24, 2015, https://betweenthebars.org/.
28. "Elizabeth's" name has been changed from the original.
29. Todd W. Burke, PhD, and Stephen S. Owen, PhD, "Cell Phones as Prison Contraband," The FBI: Federal Bureau of Investigation, July 2010, http://www.fbi.gov/stats-services/publications/law-enforcement-bulletin/july-2010/cell-phones-as-prison-contraband.
30. Ibid.
31. Vera Bergengruen, "FCC Gives Inmates Price Break on Prison Phone Calls," McClatchy D.C., Website, October 22, 2015, http://www.mcclatchydc.com/news/nation-world/national/article40881675.html.
32. Matt Clarke, "Contraband Smuggling a Problem at Prisons and Jails Nationwide," Prison Legal News, January 15, 2013, https://www.prisonlegalnews.org/%28S%28eahly1nj2ulhcizgfgfkyfjh%29%29/24817_displayArticle.aspx.
33. "Old Colony Correctional Center," Official Website of the Executive Office of Public Safety and Security, 2014, http://www.mass.gov/eopss/law-enforce-and-cj/prisons/doc-facilities/old-colony-correctional-center.html.
34. According to the Code of Massachusetts Regulations (120 CMR 302.00), "When the Parole Board Members set a parole release date, release on that date is contingent upon continued satisfactory conduct by the inmate and the absence of any new and significant adverse information not known to the parole hearing panel at the time the release decision was made"; see Massachusetts Trial Court Law Libraries, http://www.mass.gov/courts/case-legal-res/law-lib/.
35. Massachusetts Regulations, 103 CMR 430.00.

36. Members of Columbia Human Rights Law Review, "Your Rights at Prison Disciplinary Hearings," chap. 18 in A Jailhouse Lawyer's Manual, 8th ed. (New York: Columbia Human Rights Law Review, 2009), 2–3, http://www3.law.columbia.edu/hrlr/JLM/Chapter_18.pdf.
37. "Rescission and Modification of Parole," USLegal.com, accessed September 13, 2014, from http://pardonandparole.uslegal.com/scope-of-parole-power/rescission-and-modification-of-parole/.
38. Massachusetts Code of Regulations, "Rescission of Parole Date," 120 CMR 302.00, available at http://www.lawlib.state.ma.us/source/mass/cmr/cmrtext/120CMR302.pdf.
39. Commonwealth of Massachusetts Department of Correction Disciplinary Report, Karter Reed, W58026, no. 152654, Boston Pre-Release, January 14, 2009. Sent to me by Attorney Richard Neumeier, February 14, 2013.
40. Tom Vannah, "Between the Lines: Patrick's Pander," Valley Advocate, January 20, 2011. John Ellement, "Parole Board is Under Fire; Milton Officer is Called Unqualified," *Boston Globe*, June 13, 2007.

Chapter 9

1. Massachusetts Code of Regulations, "Rescission of Parole Date," 120 CMR 302.00, available at http://www.mass.gov/courts/docs/lawlib/116-130cmr/120cmr302.pdf.
2. John Caher, "Parole Is Again Denied for Inmate in Rescission Case," New York Law Journal, September 13, 2013.
3. Thomas Tracy, "Cop Killer Will Continue to Rot as Parole Denied for Man Who Murdered NYPD Officer in 1978," New York Daily News, September 4, 2013.
4. *Lewis v. Casey,* 518 US 343 (1996), available at http://www.law.cornell.edu/supct/html/94-1511.ZO.html. 518 US 343 (1996).
5. Rachel Meeropol and Ian Head, editors, "Your Right to use the Courts," The Jailhouse Lawyer's Handbook, 5th edition, (New York: The Center for Constitutional Rights and the National Lawyer's Guild, 2010) http://jailhouselaw.org/your-right-to-use-the-courts/.
6. Jonathan Abel, "Ineffective Assistance of Library: The Failings and

the Future of Prison Law Libraries," The Georgetown Law Journal 101 (2013): 1173.
7. Tessa Melvin, "Funds for Inmates Celebrated," *New York Times*, June 26, 1983.
8. Decision in the Matter of Charles Ponticelli, W50338, Revocation Review, May 2, 2013, http://www.mass.gov/eopss/docs/pb/lifer-decisions/2013/ponticellicharles5-2-13.pdf.
9. Ibid, 10.
10. "Release, Rescission and Revocation Hearings," Annual Statistical Report, 2008 (Natick, MA: Massachusetts Parole Board, n.d.), 14, http://www.mass.gov/eopss/docs/pb/2008-ar-final-web.pdf.
11. Beth Schwartzapfel, "Life Without Parole," The Marshall Project, Website, July 10, 2015, https://www.themarshallproject.org/2015/07/10/life-without-parole.
12. Massachusetts Parole Board Rescission Hearing of Karter Reed at Old Colony Correctional Center, May 18, 2009, transcript, 2, 3.
13. Ibid.
14. Ibid.
15. Ibid.
16. Massachusetts Code of Regulations, "Rescission Hearing," 120 CMR 302.08, available at http://www.mass.gov/courts/docs/lawlib/116-130cmr/120cmr302.pdf.
17. Ibid.
18. Karter Reed, "The Vision: A Conceptualization of an Effective Correctional System (and Its Implementation)," The Real Cost of Prisons Project, letter dated April 15, 2010, 7, available at http://www.realcostofprisons.org/writing/Reed_The_Vision.pdf.
19. "National Programs," The Inside-Out Center, 2014, http://www.insideoutcenter.org/national-programs.html.
20. Tabitha Cohen, "College-in-Prison for Inmates Serving Life Sentences, Morningside Review, Website, accessed by author December 27, 2015, http://morningsidereview.org/essay/college-in-prison-for-inmates-serving-life-sentences/#_edn19.
21. Ibid.
22. Jon Marc Taylor, "Pell Grants for Prisoners: Why We Should Care," Straight Low Magazine 9, no. 2 (2008): 55, available at http://realcostofprisons.org/writing/Taylor_Pell_Grants.pdf.

23. Jon Marc Taylor, "Pell Grants for Prisoners Part Deux: It's Déjà Vu All Over Again," Journal of Prisoners on Prison, nos. 1 and 2 (1997): 3–4, http://www.jpp.org/documents/forms/JPP8/Taylor.pdf.
24. Christopher Zoukis, "Pell Grants for Prisoners: New Bill Restores Hope of Reinstating College Programs," Prisoner Legal News, Website, July 31, 2015, https://www.prisonlegalnews.org/news/2015/jul/31/pell-grants-prisoners-new-bill-restores-hope-reinstating-college-programs/.
25. "Education and Vocational Training in Prison Reduces Recidivism, Improves Job Outlook," Rand Corporation, August 22, 2013, http://www.rand.org/news/press/2013/08/22.html.
26. Ibid.
27. Jean Trounstine, "Higher Education is a Key to Decarceration: Let's Pass the REAL Act,"Truthout, November 24, 2015, Website, http://www.truth-out.org/opinion/item/33767-higher-education-is-a-key-to-decarceration-let-s-pass-the-real-act.
28. Ibid.
29. John A. Grossman and Sandra McCroom, Memo titled "Cinelli," addressed to Mary Beth Heffernan, Secretary EOPSS, dated January 12, 2011, Report by the Commonwealth of Massachusetts Executive Office of Public Safety, 3–8, available at http://archives.lib.state.ma.us/bitstream/handle/2452/69729/ocn707396422.pdf.
30. Ibid.
31. Ibid.
32. Sean Thakkar, "Oversight Hearing on 2008 Criminal Justice Reforms" (paper presented to the Conn. Judiciary Committee, January 9, 2010), 1–6, available at http://www.cga.ct.gov/2010/juddata/od/00119-Criminal%20Justice%20Information%20System%20Governing%20Board-Sean%20Thakkar.pdf.
33. Trounstine, "Patrick's Folly."
34. Jean Trounstine, "Locked Up with Nowhere to Go," *Boston Magazine*, July 2013.
35. Gordon Haas, Parole Decisions for Lifers-2014, (Norfolk, Mass.: Norfolk Lifers Group, MCI-Norfolk, March 2015), 3-4, http://realcostofprisons.org/writing/haas-parole-decisions-for-lifers-2014.pdf.

36. Amanda Noss, US Census Bureau, "Household Income for States: 2010 and 2011," American Community Survey Briefs, September 2012, 1, http://www.census.gov/prod/2012pubs/acsbr11-02.pdf.
37. Newt Gingrich and Pat Dolan, "Prison Reform: A Smart Way for States to Save Money and Lives," *Washington Post*, January 7, 2011.
38. National Institute of Corrections, "The Future of Parole as a Key Partner in Assuring Public Safety," No. 024201, July 2011, 1, http://static.nicic.gov/Library/024201.pdf

Chapter 10

1. *Lanier v. Fair*, 876 F.2d 243 (1st. Cir. 1989), accessed December 12, 2011, http://www.leagle.com/decision/19891119876F2d243_11065.
2. Ibid.
3. Ibid.
4. *Lanier v. Massachusetts Parole Board & Others*, 396 Mass. 1018 (March 5, 1986), accessed December 12, 2011, http://masscases.com/cases/sjc/396/396mass1018.html.
5. Attorney Richard Neumeier, interview by author, Boston, Mass., December 2, 2013.
6. *Lanier v. Fair.*
7. Jessica Feierman, "The Power of the Pen: Jailhouse Lawyers, Literacy, and Civic Engagement," Harvard Civil Rights-Civil Liberties Law Review 4 (2006): 371; *Commonwealth v. Karter Reed*, 427 Mass. 100 (1998).
8. Similar not-for-profit prisoners' rights corporations exist in at least 24 states; see "Legal Resource Database," Prison Policy Initiative, 2013, http://www.prisonpolicy.org/resources/legal. "Can PLS Help," Prisoners' Legal Services of Massachusetts, 2013, http://www.plsma.org/can-pls-help.
9. Ashley Dunn, "Flood of Prisoner Rights Suits Brings Effort to Limit Findings," *New York Times*, March 21, 1994.
10. Margo Schlanger, "Trends in Prisoner Litigation, as the PLRA Enters Adulthood," *UC Irvine Law Review* 5, no. 1 (2015): 153-79.
11. Ibid.
12. Joe Ryan, N.J. inmates submit hundreds of lawsuits each year, despite little chance of success," NJ.com, July 25, 2010, http://www.

nj.com/news/index.ssf/2010/07/lawsuits_from_nj_inmates_are_o.html.

13. Bruce Western and Becky Pettit, "Incarceration and Social Inequality," Daedalus 139, no. 3 (2010): 9.
14. Feierman, "Power of the Pen," 373.
15. Patricia Garin and Prisoners' Legal Services (hereafter PLS), "White Paper: The Current State of Parole in Massachusetts," February 2013, 7, http://www.plsma.org/critical-current-legislation/parole-white-paper.
16. *Reed v. Massachusetts Parole Board,* No. 11-02408H, Suffolk County Superior Court (May 10, 2012), 7.
17. Garin and PLS, "White Paper," 10–12.
18. Ibid., 11.
19. Ibid.
20. Karter Reed, Letter to Michael Rezendes, reporter at *Boston Globe*, dated July 1, 2011, available at http://realcostofprisons.org/writing/reed_rezendes.pdf.
21. Reggie Sheffield, "Ferrer Gets at Least 15 Years for Shooting at Fourteen," New Bedford Standard-Times, May 11, 1995.
22. Massachusetts Parole Board, Antonio Ferrer Record of Decision W58563, September 20, 2011, accessed February 15, 2013, http://www.mass.gov/eopss/docs/pb/lifer-decisions/2013/ferrerantonio4-19-13.pdf.
23. Garin and PLS, "White Paper," 6.
24. Jean Trounstine, "Why Josh Wall Should Not be Judge, Part II," jeantrounstine.com, September 25, 2014, http://jeantrounstine.com/?p=2149.
25. Michael Rezendes, "Backlog Follows Parole Overhaul," *Boston Globe*, Mar 26, 2012.
26. Ibid.
27. "Gov. Council Public Policy Forum with Dr. Charlene Bonner chair of Mass Parole Board" (Governors Council meeting, State House, Boston,MA,April8,2015),notesbyWayneR.Perry,availableathttps://www.linkedin.com/pulse/gov-council-public-policy-forum-dr-charlene-bonner-chair-perry.
28. Tatum Pritchard et al., *Three Strikes: The Wrong Way to Justice: A Report on Massachusetts' Habitual Offender Proposed Legislation* (Cambridge, MA: Charles Hamilton Houston Institute for

Race and Justice, Harvard Law School, June 26, 2012), 6, http://www.prisonpolicy.org/scans/HHIRJ_203_20Strikes_20Report-Merged.pdf; M.G.L. c.279, s.

29. Ibid, 24.
30. American Civil Liberties Union, "10 Reasons to Oppose '3 Strikes, You're Out,'" Website, accessed by author December 31, 2015, https://www.aclu.org/10-reasons-oppose-3-strikes-youre-out.
31. Neumeier, interview.
32. Merriam-Webster Online, s.v. "deposition," http://www.merriam-webster.com/dictionary/deposition.
33. Neumeier, interview.
34. Ibid.
35. Sarah Schweitzer and Michael Levenson, "Mass SJC Bars No-Parole Life Terms for Youth," *Boston Globe*, December 24, 2013.
36. *Reed v. Massachusetts Parole Board,* 30(b) (6) Deposition of L. Ferraris (October 10, 2012), transcript, 1:4.
37. Ibid., 42-45.
38. Ibid., 42–45.
39. Amy Burroughs, "Top Women of Law 2013," Massachusetts Lawyers Weekly, October 31, 2012, 30.
40. Attorney Richard Neumeier, telephone interview by author, April 16, 2013.
41. Ibid.

Chapter 11

1. *Reed v. Massachusetts Parole Board,* No. 2011-02408, Suffolk Superior Court (May 1, 2013), Transcript.
2. Attorney Richard Neumeier, telephone interview by author, June 5, 2014.
3. Caterina Gouvis Roman and Jeremy Travis, Taking Stock: Housing, Homelessness, and Prisoner Reentry, Final Report (Washington, DC: Urban Institute, Justice Policy Center, March 8, 2004), iv, http://www.urban.org/UploadedPDF/411096_taking_stock.pdf.
4. National Council on Crime and Delinquency, "What is Restorative Justice?" nccdglobal.org, 2015, http://nccdglobal.org/what-we-do/major-projects/restorative-justice-project.

5. Paul Tullis, "Can Forgiveness Play a Role in Criminal Justice," *New York Times*, January 4, 2013.
6. Talk of The Nation, "Victims Confront Offenders Face to Face," NPR.org, July 28, 2011, http://www.npr.org/2011/07/28/138791912/victims-confront-offenders-face-to-face.
7. Ibid.
8. Ibid.
9. Demelza Baer et al., Understanding the Challenges of Prisoner Reentry: Research Findings from the Urban Institute's Prisoner Reentry Portfolio (Washington, DC: Urban Institute, Justice Policy Center, January 2006), 8–9, http://www.urban.org/UploadedPDF/411289_reentry_portfolio.pdf.
10. Ibid.
11. Kira Dunn and Stephanie Coughlin, "Housing after Prison: The Massachusetts Parole Board Model," American Probation and Parole Association's Perspectives Journal (Summer 2008): 9–16, http://www.mass.gov/eopss/docs/pb/appaarticle.pdf.
12. Roman and Travis, Taking Stock, 14.
13. Ibid.
14. Derek Gilna, "When Halfway Houses Pose Full-Time Problems," Prison Legal News, Website, January 10, 2015, https://www.prisonlegalnews.org/news/2015/jan/10/when-halfway-houses-pose-full-time-problems/.
15. Ibid.
16. "How it All Began," Dismas House, 2013, http://dismashouse.org/about-us/history/
17. "Mar. 25, St. Dismas, The Good Thief," CatholicIreland.net, 2015, http://www.catholicireland.net/saintoftheday/st-dismas-the-good-thief/.
18. "Education, Employment and Support," Dismas.com, 2013, http://www.dismas.com/about/programs-and-services/.
19. Denise A. Hines et al., The Great Recession and Its Impact on Families: 2010 Massachusetts Family Impact Seminar; (Worcester: The Mosakowski Institute for Public Enterprise, Clark University, 2010), 11-16; http://www.clarku.edu/faculty/dhines/_Family_Impact_Report.pdf; Chris Isidore, "It's Official: Recession since Dec. 2007," CNN Money, December 1, 2008, http://money.cnn.com/2008/12/01/news/economy/recession.

20. "Dismas House Fact Sheet," Dismas House, 2013, http://dismashouse.org/about-us/apply.
21. "MassHealth Eligibility Requirements," Community Information Resources, accessed January 5, 2014, http://www.massresources.org/masshealth-general-eligibility.html.
22. Challenges of Prisoner Reentry, 12.
23. Reed, interview.
24. Ibid.
25. Kate J. Wilson, State Policies and Procedures Regarding "Gate Money": A Report Prepared for the California Department of Corrections and Rehabilitation (Davis: University of California–Davis, Center for Public Policy Research, June 2007), 3, http://www.cdcr.ca.gov/adult_research_branch/research_documents/gate_money_oct_2007.pdf.
26. Reed, interview.
27. Massachusetts Legislature General Laws. c.127, §149A, accessed January 5, 2014, https://malegislature.gov/Laws/GeneralLaws/PartI/TitleXVIII/Chapter127/Section149.
28. Shawna M. Anderson, Trends in Revocation among Massachusetts Parolees, Massachusetts Parole Board Special Report, October 2013, 1–3, http://www.mass.gov/eopss/docs/pb/trendsinrevocationamongmassachusettsparolees.pdf.
29. Shauna M. Anderson, 2013 Parole Board Massachusetts Annual Statistical Report, September 2014, 73, available at http://archives.lib.state.ma.us/handle/2452/238516.
30. Reed, interview.
31. Larry K. Gaines and Roger LeRoy Miller, Criminal Justice in Action, (Belmont: Thomson Wadsworth, 2007), 476.
32. Shauna M. Anderson, 2012 Parole Board Massachusetts Annual Statistical Report, March 2014, 54, http://www.mass.gov/eopss/docs/pb/2012annualstatisticalreport.pdf.
33. Jeremy Travis, Amy L. Solomon, and Michelle Waul, From Prison to Home: The Dimensions and Consequences of Prisoner Reentry (Washington, DC: The Urban Institue, Justice Policy Center, June 2001), 31, http://www.urban.org/pdfs/from_prison_to_home.pdf.
34. Ibid.
35. "Hiring Ex-Convicts: Between a rock and a Lawsuit," *The Economist*, June 22, 2103.

36. Binyamin Appelbaum, "Out of Trouble, but Criminal Records Keep Men Out of Work," *New York Times*, February 28, 2015.
37. Travis et al., From Prison to Home, 31.
38. Appelbaum, "Out of Trouble."
39. "BMW to Pay $1.6 Million and Offer Jobs to Settle Federal Race Discrimination Lawsuit," US Equal Opportunity Employment Commission, Website, September 8, 2015, http://www.eeoc.gov/eeoc/newsroom/release/9-8-15.cfm.
40. Jhaneel Lockhart, "4 Reasons Why Your Small Business Should Hire an Ex-Offender," Business Insider, Website, January 13, 2012, http://www.businessinsider.com/benefits-of-hiring-ex-convicts-for-small-business-owners-2012-1.
41. "Work Opportunity Tax Credit," United States Department of Labor Employment and Training Administration, Website, March 13, 2015, https://www.doleta.gov/business/incentives/opptax/eligible.cfm#Ex-felons.
42. Jeffrey Gilbreath and Gary Olberstein, "Massachusetts Bans Criminal History Questions on Job Application Forms: Employers Must Take Action or Risk Noncompliance," Nixon-Peabody, August 12, 2010, http://www.nixonpeabody.com/118509.
43. Amy L. Solomon, "In Search of a Job: Criminal Records as Barriers to Employment," National Institute of Justice Journal 270, June 2012, 47-8, http://www.crime-scene-investigator.net/NIJ-JobCriminalRecords.pdf.
44. Michelle Natividad Rodriguez and Nayantara Mehta, "Ban the Box: US Cities, Counties, and States Adopt Fair Hiring Practices," National Employment Law Project, Website, December 1, 2015, http://www.nelp.org/publication/ban-the-box-fair-chance-hiring-state-and-local-guide/.
45. Massachusetts did raise the minimum wage soon thereafter: Dan Ring, "Massachusetts Senate Overwhelmingly Approves Minimum Wage Increase to $11.00 an Hour," Springfield Republican, November 19, 2013.
46. "One-Stop Career Center Ex-Offender Services," MassResources.org, Website, accessed by author January 5, 2013, http://www.massresources.org/exoffender-career-center.html.

Afterword

1. Governor Dannel P. Malloy, "Gov. Malloy's Prepared Remarks Today on Criminal Justice Reform," (Connecticut Law Review Symposium, Hartford, CT, UConn School of Law, November 6, 2015), http://portal.ct.gov/Departments_and_Agencies/Office_of_the_Governor/Press_Room/Press_Releases/2015/11-2015/Gov__Malloy_s_Prepared_Remarks_Today_on_Criminal_Justice_Reform/.
2. Vincent Schirildi, "Raise the Minimum Age a Juvenile Can Be Tried as an Adult to 21," *New York Times*, December 14, 2015.
3. Christopher Keating, "Connecticut To Open Prison For 18- To 25-Year-Olds," http://www.courant.com/news/connecticut/hc-connecticut-prison-young-inmates-1218-20151217-story.html.
4. Vincent Schiraldi and Bruce Western, "Why 21 Year-Old Offenders Should be Tried in Family Court," *Washington Post*, October 2, 2015
5. Ibid.
6. "YJAM Recap 2015: Sharing Stories, Why we start with stories, and move them to Action," Campaign for Youth Justice, Website, October 29, 2015, http://cfyj.org/news/blog/item/yjam-recap-2015-sharing-stories-why-we-start-with-stories-and-move-them-to-action.
7. Jennifer Emily and Diane Jenning, "Kids of Criminals: Raised Behind Bars," *Dallas Morning News*, August 27, 2015, http://interactives.dallasnews.com/2015/kids-or-criminals/part1.html.
8. Elias Isquith, "Juvenile Incarceration is a Dickensian Nightmare: The Shameful Ravages of Mass Incarceration," Salon, November 17, 2015, http://www.salon.com/2015/11/17/juvenile_incarceration_is_a_dickensian_nightmare_the_shameful_ravages_of_mass_incarceration/.
9. Fox Butterfield, "Dedication," *All God's Children: The Bosket Family and the American Tradition of Violence*, (New York: Vintage, 1995).